ISLAM AND HUMAN RIGHTS

ISLAM AND HUMAN RIGHTS

Tradition and Politics

Ann Elizabeth Mayer

WESTVIEW PRESS • Boulder and San Francisco
PINTER PUBLISHERS • London

Copyright © 1991 by Westview Press, Inc.

Published in 1991 in the United States of America by Westview Press, Inc., 5500 Central Avenue, Boulder, Colorado 80301.

Published in 1991 in the United Kingdom by Pinter Publishers, Ltd., 25 Floral Street, Covent Garden, London WC2E 9DS.

Library of Congress Cataloging-in-Publication Data
Mayer, Ann Elizabeth.
    Islam and human rights : tradition and politics / Ann Mayer.
      p. cm.
    ISBN 0-8133-8091-X
    1. Civil rights (Islamic law).   2. Human rights—Religious aspects—
Islam.   I. Title.
LAW
342′.085′0917671—dc20
[342.2850917671]   90-19921
                                                                                   CIP

British Library Cataloguing-in-Publication Data
A CIP catalogue record for this book is available from the
British Library.
    ISBN 0-86187-091-3

Printed and bound in the United States of America

  The paper used in this publication meets the requirements
       of the American National Standard for Permanence of Paper
       for Printed Library Materials Z39.48-1984.

10   9   8   7   6   5   4   3   2

To my mother
and her mother

Contents

Preface

Perspicacious readers will probably note that the title of this book is a misnomer. A more accurate title might be "A Comparison of Selected Civil and Political Rights Formulations in International Law and in Actual and Proposed Rights Schemes Purporting to Embody Islamic Principles, with a Critical Appraisal of the Latter in Terms of International Law and Islamic Jurisprudence." I confess that the actual title stands as it is simply because it is the kind of rubric that people tend to consult when looking for material on human rights in Muslim countries. That is, it has been selected for purely practical reasons despite its not being very informative.

The reference to "Islam" in the book title is potentially misleading, since I repudiate the commonly held view that Islam by itself determines the attitudes one finds in the Muslim world on human rights issues. In fact, I see Islam as only one factor in the reception of human rights in the Middle East. The reason why this book focuses on Islamic responses to international human rights principles is that my own research interests happen to center on the role of Islamic law in contemporary Middle Eastern societies.

A central thesis of this book is that one should not speak of "Islam" and human rights as if Islam were a monolith or as if there existed one settled Islamic human rights philosophy that caused all Muslims to look at rights in a particular way. The precepts of Islam, like those of Christianity, Hinduism, Judaism, and other major religions possessed of long and complex traditions, are susceptible of interpretations that can and do create conflicts between religious doctrine and human rights norms or that reconcile the two. In reality, one cannot predict the position that a person will take on a human rights problem simply on the basis of the person's religious affiliation—and this is as true of Muslims as of members of other faiths. Even where the discussion is limited, as it is here, to Muslims living in the area stretching from North Africa to Pakistan, Muslims' attitudes toward human rights run the gamut from total rejection to wholehearted embrace.

What currently differentiates Muslims' approaches to rights from discussions of rights in secularized Western milieus is the tendency of the former to rely heavily on religious principles and interpretations of Islamic sources to develop their positions supporting or condemning rights. Under present conditions, questions of human rights, like other great political issues facing Muslim societies, cannot easily be severed from disputes that are raging about the implications of Islamic theology and law for contemporary problems. "Islam" has become the vehicle both for political protest against undemocratic regimes and for the repression meted out by such regimes, simultaneously expressing aspirations for democracy and equality and providing rationales for campaigns to crush democratic freedoms and perpetuate old patterns of discrimination.

At a time when Islamic themes and terminology dominate political discourse, it can be difficult for persons both inside and outside Muslim societies to distinguish neatly between political and religious issues. Nonetheless, when the substantive issues being contested are compared with matters in dispute in non-Muslim societies, it is possible to discern that under the surface of the debates about "Islam," political struggles are going on that have much in common with the history of campaigns for democracy and equality in non-Muslim countries. In the West, analogous debates on rights have been carried out in secular terms— as indeed they were for decades in many Muslim milieus before the onset of the Islamic resurgence after 1967.

In this book I evaluate the significance of some uses of Islamic law since World War II in formulations of distinctive Islamic approaches to human rights. Analyses of these contemporary uses of Islam must be differentiated from analyses of the Islamic sources and the core doctrines of Islam as a religious faith, none of which are being subjected to critical assessment in this study. Instead, my appraisals of Islamic rationales that have recently been put forward for various positions on rights entail critiques of the application of human reason to extrapolate rules from the Islamic sources and to apply them to rights problems.

I take issue with many of the interpretations embodied in Islamic human rights schemes where I have identified inadequacies and confusion in their authors' reasoning and command of the relevant material. The deficiencies that I discuss include misrepresentations of comparative legal history, failure to take into account the impact of the nation-state on the contemporary rights situation, ignoring the significance of the disintegration of the institutions of traditional societies under the impact of the development process, insufficient grasp of international rights principles, imprecise legal methodologies, evasive and ambiguous formulations, and misleading terminology. All these flaws are attributable solely to the human authors' own failings in the task of interpreting Islamic requirements.

The emphasis placed here on the problems of interpreting and applying the Islamic sources, problems central to the production of Islamic human rights schemes, resembles the emphasis placed on issues of methodology by the premodern jurists of Islam. Islam has historically been a very decentralized religion hosting a wide range of dissimilar opinions and competing schools of law, and one could say that the Islamic legal tradition has historically been a culture of argument. Critical appraisals of interpretations of the Islamic sources preoccupied the jurists, who argued endlessly in their treatises about what the right techniques were for deriving rules of law. This disagreement among the jurists was accepted as an integral feature of the Islamic tradition. Unfortunately, this tradition of tolerance of debate and argument about the meanings of the Islamic sources has been repudiated by many persons today. There are ideologues of Islamic revival and academicians in the West who show a disposition to confuse criticisms of contemporary interpretations of the Islamic sources, which include policies of governments that are officially based on Islamic law, with attempts to discredit the Islamic religion or with a lack of respect or sympathy for the views of its adherents. Attitudes like these have had consequences for trends in scholarship on human rights in Islam.

Most of the secondary literature currently available in the West on the relationship of Islam and human rights is informed by an uncritical approach and contributes little to an understanding of the subject. Rather than try to present a catalogue of the deficiencies plaguing most articles and books on this subject, I have preferred to point out where secondary sources offer sound methodologies or valuable assessments of rights issues. However, in many ways the approach taken in this book has been inspired by the defects in the secondary literature and is intended to compensate for its gaps and its prevailing uncritical quality. Since I am consciously endeavoring to respond to what I see as defects in the secondary literature, these defects should be summarized.

The authors of most of the works in the secondary literature on Islam and human rights fail to analyze and explain the criteria that are being employed to decide what qualifies as "Islamic law." They seem to perceive no need to distinguish between principles set forth in the Islamic sources and the historical patterns of interpreting these sources according to criteria set by various schools of law or sects. They do not address evolutions and reforms in interpretations of texts that have taken place over time. The disparities in views among contemporary Muslims on rights questions are rarely given their due. Generally, the authors of the secondary literature do not assess the significance of the fact that the idea of human rights is a recent legal transplant and one that requires many adjustments to accommodate within the framework of premodern Islamic legal doctrines. They likewise neglect to differentiate between moral values or ideal prescriptive norms of Islam and the actual laws and legal institutions in place in Muslim countries. In particular, there is a disinclination to take into account the skewed balance of power between the government and the governed in the political systems in the contemporary Middle East and the implications of that situation for rights problems. The presentations rarely demonstrate a firm grasp of international rights principles and their philosophical underpinnings. Comparisons of Islamic rights standards with their international counterparts tend to be careless and underdeveloped. Specific analyses of rights issues are usually wanting, so that discussion remains at a level of abstraction and vague generalization.

The weaknesses in the secondary literature correlate with the tendency one finds in the work of the average Western student of the Middle East and Islam to accept at face value Islamic rationales for denying human rights. A curious assumption underlying this attitude seems to be that the proper empathy for Muslims and their beliefs requires uncritically accepting the "Islamic" rubrics for legal rules and policies that deny human rights to Muslims. In contrast, among Muslims, skeptical scrutiny of official rhetoric and Islamic rationales for policies of disregarding international human rights norms is common. Thus, although governments may claim that their opposition to international human rights is justified by Islamic authority, Muslims may dismiss such claims as cynical appeals to religious sentiment, made with an intent to legitimize governmental policies violative of rights. At the same time well-meaning Western observers are inclined to treat those very governmental rights policies as necessary and normal concomitants of any Islamic order.

A specific example from my own experience may illustrate what I have in mind. I have gotten the impression that academics in the West who specialize in Islam or the Middle East think that critical appraisals of Sudanese President Ja'far al-Nimeiri's Islamization policy must be motivated by a lack of sympathy for Islam or a failure to grasp standards of cultural relativism. Such reactions are hard to reconcile with evidence that Nimeiri's Islamization program was overwhelmingly rejected by Muslim Sudanese, on the grounds that it violated international human rights standards and that it was not in conformity with true precepts of Islamic law. It is interesting that the opinions of those Muslims who decry the abuses and vagaries of Islamization measures and call for the realization of the standards of democracy and human rights that are enjoyed in the West tend to be discounted by many academics in the West, who seem to be committed to irrebuttable presumptions about the distinctive mindsets of peoples from non-Western cultures and the absolute nontransferability of Western norms and attitudes.

I often recall one sign of the Sudanese reaction to Nimeiri's Islamization program. On a research trip of mine to Khartoum in December 1984 and January 1985, during which I made frequent visits to Khartoum University Law School, I kept encountering a cartoon poster of President Ja'far al-Nimeiri that had been displayed right in the front entrance. It portrayed Nimeiri seated, wearing traditional dress and a turban, apparently sermonizing about Islam, as he often did in the period when he was pressing Islamization. In the cartoon, Nimeiri was surrounded by Islamic clerics, apparently looking on in approval. On one side of Nimeiri there was a severed arm oozing blood, representative of the many amputations—as penalties for criminal offenses—carried out under his Islamization program. The caption at the base of the poster was "Satan preaches." I was amazed that the cartoonist's subversive characterization stayed on display at a time when lawyers and law professors had been jailed for denouncing rights abuses under Nimeiri's Islamization program. The sentiments on the poster must have been approved by the law school community for it to remain intact and on display for so long. It seems that Sudanese specializing in the study of law had no difficulty discerning that it was not Islam that the poster attacked, but Nimeiri's hypocritical and cruel version of Islamization. Indeed, in my conversations with Sudanese at the law school, I encountered no one who was impressed by Nimeiri's Islamization campaign or his posturing as a pious Muslim. It was curious, then, to encounter academics subsequently in the West who disallowed the legitimacy of criticisms of Nimeiri's Islamization measures as necessarily involving the application of "alien" standards to judge Islamic culture and institutions.

I am inclined to be critical of government's claims that unimpeachable Islamic authority lies behind their violations of human rights, even though I understand that individual Muslims may freely decide to accept the authority of interpretations of Islamic sources that place Islamic law at odds with the international rights norms. Some Muslims may have sincere religious convictions that lead them to believe that their religious tradition requires deviations from international norms, and their right to have such private convictions must be respected. However, the situation becomes different where assertions that Islamic rules call for disregarding human rights lead to programs designed to deprive others of human rights or to the adoption by governments of laws and policies that violate the International Bill of Human Rights. The resulting conflicts over religious justifications for curbs on rights and freedoms go well beyond the realm of protected private beliefs and enter the domains of politics and international law.

Where Islamic rationales appear to be factors in the formulation of governmental policies denying internationally guaranteed human rights, they must be open to scrutiny. Any Islamic rationales offered for violating international law should be examined in the light of Islamic jurisprudence, and if they turn out to be less than compelling or only tenuously connected to central values and principles of the Islamic religion, there may be reason to doubt that they are determined solely by religious criteria. It is also legitimate to investigate what reasons other than religion may lie behind the policies, particularly where the policies serve the interests of powerful groups already enjoying privileged positions. In this regard, it is noteworthy that the practical results of rights policies associated with governmental Islamization programs have simply replicated patterns of rights violations common in undemocratic countries outside the Muslim world, violations that gave rise to the current principles of international human rights. The patterns of discrimination against women and religious minorities that proponents of Islamization insist are mandated by rules of Islamic law likewise mimic patterns of discrimination found outside the Muslim world. This is particularly apparent to anyone who reviews the historical record of treatment of women and religious minorities in premodern societies.

In assessing Islamic human rights schemes I have endeavored to treat all sources and arguments objectively, but that does not mean that I feel obligated to withhold judgment or to suppress my own opinions. My own views—with supporting reasoning—are expressed at various points in the following book. On human rights questions, I do not consider that it is possible or even advisable to withhold all judgment on the moral rightness of positions. In clarification, I would say that one can write on questions of slavery in a serious and fair manner without withholding all judgment about whether slavery is a benign or an evil institution. Similarly, one should be able to offer scholarly assessments of torture without having to adopt the attitude that torture is a morally neutral phenomenon. On the same grounds, I also believe that it is possible to give a fair appraisal of conflicts on rights issues without being obliged to deny all philosophical convictions about whether human beings possess rights that deserve respect or whether governmental rights violations are blameworthy.

I feel no need to disguise my own belief in the normative character of the human rights principles set forth in international law and in their universality. Believing these are universal, I naturally also believe that Muslims are entitled to the full measure of human rights protections accorded under international law. This inclines me to be critical of any actual or proposed governmental rights policies that have the effect of violating international human rights, regardless of whether they employ secular rationales or formulations of Islamic doctrines to legitimize the deviations from international norms. Conversely, I am pleased to see the emergence of serious human rights movements in Middle Eastern countries and the growing tendency to interpret the Islamic sources in ways that harmonize Islamic law and international human rights. As a supporter of international law and an advocate of respect for human rights, I readily concede that I regard the liberal reformist trend in Islamic thought as a positive development. Since the ideas of liberal reformist Muslims are under constant attack by powerful conservative forces determined to discredit them and delegitimize their programs, there is no cause to worry that their beleaguered positions will escape being subjected to the harshest possible critical scrutiny. In consequence, it will be largely the positions of Muslim conservatives hostile to rights, positions that people in Middle Eastern countries can assail only at great risk to their personal safety and freedom, that will be critically examined here.

I consider the use of international human rights standards to evaluate Islamic schemes of rights entirely appropriate, as these standards have won a wide following among Muslims. It is worth pointing out that international human rights norms assume far greater importance for the inhabitants of Muslim societies than they do for citizens of Western liberal democracies, who rarely think about trying to secure protections for their rights by appeals to international law. In general, provisions in the International Bill of Human Rights enjoy more prestige and moral authority in Muslim milieus than they do in the West, where average persons, when deprived of rights, tend to think in terms of vindicating claims under domestic legal standards of civil or constitutional rights. Thus, an American with a rights claim would normally seek relief exclusively under domestic laws like provisions of the Bill of Rights in the U.S. Constitution, discounting the utility of any appeal to international norms. In contrast, a Muslim in the Middle East may well know that there is no realistic possibility of obtaining redress for rights violations by appeals to domestic legal standards and may use international rights concepts set forth in instruments like the Universal Declaration of Human Rights to try to pressure the local government to recognize the legitimacy of a rights claim.

I know about Muslims' growing reliance on international human rights norms because, largely as a result of the efforts of Muslim friends to draw me into human rights networks, I have become a member of a number of international human rights advocacy groups. I have worked in association with persons and groups concerned with helping victims of governmental rights violations, and I have participated in a variety of efforts to try to secure greater respect for human rights in Middle Eastern countries—and not just in those countries pursuing Islamization. Even without studying the question of how Islam relates to human rights issues, my experience in work on behalf of the cause of human rights would have sufficed to convince me that Islam is not the cause of the human rights problems endemic to the Middle East. Human rights abuses are every bit as prevalent and just as severe in countries where Islamic law is in abeyance or consciously violated as in countries where it is, at least officially, the legal norm. For example, as I am on the list of persons who are routinely informed regarding rights violations in the Middle East, I receive materials from the North African Students for Freedom of Action, a group that seems particularly interested in protesting denials of freedoms experienced by Islamic activists in contemporary Tunisia. Of course, Islamic activists in Tunisia have suffered under secular regimes that have endeavored to suppress the political challenges being mounted by Islamic fundamentalism. One must recognize that, depending on the political context, supporters of Islamization may easily turn out to be the victims of rights violations committed by secular regimes, and I believe that the violations of their human rights must be taken as seriously as any other rights violations. However, rights violations by secular regimes do not take place under the rubric of applying Islamic law, and they will not be dealt with here.

This study focuses on the legal dimensions of human rights problems, examining the questions within the framework of comparative law and comparative legal history. Given the centrality of law in the Islamic tradition, the legal emphasis is warranted. However, there is no intention to imply that Islam is exclusively a legal tradition or that comparative legal history is the only legitimate way to approach this topic. In a more comprehensive study on the relationship of Islam to human rights, one would ideally want to include analysis of how principles of Islamic theology, philosophy, and ethics tie in with the treatment of human rights. This would carry one into areas beyond the domain of legal provisions affecting civil and political rights, which are the sole concern of this study. The reader who conscientiously attempts to follow all the arguments and the specific comparisons of legal provisions that I will be making will probably concur that the task of sorting out the details of the relationship of the treatment of selected civil and political rights in Islamic human rights schemes and in international law is sufficiently arduous to justify restricting the scope of this particular study. More-over, the legal emphasis is warranted on the grounds that the greatest concern of contemporary Muslims seems to be examining international human rights principles in terms of Islamic law.

Ann Elizabeth Mayer

Acknowledgments

The genesis of this book was my experience during almost three decades of study of Middle Eastern history and law, as well as research trips to Egypt, Libya, Pakistan, and the Sudan. My interest in the subject of human rights in the Middle East emerged only belatedly, stimulated by talks with Middle Easterners, whose ideas about human rights and democracy continually intruded into discussions that I initiated regarding other research interests. The attitudes that Muslims expressed on human rights struck me as being different from what my academic training in the West had led me to expect and were often hard to reconcile with the descriptions of Middle Eastern culture and Islamic political thought in scholarly literature written by Westerners. I became intrigued by the comments Muslims made about their aspirations for democratic freedoms. I noticed a common—though not unanimous—tendency to demand the same kinds of democratic institutions that exist in liberal democracies in the West and a general impatience with all official rationales that governments exploited to justify repression. I was ultimately brought to the conclusion that Muslims' ideas of human rights deserved more systematic investigation, and I reoriented my research accordingly.

There are so many Middle Eastern friends, colleagues, and acquaintances to whom I owe debts of gratitude for their generous efforts over twenty-seven years to enlighten me about their political attitudes, their understanding of the Islamic tradition, and their ideas of human rights that it would be impossible to list them all here. It might also be inadvisable to mention names in a book on this sensitive topic at a time like the present, when human rights issues are so bitterly contested. Several leading Muslim advocates of human rights whom I would like to thank are now forced to live in exile in the West because of the risks that would be involved in advocating their ideas in their home countries. One friend who did much to enhance my awareness of the dimensions of the struggle for human rights has been imprisoned since 1989 by the Bashir regime in the Sudan precisely because of his tenacious public defense of international human rights principles. In the present political climate, I would do such persons no service by citing their names, but I hope they know that I acknowledge owing them a great debt.

In addition, I wish to express my appreciation to Deloris Jones, Lauretta Tomasco, and Anita Zelinski for their expert help, kindness, and patience in the work on the preparation of this manuscript for publication.

A.E.M.

CHAPTER 1

Comparisons of Rights Across Countries

In the Muslim Middle East there has been a strong but mixed response to the ideals of human rights. Formulations of human rights both on the individual and the governmental levels have often been in Islamic terms, suggesting that Islam is a critical factor affecting Muslims' receptivity to human rights concepts. It is this Islamic dimension of the reaction that is analyzed here.

The Islamic religion was a deeply ingrained feature of the culture of the traditional Middle East. In the course of the difficult modernization process to which all Muslim countries have been subjected, traditional societies in the Middle East have been undergoing transformations that have affected both those societies and their Islamic institutions. Even as the societies involved move through transitional stages en route to modernization, Islam retains great influence, so that the confrontation of modernity on the social level has also become a confrontation of Islam and modernity on the theological and ideological levels.[1] International human rights have percolated through Middle Eastern societies at a time when traditional Islam is being challenged by new formulations of Islamic doctrine. Responsive to the changing realities in the Muslim world, these new formulations accommodate the evolving attitudes and aspirations of Islam's followers, which include hopes of greater freedom. The advances of the modernization process have exacerbated Muslims' resentment of the arbitrary, repressive, and despotic governments of their countries and have prompted the growth of movements supporting democratization and human rights.[2]

The issue of the relationship between the Islamic legal tradition and human rights, which is of great theoretical interest, has gained in practical significance in the wake of the Islamic resurgence that began after the Arab-Israeli war of 1967. Prior to that time, the issue seemed to be academic because the movement toward secularization of legal systems had been very consistent, leaving only small islands of Islamic substantive rules in what were basically modern, secularized legal systems. In a dramatic turnabout, the fate of imported Western legal systems became uncertain as the Islamic resurgence shaped both private and governmental attitudes in ways that led to rejection of Western legal models and searches for indigenous replacements based on Islamic models. The consequences of official Islamization programs in many Muslim countries were changes in the legal systems that adversely affected the recognition and protection of human rights. Indeed, the applicability of international versus newly coined Islamic versions of rights became one of the main areas of controversy in the Islamization drives that ensued.

Muslims who opposed international human rights and demanded their replacement by Islamic norms have not done so because they conceived of Islam affording more extensive protections for human rights than are provided by the international standards. As will be shown in the discussion of Islamic human rights schemes, distinctive Islamic criteria have consistently been used to cut back on the freedoms guaranteed in international law. That is, Muslims who reject the applicability of international human rights law act on the grounds that the international guarantees exceed the limits of rights and freedoms permitted by Islam.

A distinction must be maintained between Islam as a world religion, the doctrines of which are not being subject to critical analysis here, and the new proposals and legislation mandating distinctive Islamic treatments of rights. It is those treatments that are in conflict with international norms that are being critically analyzed.

The schemes for Islamization of rights that have been proposed or enacted into law are diverse. They do not conform to any single, settled Islamic model accepted as authoritative by universal Muslim consensus but reflect a variety of political philosophies as well as the local contexts in which they have arisen. When one discusses Islamization measures taken by contemporary regimes, one is not speaking of Islam per se, but rather of the uses to which Islamic doctrines and symbols are being put in the service of specific political agendas and in shaping the positive laws of various separate national legal systems.

There are differences of opinion among Muslims regarding the existence of a real Islamic warrant for these national Islamization programs. These differences are mirrored at the theoretical level in the disputes about Islam and human rights that one finds in the literature by Muslims on the relationship of Islamic and international law. This literature, which arose after the emergence of the international law of human rights in the wake of World War II, betokens a strong interest on the part of Muslims in comparisons of Islamic law and international human rights principles. Muslims have espoused a wide range of opinions on rights—from the assertion that international human rights are fully compatible with Islam to the claim that international human rights are products of alien, Western culture and represent values that are repugnant to Islam. In between these extremes, one finds compromise positions that in effect maintain that Islam accepts many but not all aspects of international human rights or that it endorses human rights with certain reservations and qualifications.

Views that are representative of this middle ground will constitute the focus of attention of this study. In this connection, I will present analyses of specific aspects of Islamic human rights schemes. These schemes, promoted by members of the educated elites and by certain governments, purport to represent definitive Islamic countermodels of human rights that Muslims should follow in lieu of the international formulas. Islamic human rights schemes cover a broad area, but the scope of this study has been limited to the realm of political and civil rights—to keep the treatment from becoming too superficial. Those rights are particularly important in the debates on Islam and human rights, since it has been in the area of political and civil rights that international human rights tenets have been most vigorously challenged by extensive recourse to Islam. Political and civil rights have also been of particular concern to Muslims involved in human rights work.

The fact that the middle-ground positions are being emphasized in this study does not mean that they are more authentically Islamic than the others. They are simply more attractive subjects for investigation because they reveal the conflicting trends presently at work, shaping distinctive Islamic provisions on human rights. Middle-ground positions illustrate the problems of transplanting legal institutions from a culture in which they originally grew, to another culture, where they may face culture-based resistance. Such positions are also of practical importance for understanding rights treatments in contemporary governmental Islamization programs. The literature arguing that Muslims must reject international rights norms and instead follow distinctive Islamic rights principles, which limit freedoms and restrict rights, provides the theoretical rationales for many of the steps that governments have taken and are likely to continue to take in the course of Islamization programs. The distinctive Islamic positions on rights in that literature are reflected in features of Islamization measures in Iran, Pakistan, and the Sudan, which are thus far the major field experiments in the revival of Islamic law. For that reason we shall examine Islamization in those three countries.

When Islamization occurs, it is necessary to consider the Islamic models of rights proposed as local alternatives to international human rights norms. Cross-comparisons between what has been or is being implemented in several countries under the rubric of Islamization and the relevant Islamic human rights formulations will be presented here. The latter, in turn, will be compared with international human rights standards to elucidate where international standards and the various Islamic standards and Islamization measures coincide or diverge. In addition, Islamic human rights formulations will be discussed in the light of relevant aspects of Islamic intellectual history and current disputes about how Muslims should treat their premodern legal heritage.

Comparative legal history, with which this study is primarily concerned, is an academic field where major political controversies are rarely encountered. As an eminent comparatist has stated, comparative law looks at the relationships among legal systems and their rules, and ultimately, it is concerned with similarities and differences in legal systems and rules in the context of historical relationships.[3] In the main, scholars in the West can expect such studies to be of interest to specialists and will be justified in assuming that any controversies they may provoke will center on issues of scholarship. If scholars are comparing, say, the influence of German law on Japanese law, the relationship between Spanish law and family law in California, the influence of Islamic law on the English law of trusts, or the reception of Roman law in European legal systems, they do not expect the mere undertaking of such comparisons to be condemned by their academic peers. Nor do they expect that their work will be denounced as politically unsound if they objectively record the similarities and differences that they have uncovered or state whether aspects of one system were historically derived from the other. Those writing on comparative legal history in the West are used to working in a discipline free from ideologically inspired precensorship. Thus, they are not inhibited in their scholarly inquiry and may express the conclusions to which their research and analysis have brought them without having to adjust their conclusions to fit prevailing canons of an established political orthodoxy.

It would seem that there should be no bar to evaluating Islamic human rights norms and Islamization measures, along with their theoretical underpinnings, by the standards of international human rights. Since the study of the relationship between contemporary efforts to formulate Islamic rights provisions and their counterparts in contemporary international human rights law is a proper and even conventional topic in the field of comparative legal history, one would not expect that researching and commenting on it would be like stepping into an ideological minefield. In actuality, one discovers that the mere project of undertaking a critical assessment of Islamic approaches to rights will be widely denounced as a venture necessarily motivated by ethnocentric biases and designed to promote political objectives associated with Orientalism and Western imperialism. It therefore is important both to offer a preliminary response to the kinds of objections that can be anticipated and to establish the nature and goals of a comparative legal study like the one being attempted here.

The pressures to precensor discussions of this topic may in part account for the fact that there is a paucity of literature available in the West offering critical comparisons of Islamic law and international law on human rights.[4] Much of what has been written in this area is characterized by superficiality and an unwillingness to tackle real problems using scholarly tools of comparative legal analysis. Western scholars who perceive this gap and venture to undertake such analysis will quickly discover why it is a path that others have feared to tread. If they persist, the misunderstandings and hostility that they will encounter are likely to be daunting.

Obstacles to Comparison

What are the reasons why this topic has been effectively ruled off limits for any critical scholarly inquiry? The impetus behind this informal but effective censorship does not come from scholars in the fields of international and comparative law. It comes, instead, from specialists in area studies like the study of the Middle East, where Islamology is a major subject.[5] Islamologists and specialists in Middle East studies tend to become acculturated to and socialized by the academic milieus in which they operate in ways that lead them to conclude that such comparisons are objectionable. Because many Third World spokespersons reject the idea of the universality of human rights and defend local schemes of culture-based resistance to international rights standards, these perspectives may be uncritically assimilated by scholars studying areas of the Third World. Scholars who are conscientiously seeking to understand the cultural background of indigenous attitudes toward Western institutions may develop personal sympathies for Third World perspectives. A critical perspective that could reflect Western biases will tend to be discarded in the process as an impediment to understanding the societies under study. In contrast, the present study will try to demonstrate that a critical and even skeptical perspective should be maintained in the face of assertions that human rights norms are not applicable to the Third World.

A factor underlying objections to Western critiques of human rights in the Third World is that the criticism is seen as inevitably tinged with hypocrisy. The West does have its own history of egregious human rights violations—including an extensive record of patterns of torture, genocide, religious persecution, racism, and centuries of slavery—as well as a record of disregarding the rights of the inhabitants of the Third World societies that it ruled and exploited in the era of Western colonialism. This history prompts arguments that Westerners should be disqualified from acting as the judges of rights records of independent Third World countries.

The most frequently cited example of contemporary Western hypocrisy in judging rights records of Middle Eastern countries is the Western reaction to rights violations in Iran. Current Western criticism of Iran's rights record is rejected because of the disparity between the Western response to human rights abuses under the shah of Iran and under the subsequent Khomeini regime. The West is deemed to be outrageously hypocritical: Its toleration of grievous rights abuses under the shah proves that its professions of deep concern for the rights of people in Iran after the Islamic Revolution cannot be genuine. The inference is drawn that the West condones or ignores human rights abuses by friendly pro-Western regimes and brings up human rights issues only to discredit regimes that defy Western hegemony and reject Western cultural values.

In the case of Iran, there is no disputing the fact that the West generally and United States in particular played a major role in propping up the shah's brutal regime and that while paying lip service to human rights ideals, the West demonstrated a lack of real concern for ending the human rights violations perpetrated under his rule. It is a matter of public record that U.S. apologists for the shah's regime rationalized his oppressive practices in ingenious ways. To such apologists, practices that were ingrained under the Pahlavis suddenly became reprehensible after the Khomeini regime overthrew the Pahlavi monarchy and adopted an anti-Western stance. Their subsequent expressions of concern for the human rights of Iranians obviously have little credibility.

However, having conceded this, one does not see why the U.S. government's record of hypocrisy and double standards in the human rights area should bar independent scholars in the West from looking at human rights issues in Muslim countries. In fact, if the hypocrisy of the foreign policy of a scholar's home government were a disqualification for pursuing study of other societies and cultures, most scholarship would be barred. The evidence is that all governments, whether in the West or in the East, have followed and do follow double standards in the conduct of foreign relations, including dealing with human rights concerns as part of foreign policy, and it is true that governments are generally much more critical of the conduct of their foes than of their allies or client states.

The argument that private criticisms of the treatment of rights in Islamic milieus are of a piece with hypocritical governmental policy is especially weak in the case of this study, which focuses on Pakistan and the Sudan in the period 1983–1985 in addition to Iran. With respect to Pakistan and the Sudan, the United States was hypocritical not in the sense of denouncing human rights abuses perpetrated under Islamization programs or judging them particularly harshly but, rather, the reverse—it glossed over human rights abuses caused by Islamization programs because they were committed by strategically important allied governments.

The United States provided the strongest military and economic support for President Zia's regime in Pakistan from his 1977 coup until his death in 1988. He died together with the U.S. ambassador in an airplane crash—symbolic of the close links between his fortunes and U.S. policy in the region. The United States has excoriated the rights violations under the secular, leftist regimes in the region, but it was relatively silent about the rights violations perpetrated under Islamization in Pakistan. The same U.S. reticence can be seen in the stance taken vis-à-vis rights abuses by conservative Islamic forces fighting on the side of the Afghan *mujahidin,* including the archfundamentalist faction led by Gulbedin Hekmatyar, who have been financed and supplied by the United States notwithstanding the evidence of their disregard for human rights and human life. Furthermore, in the case of the Sudan, the United States was the strong mainstay of the highly unpopular Nimeiri government in 1983–1985, the period in which the latter was pursuing its Islamization campaign. Whatever the U.S. pressures on Ja'far Nimeiri to mitigate the harshness of his version of Islamic justice may have been, they were not strong enough to oblige him to terminate the human rights violations that were rife under the program. In fact, Ronald Reagan gave President Nimeiri a cordial reception in the White House in March 1985 after Nimeiri had ordered the execution of a seventy-six-year-old Sudanese religious leader as a "heretic."

Such treatment indicated that the government of the United States was quite willing to go along with Islamization programs that meant gross violations of human rights—as long as the victims were not persons in whom policymakers had a political investment. It also illustrated how the lives of Muslims and non-Western peoples are devalued in the calculations of Washington officialdom in charge of U.S. human rights policy. Thus, critical appraisals of the consequences for human rights of Islamization in the Sudan and Pakistan hardly correlate with or serve the ends of any hypocritical policies on the part of the U.S. government.

Another reason why people concerned with the Middle East and the study of Islam have been inclined to condemn critical comparisons of Islamic and international human rights is that they see sinister political objectives in Western criticisms of rights violations related to Islamic institutions. Some consider Western critiques of the human rights records of Muslim societies part of an effort to whitewash the Western record on rights and tarnish the image of Islam and to portray Islamic culture as primitive and cruel. The ultimate goal in this regard is thought to be that of establishing that Western culture is advanced and inherently superior, and showing that Western political, economic, and cultural hegemony was and is a natural and beneficial phenomenon for humankind. Criticisms of Islamic institutions have been historically associated with attempts by Western governments to justify their interference in the politics of countries in the Muslim world. Thus, critiques of the treatment of rights in Islamization programs may be regarded as indicative of neocolonialist attitudes that show a lack of respect for the sovereignty of Muslim countries. In particular, such critiques may be understood as an effort to demonstrate that Western domination of Muslim countries in the past was justified in the light of the fact that after Muslim countries obtained their independence they did not develop institutions that complied with international rights standards.

Western specialists in the Muslim world and Islam are predisposed to attack scholarly projects that appear to be inspired by neocolonialist attitudes and designed to further an effort to rehabilitate the imperialist enterprise retroactively. Their sensibilities in this regard have been exacerbated by the pervasive influence of Edward Said's seminal book, *Orientalism.*[6] In this book Said argued that much of Western scholarship on the Orient, meaning the Islamic Middle East, is not conducted in a spirit of scientific research but is based on a racist assumption of fundamental Western superiority and Oriental inferiority. By positing ineradicable distinctions between the West and the Orient, Orientalist scholarship, in Said's view, obscures the common humanity of people in the West and the Orient and thereby dehumanizes Orientals in a way that serves the goals of Western imperialism.

Although Said is not a lawyer and did not analyze legal scholarship, people influenced by his arguments tend to expand them to include legal scholarship, and although Said did not assert that all critical examination of Islamic institutions is infected by Orientalist biases, his disciples seem inclined to draw this inference from his book. In consequence, they may perceive projects for comparative legal analysis of

Islamic law and international law—the latter being identified with the West—as Orientalist in a pejorative sense, particularly in cases where they anticipate that the analysis will expose disparities between Islamic and international law. This perception is unjustified.

The use of international rights standards as norms in critical examinations of Islamic human rights schemes and restrictions on human rights imposed by governments in the Muslim world does not necessarily reflect a racist assumption of Western superiority. Rather, such use may rest on the premise that peoples in the West and the East share a common humanity, which means that they are equally deserving of rights and freedoms. To maintain that human rights norms are inapplicable in Islamic milieus is to accept the quintessentially Orientalist notion that the concepts and categories employed in the West to understand societies and cultures are irrelevant and inapplicable in the East. To believe that Islam precludes Orientals from claiming the same rights and freedoms as people in the West is to commit oneself to perpetuating the Orientalist tenet that Islam is a stable, unique regulatory scheme that dominates Oriental society, the coherence and continuity of which should not be imperiled by foreign intrusions like democratic ideas and human rights principles disseminated by "Westernized" intellectuals.[7] Those who charge that comparisons of international and Islamic law on human rights issues are Orientalist implicitly endorse the same elitist stance as the cultural relativists, discussed below—that international human rights are the sole prerogative of members of Western societies. Therefore, they are distorting Said's message, which was, ultimately, that categories like "Islam" and "Oriental" should not be allowed to obscure the common humanity of peoples in the East and in the West.

Cultural Relativism

At the core of most efforts to delegitimize comparisons of Islamic and international law is the conviction that they violate the principles of cultural relativism. Not all cultural relativists approach questions in an identical fashion, but in general they are inclined to condemn the notions that there are universal standards by which all cultures may be judged and to deny the legitimacy of using values taken from Western culture to judge institutions of non-Western cultures. They also tend to oppose the idea that human rights norms are universal.[8] To impose on Third World societies norms taken from the Universal Declaration of Human Rights involves, according to this perspective, "moral chauvinism and ethnocentric bias."[9] For strong cultural relativists, evaluative comparisons of Islamic rights concepts and international ones are impermissible because such comparisons are believed to involve judging Islamic norms by the criteria of international law, which the relativists view as an alien, Western system.

Cultural relativists seeking support for their position might take comfort from statements like that of Iran's UN representative, Said Rajaie-Khorassani, defending Iran from charges that Iran was violating human rights. His argument that international standards could not be used to judge Iran's human rights record was paraphrased as follows:

> The new political order was . . . in full accordance and harmony with the deepest moral and religious convictions of the people and therefore most representative of the traditional, cultural, moral and religious beliefs of Iranian society. It recognized no authority . . . apart from Islamic law . . . conventions, declarations and resolutions or decisions of international organizations, which were contrary to Islam, had no validity in the Islamic Republic of Iran. . . . The Universal Declaration of Human Rights, which represented secular understanding of the Judaeo-Christian tradition, could not be implemented by Muslims and did not accord with the system of values recognized by the Islamic Republic of Iran; his country would therefore not hesitate to violate its provisions.[10]

It is significant that Rajaie-Khorassani identified the official position of the Iranian government with the Islamic religion and traditional culture. Similar assertions that governmental resistance to international human rights represents a defense of traditional culture and morality have been made by other governmental spokespersons for Muslim countries in attempts to defend governmental records of human rights violations, thereby demonstrating the political usefulness of the cultural relativist stance.

Taking a cultural relativist stance to deny the universality of human rights and to challenge the validity of comparative examination of international and Islamic versions of rights is problematic for several reasons. An initial point that needs to be made is that cultural relativism, like Said's idea of Orientalism, is not a concept developed for application in the field of law or for evaluating whether governments of nations are adhering to international legal norms. Instead, it is a term that was developed for use in anthropology and moral philosophy.[11] As will be explained, the developments examined here are not simple manifestations of local cultural preferences and moral choices that fall within the realms of anthropology and moral philosophy. In this study, the concern is actual or proposed changes in national legislation and governmental policy pursuant to Islamization, and the focus is on the position of the state vis-à-vis human rights issues.

As Donnelly has noted, the interesting issue for cultural relativists is the situation where there are practices that are internally defensible within the cultural system but unacceptable by external standards.[12] This is, of course, the very issue raised by Rajaie-Khorassani's comments. Cultural relativists tend to endorse the legitimacy of rules that are produced within a given cultural system. It is important to note that the opposition of cultural relativists to critical comparisons of Islamic and international rights concepts rests on an assumption that the curbs on rights in Islamic rights schemes constitute authentic products of Islamic culture, the authority of which is accepted by Muslims—with the corollaries that Muslims do not think as Westerners do about rights and do not aspire to have them on the same terms. That is, cultural relativists assume that there is an authoritative, identifiably "Islamic" cultural position on rights issues corresponding to official rationales offered for opposition to rights, that the internal Islamic position entails practices that are violative of external international norms but defensible within the framework of Islamic culture. But when one examines that assumption, one sees that it is based on a prejudgment rather than on conclusions that could emerge only after analysis establishing how human rights are actually treated in Islamic culture and after comparisons with the external standards to ascertain whether they differ.

Muslim Positions on Human Rights

Precisely such comparisons are being pressed by Muslims, who in the 1980s produced a large literature trying to define the Islamic norms affecting rights and comparing Islamic and international human rights. The very existence of this literature demonstrates that Muslims believe that such comparisons are both timely and legitimate. The frequent references to normative criteria of international human rights even by Muslims who quarrel with features of those norms show that international human rights concepts exist not only outside the Islamic tradition; the evidence shows that they are already percolating through that tradition and becoming part of the apparatus that Muslims use internally to determine what practices are or are not acceptable and to judge the adequacy of positive laws. A survey of this literature will quickly disabuse anyone of the assumption that there is a monolithic Islamic cultural standard. Muslims do not have a common belief about what the Islamic position on human rights is or the relationship of their cultural tradition to international human rights norms. Muslims have taken many differing positions on human rights, including the unqualified endorsement of international human rights standards as fully compatible with their culture and religion.

It is natural that rights concepts should have become a preoccupation of contemporary Islamic thought because they are intimately related to the actual political and legal changes brought about by the modernization process, which all Muslim societies have had to undergo and which has substantially undermined traditional culture and society. Concepts of human rights are just one part of a cluster of institutions transplanted since the nineteenth century from the West, the foremost of which was the model of the modern nation-state. This institution, with its great, centralized power over society and its monopoly of control over resources, had never before existed in Islamic history and had not been contemplated in Islamic jurisprudence. The nation-state is now ubiquitous in the Muslim world, and it was inevitable that the legal institutions associated with it should also be transplanted. These legal institutions included constitutionalism and the scheme of protection for rights of citizens, which later became known as human rights—actually, legal constraints on the power of the modern nation-state. It is also natural that contemporary international human rights formulations should have counterparts in the principles of the domestic legal systems and constitutional provisions in almost all Muslim countries.

Thus, when one compares Islamic human rights concepts with international law, one is not judging an institution of an intact traditional culture by alien Western standards but examining Muslims' reactions to imported legal concepts and to transplants in national legal systems, imports and transplants that they have dealt with for decades. One refers to the international rights standards to see how the original rights concepts have been received and modified in their new settings. It should be borne in mind that rights adopted in the national legal systems are institutions that independent Muslim countries have freely chosen to include in their laws.[13] Thus, to maintain at this stage in history that rights are somehow external to Islamic culture entails accepting the notion that Islamic culture froze in its premodern formulation and taking the position that Islam rejects both the political changes wrought by modernization and the adoption of new ideas that accompanied the process. This is a fringe view, acceptable to only a few extremely conservative rejectionist groups in the Muslim world.

The positions occasionally taken by governments in the Muslim world that justify their rejection of international human rights norms on the basis of their alleged concern for Islamic principles are paradoxical, for those governments have already indicated in various ways their acceptance of international law as the law of nations. Since Muslim countries have, without exception, joined the international community of nations

formed under UN auspices, they have agreed to be bound by international law. Muslim, like other nations, contribute to the formulation
of public international law in such capacities as working with other
nations in the United Nations and its affiliated organizations and in
drawing up and ratifying treaties and conventions.

With regard to the present system of international law, it would be
difficult to maintain that Muslim countries were in any sense outsiders.
Several Muslim countries were among the founding members of the
United Nations and participated in deciding on the terms of the UN
Charter, which in Article 1 affirms the members' commitment to
promote and encourage respect for human rights. Muslim countries
also worked on the drafting of the Universal Declaration of Human
Rights (UDHR) of 1948. In that period, Saudi Arabia was the only
Muslim country to reject formally some principles set forth in the
UDHR on the grounds of conflicts with Islamic law. It is worth
reviewing how Saudi Arabia wound up being isolated in its rejectionist
position.

The Saudi representative condemned the UDHR on the grounds that
it reflected Western culture and was "at variance with patterns of
culture of Eastern States" and on the grounds that the provisions for
religious liberty violated Islamic law.[14] On the latter point, his comments
provoked sharp dissent from the representative of Pakistan, who took
the position that Islam unequivocally endorsed freedom of conscience.[15]
The debate on whether Muslim countries could approve the UDHR
thus presaged decades of subsequent disputes in the Muslim world
about whether in endorsing international human rights Muslims were
betraying Islamic law and accepting domination by Western culture. In
the end, when it came time to vote on the UDHR, Saudi Arabia was
alone among Muslim countries in abstaining, being joined only by
South Africa and various East Bloc countries.

In the main there has been little to distinguish the approach of the
governments of Muslim countries to international human rights principles from that of non-Muslim nations. Muslim countries do have an
uneven record of ratifying the major human rights conventions, with
some countries having ratified most conventions and others, few, but
the very unevenness and dissimilarities in the patterns of ratification
and nonratification indicate that, from the governmental perspective,
there is no single, definitive interpretation of Islamic rights principles
standing in the way of accepting international human rights. It is worth
noting that various non-Muslim countries, including Angola, Belize,
China, Japan, Liechtenstein, Luxembourg, Singapore, and the United
States, as well as the Vatican, have relatively poor records of ratifying
these conventions. Muslim countries can hardly be said to be less likely

to ratify than non-Muslim countries when the ratification records of Algeria, Egypt, Iran, Iraq, Jordan, Mali, Morocco, Niger, Syria, and Tunisia compare favorably with that of the United States, which has been reluctant to commit itself to international human rights principles. Even Saudi Arabia, which found itself unable to endorse the UDHR, has subsequently ratified fourteen of the specific conventions.

The 1972 Charter of the Islamic Conference, the international organization to which all Muslim countries belong, expressly endorses international law and fundamental human rights, treating them as compatible with Islamic values. In the Preamble of the charter, two adjacent paragraphs assert that the members are

> RESOLVED to preserve Islamic spiritual, ethical, social and economic values, which will remain one of the important factors of achieving progress for mankind;
> REAFFIRMING their commitment to the UN Charter and fundamental Human Rights, the purposes and principles of which provide the basis for fruitful co-operation amongst all people.

That is, the formal position of Muslim states justifies the conclusion that the international human rights standards developed in the United Nations are regarded as compatible with Islamic law by the very actors—governments—whose conduct is subject to regulation by international human rights principles.

Having formally accepted international human rights norms, governments of Muslim countries are bound by these norms and are also subject to being judged under them. Furthermore, support is growing for the notion that at least some principles of international human rights, because they have been subsumed over time as features of customary international law, are binding on all states regardless of their ratification of individual conventions. International law does not cease to bind states when their representatives formally comment, as Saudi Arabia's and Iran's have done, that the states' adherence to Islamic law justifies diverging from the standards of international law. Countries are not permitted to opt out of their international legal obligations at will or on pretexts of their own devising. Derogation from international human rights standards is permitted only under specific, narrow conditions, which do not include denying people human rights by appeal to the standards of any particular religion.

Given Muslim governments' having chosen to join the international system and to commit themselves in various ways to the observance of international human rights, it is surprising that cultural relativists seem to be so easily impressed when governmental spokespersons invoke "Islam" and "Eastern culture" to justify their denial of human rights. Even though no government of a nation-state can speak with unquestioned authority on matters of Islamic doctrine and Muslim governments differ among themselves regarding what Islam calls for, cultural relativists seem disposed to accord more deference to governmental assertions that their fidelity to Islam precludes the acceptance of "Western" international human rights than to the positions of the individual Muslims who have been harmed by their governments' abuses of human rights. The latter have vigorously rejected the Islamic rationales offered by governments for oppressing them.[16] Muslims who enthusiastically support international human rights risk being dismissively treated by cultural relativists on the grounds that advocates of human rights must be Westernized or alienated from their own traditions or, even worse, traitors to their own culture. In this the cultural relativists betray their Orientalist proclivities that, as discussed above, dispose them to view the Orient and Occident as having inherently different natures and traits and to consider the adoption of Occidental ideas and institutions by Orientals as somehow incongruous and unnatural.

It should be stressed that the attitude of cultural relativists is relevant not just to Islamic cultural justifications for resisting human rights principles but also to Western approaches to rights issues in Third World settings generally. As an Argentinean observer of the attitudes of American cultural relativists has noted, their position implies that

> countries that do not spring from a Western tradition may somehow be excused from complying with the international law of human rights. This elitist theory of human rights holds that human rights are good for the West but not for much of the non-Western world. Surprisingly, the elitist theory of human rights is very popular in the democratic West, not only in conservative circles but also, and even more often, among liberal and radical groups. The right-wing version of elitism embodies the position, closely associated with colonialism, that backward peoples cannot govern themselves and that democracy only works for superior cultures. The left-wing version, often articulated by liberals who stand for civil rights in Western countries but support leftist dictatorships abroad, reflects a belief that we should be tolerant of and respect the cultural identity and political self-determination of Third World countries (although, of course, it is seldom the people who choose to have dictators; more often the dictators decide for them).
>
> The position of relativist scholars who are human rights advocates illustrates an eloquent example of concealed elitism.
>
> Such persons find themselves in an impossible dilemma. On the one hand they are anxious to articulate an international human rights stan-

dard, while on the other they wish to respect the autonomy of individual
cultures. The result is a vague warning against "ethnocentrism," and
well-intentioned proposals that are deferential to tyrannical governments
and insufficiently concerned with human suffering. Because the consequence of either version of elitism is that certain national or ethnic groups
are somehow less entitled than others to the enjoyment of human rights,
the theory is fundamentally immoral and replete with racist overtones.[17]

The elitist approach underlying the cultural relativist position vis-à-
vis the Muslim world implies that Muslims, because of their non-
Western cultural identity, are outside the realm where international
human rights should be applied. This is hard to reconcile with the
universal endorsement of international human rights by Muslim governments and flies in the face of growing evidence that Muslims find
the observance of international human rights standards perfectly compatible with their tradition and enthusiastically embrace them.

One also is entitled to doubt that the governmental policies of denying
human rights under the guise of Islamization stem from what may be
accurately called tradition. When a state, in order to enforce its policies,
has to resort to measures like beatings, jailings, torture, and executions—routinely used in countries like Iran to enforce compliance with
official codifications of Islamic tradition—those policies cannot embody
an authentic tradition. Authentic tradition imposes itself on its own
authority and is normative because it has authority.[18] Thus, authentic
living tradition is automatically accepted as such and does not have to
be imposed with police-state tactics on a resisting population. What
Islamization policies represent is more like "traditionalism," or the
ideology of tradition. However, cultural relativists, when dealing with
rights in Muslim countries, do seem to mistake official, ideologized
representations of Islamic culture for authentic manifestations of indigenous tradition.

As Donnelly has noted, there is irony in the largely Westernized
elites in the Third World warning against the values and practices that
they themselves espouse. He reminded the reader that it may be necessary for today's supposedly "traditional" models—like Tanzania's vil-
lagization—to be imposed by force over the intense objections of the
supposedly "traditional" population.[19] He has pointed out the hypocrisy
of members of Third World elites in praising traditional communities
and values, which they themselves have long since escaped, while
asserting their prerogatives to "wield arbitrary power antithetical to
traditional values, pursue development policies that systematically undermine traditional communities, and replace traditional leaders with
corrupt cronies."[20] Such remarks apply with great force to Muslim

countries, where governments eager to impose an ideologized, uniform version of national culture have shown little inclination to respect cultural diversity and distinct local traditions.

If supposedly traditional Islamic values are in fact being manipulated for political ends by governments, this should be seen as part of a broader recent phenomenon in the Third World. The remarks of Donnelly are worth citing in this connection. He warned that "while recognizing the legitimate claims of self determination and cultural relativism, we must be alert to cynical manipulations of a dying, lost, or mythical cultural past," and commented:

> In the Third World today, more often than not we see dual societies and patchwork practices that seek to accommodate seemingly irreconcilable old and new ways. Rather than the persistence of traditional culture in the face of modern intrusions, or even the development of syncretic cultures and values, we usually see instead a disruptive and incomplete westernization, cultural confusion, or the enthusiastic embrace of "modern" practices and values.[21]

Muslims impatient with the lack of progress toward democracy are clearly unimpressed by the explanations of governments that their aspirations for human rights cannot be reconciled with respect for traditional culture. Organizations committed to the furtherance and protection of human rights according to international standards have proliferated throughout the Muslim world, sometimes even in very hostile political environments and under extremely dangerous conditions.[22] Many Muslims have risked death and imprisonment to stand up for the same human rights principles that cultural relativists would maintain are not suited for application in the Muslim world because of its dissimilar culture. Cultural relativists may fail to perceive how rapid urbanization, industrialization, and factors like the growing power of the state are creating awareness of the need for human rights guarantees in non-Western cultures.

As evidence that the human rights movement is now powerful enough at the grass-roots level to be a factor to be reckoned with in politics, one could point to steps recently taken by governments in the Muslim world that indicate their awareness of the mounting popularity that human rights enjoy. Concerned about their own popularity, several have found it prudent to make concessions to their citizens' demands for the observance of international human rights. For example, in June 1988, after years of trampling on the human rights of Libyans, Mu'ammar al-Qadhdhafi, assuming the posture of an advocate of human rights, issued a Libyan human rights charter, released hundreds of political prisoners, and denounced the human rights abuses that had previously been carried out by representative institutions of his regime. He also indicated a willingness to establish ties with Amnesty International. In Tunisia, after the overthrow of the increasingly autocratic and arbitrary Bourguiba regime in 1987, one of the early steps of the new government was to announce in 1988 a policy of respect for human rights and to authorize the establishment of a chapter of Amnesty International, the first one permitted to operate in the Arab world. The authoritarian Algerian government, shaken by riots and popular demonstrations in the autumn of 1988, offered Algerians a new constitution in February 1989 with rights provisions formulated along international lines and without Islamic qualifications and accepted the innovation of an express constitutional guarantee of protection for human rights advocacy.[23]

The Algerian case is fascinating because it illustrates the potency of grass-roots pressures for enhanced protections for human rights that are being exerted simultaneously with opposition groups' pressures on behalf of Islamization, another cause with demonstrable support among the masses. The Algerian regime felt compelled to offer concessions making the constitution more Islamic than the previous secular and socialist model. While appearing more Islamic, the text of the rewritten constitution avoided specification of the degree to which Islamic law would be adhered to.[24]

In the June 1990 elections for municipal offices in Algeria, candidates supporting the Islamic fundamentalist cause won in most municipalities, and the secular, socialist Front de Libération Nationale (FLN), which had dominated the country since its 1962 independence, was humiliatingly defeated. However, the full spectrum of parties was not represented because the election was boycotted by important secular political opposition parties. Thus, it is not yet clear whether in the 1990 Algerian ballot the impressive victories of candidates endorsing Islamization revealed a general popular mandate for Islamization or was simply intended to communicate the depth of voters' alienation from the discredited, secular FLN government.

One must bear in mind that in Algeria, Tunisia, and Libya—and in Muslim countries generally—Islam has become the primary and most potent language of political protest against oppressive dictatorships and military regimes. Popular support for groups calling for "Islamization" in situations where undemocratic and corrupt secular governments stubbornly cling to power may signal more a repudiation of their policies than the intent to support the specifics of the Islamization programs that are pursued by fundamentalist groups once they come to power and, as in Iran, prove unwilling to tolerate the democratic freedoms that they clamored for while still united with the opposition forces. In these circumstances, the existence of a popular mandate for Islamization at the expense of democratic freedoms is doubtful.

What Islamization programs mean in practice becomes clear only once their proponents have the chance to implement them. Once in power, they have not been able to trust the voting public to keep them there. In Iran, the clerical leadership has not tolerated any political opposition that could mount a challenge to the official Islamization policy, and in Pakistan and the Sudan, results of relatively free elections held after the countries had had actual experience of what Islamization entailed revealed voter disenchantment.

In Iran since the Islamic Revolution the population has not been permitted to vote freely to choose or to reject the official version of Islamization because no parties have been allowed to operate on the Iranian political scene unless they endorsed the official Islamic ideology and were acceptable to Iran's clerical leadership. The Iranian secular, leftist opposition has meanwhile been rendered unable to mount effective challenges to the dominance of the clerical establishment that rules the country, having been systematically decimated by government measures, including censorship, persecution, jailings, torture, and executions.

In Pakistan, during his years in power, President Zia never allowed free elections, which could have tested whether he was able to withstand a challenge from the Pakistan People's party. In the November 1988 elections, held three months after Zia's death, the voters gave a large electoral mandate to the Pakistan People's party and its leader Benazir Bhutto, President Zia's longtime political nemesis. Bhutto won the prime ministership by decrying the abuses of the military regime, campaigning on a platform opposing Islamization and calling for the restoration of rights embodied in the 1973 Pakistani Constitution. The Jama'at-i-Islami, the best-known of the Islamic fundamentalist groups calling for Islamization in Pakistan, was able to win only three seats in parliament and was further humiliated by failing to persuade the parliament to support the position that a woman should not be allowed to lead a Muslim country.[25]

Although Bhutto's electoral triumph was initially heartening to Muslim feminists, human rights advocates, and proponents of democratization, her performance during her brief tenure in office proved a great disappointment to her erstwhile supporters. She did nothing to roll back Islamization measures, contrary to her promises while she was in the opposition, and she seemed unequal to the task of effectively tackling the myriad grave political and economic problems facing the country, which included growing urban unrest and rising tensions among ethnic groups. Moreover, it was widely believed that she was closing her eyes to patterns of corruption on the part of persons close to her.

In the light of the disillusionment with Bhutto's leadership, her enemies believed that it would be politically safe to remove her, and the president abruptly dismissed her from office on August 6, 1990, on the grounds that her government had been corrupt and nepotistic. Although Bhutto was able to regain her seat in parliament in the October 1990 elections, candidates of her party did poorly in most areas of the country, and the prime ministership went to her archrival and a political ally of Zia, Nawaz Sharif, who was the leader of the conservative coalition known as the Islamic Democratic Alliance.

In the Sudan, President Nimeiri never allowed the country to have free elections to test the depth of support for his Islamization policy. He was overthrown in April 1985 after mass demonstrations against his government led to a popular revolution prompted in part by outrage at the human rights abuses that Nimeiri's version of Islamization had entailed. In the elections in 1986, Islamic fundamentalists made a poor showing, and they were able to come back to power in 1989 only by forging a second coalition with a military dictatorship.

If there were regular free elections in the Muslim world, one would have a better basis for saying exactly what policies do enjoy popular support and to what degree. Unfortunately, relatively free elections are a rarity in Muslim countries, so one does not have an accurate record of how people would vote about governmental Islamization programs. However, one can conclude from the patterns of holding and not holding elections in Pakistan and the Sudan that the official Islamization programs were not undertaken on the basis of any electoral mandate and that they were repudiated by a majority of voters once the military dictators imposing them were removed from power. The fact that democratization has been consistently seen as a threat by regimes committed to Islamization suggests that cultural relativists who assume that official Islamization measures necessarily express popular mandates for a revival of traditional local culture are mistaken.

The fact that the record shows that Muslims aspire to rights does not mean that they want rights and freedoms defined and protected in exactly the same way as they are protected, say, in the United States. It is possible that Muslims, when they are given real freedom to work out Islamic schemes for human rights genuinely reflecting their aspirations and cultural values, may produce ones that differ from U.S. counterparts in many details. But that would be hardly astonishing given the significant differences in concepts of rights and rights protections even between countries as closely linked as the United States and Canada. Respect for international human rights law does not require that every culture use an identical approach, but it does require that human rights be defined and protected in a manner consonant with international principles. One Muslim scholar who has offered a thoughtful critique of typical misuses of cultural relativism in the rights sphere suggested that a proper respect for cultural relativism means that we should accept "the right of all people to choose among alternatives equally respectful of human rights," and that the latter must include the rights of life, liberty, and dignity for every person or group of people.[26]

The kind of cultural relativism that demands tolerance for dissimilar ways of resolving rights problems in different cultures seems legitimate. Likewise, the cultural relativism that calls for the West to forbear condemning intact traditional societies as defective because they fail to protect human rights according to modern international standards seems justifiable. What does not seem defensible is cultural relativism that would insulate the conduct of modern nation-states from critical scrutiny simply because the states claimed to be following the dictates of a religion or a local culture that exempted them from the duty to abide by the standards of international human rights. The great problems of human rights in Muslim countries are not ones created by the increasingly rare survival of traditional cultures: They are ones created by governmental policies and laws inimical to rights and democratic freedoms—and, in the case of Islamic human rights schemes examined here, by policies and laws that are designed to be implemented by states at the expense of the rights and freedoms of the individual. The way governments of countries treat those they govern should not be ruled off-limits to critical scholarly inquiry, and judging Islamic schemes of human rights by the standards of the international human rights norms that they seek to replace is entirely appropriate.

CHAPTER 2

International and
Islamic Human Rights

International Human Rights: Sources

Even with a focus narrowed to civil and political rights, the range of potential sources regarding international standards for those rights is too vast to permit exhaustive citation and examination in the course of the present study. In part for simplicity's sake, my examination of international human rights will largely leave aside the voluminous academic literature on international human rights, relying instead primarily on principles taken from the so-called International Bill of Human Rights, which will be treated as exemplifying the standards of public international law on civil and political rights.

The International Bill of Human Rights consists of the Universal Declaration of Human Rights (UDHR), of 1948, the International Covenant on Economic, Social, and Cultural Rights (ICESCR), of 1966, and the International Covenant on Civil and Political Rights (ICCPR), also of 1966, along with the Optional Protocol of the latter. The 1966 covenants entered into force in 1976. The universal declaration has, since its adoption by the UN General Assembly, achieved great international renown as an authoritative statement of the modern standards of human rights protections and is the single most influential statement of international human rights principles.

In choosing to rely on the International Bill of Human Rights in the comparisons that will be made here, I do not pretend that there are no controversies about what international human rights entail, nor do I claim that the International Bill of Human Rights is universally acknowledged by legal scholars and philosophers to constitute a perfect summation of human rights norms. Some academic specialists have questioned the authoritativeness of these documents, and they may be criticized for inadequacies and lack of balance.

One should also remember that there are many countries that have refused to ratify one or more of the conventions involved and that a number of Muslim countries have elected not to ratify human rights conventions. Among Middle Eastern Muslim countries not ratifying the ICCPR and the ICESCR, one finds Kuwait, Pakistan, Saudi Arabia, Turkey, and the United Arab Emirates (UAE). On the other hand, such diverse countries as Afghanistan, Egypt, Iran (here it is undoubtedly significant that the issue of Iran's ratification came up prior to the Islamic Revolution), Iraq, Jordan, Libya, Morocco, the Sudan (during 1985–1989, the brief period of democracy between military regimes committed to Islamization), Syria, and Tunisia have ratified the same covenants, and Algeria has become a signatory, indicating its intent to ratify.[1] Acknowledging that there is not full academic or political consensus regarding the authority of individual rights formulations constituting the International Bill of Human Rights, one can nonetheless maintain that they are representative, if perhaps not ultimately definitive, statements of what a broad segment of international opinion believes that human rights entail. In addition, some scholars of human rights would maintain that because of the general recognition of their validity in state practice—in which they are commonly referred to as normative standards—those formulations express principles that have come to be international customary law and, as such, are binding on states regardless of whether they have ratified the individual conventions.

Another reason for this study's use of these international human rights documents is that their formulations of human rights principles are succinct enough to allow easy comparisons with principles in Islamic human rights documents. The broad outlines of the Islamic documents in many instances are clearly inspired by provisions in the International Bill of Human Rights, even though they may differ from the latter in important respects. In particular, the UDHR is more familiar to people in the Middle East than other sources of international human rights law. In contrast, one does not sense that the authors of the Islamic human rights schemes that will be discussed here follow the specialist-oriented academic literature on human rights.

Islamic Human Rights: Sources

The materials by Muslims dealing with the relationship of Islam and human rights are extensive, and only a small fraction of the literature can be covered here. Selected provisions in the international bill will be compared with principles set forth in a number of Islamic human rights schemes and in rights provisions in Islamic constitutions that embody distinctive, Islamic treatments of rights issues. By "Islamic constitutions," I mean constitutions that are purportedly based on Islamic principles, not merely constitutions in force in countries where the inhabitants are predominantly Muslim. The treatment of human rights in Islamic constitutions exemplifies the degree to which the drafters are willing to make the rights provisions in national legal systems conform to international standards. This is critical, because international human rights law relies for its implementation on national laws and institutions; the international standards are meant to serve as models for the schemes of human rights protected under the constitutions and legal systems of the separate countries of the international community.[2]

The works that will be examined in detail have been written by Muslims representing a variety of countries and backgrounds, but all are from the Middle East and North Africa, and the comparisons will not go beyond these regions. In selecting the material to be surveyed, I have emphasized Islamic approaches to human rights that have been presented by major Islamic institutions and influential figures as well as ones adopted by governments. The exception is Sultanhussein Tabandeh, who is a relatively minor figure but who is interesting because of his candor and his detailed responses to various UDHR provisions. The material selected represents views of Muslims from both the Sunni and Shi'i traditions, from inside and outside governments, and from several important countries. The range of material surveyed is, therefore, broad enough to permit some generalizations to be made.

A word needs to be said at this point about the way different rights positions will be characterized. It will be necessary to distinguish between the views of Muslims who favor and those who oppose adherence to international human rights standards. It is not the purpose of this study to catalogue exhaustively the political divisions among different factions of Muslim opinion, but only to contrast the views of Muslims who fall on one or the other side of the line in this dispute. For purposes of this study, only two categories need to be designated.

Here and throughout, the terms *liberal* and *conservative* will be used in their dictionary senses, "liberal" denoting views favoring reform and progress toward democracy, and "conservative" denoting views calling for the preservation of established institutions and opposing any changes in these. Here liberal Muslims are those who tend to embrace international human rights norms, and conservative Muslims are those who oppose democratization, resisting human rights insofar as they appear to threaten the established order, including premodern Islamic institutions. These are the classifications that are most useful for characterizing Muslims' attitudes toward human rights. Obviously, many finer distinctions between different political groupings could be drawn, but they would only burden a work that is already heavily weighted down by discussions of very specific distinctions.

One of the documents assessed will be *A Muslim Commentary on the Universal Declaration of Human Rights,* by Sultanhussein Tabandeh (Sultan Hussain Tabanda), a conservative. His pamphlet was originally published in Persian in 1966, appearing in an English translation in 1970. Tabandeh, who was born in northeastern Iran in 1914, inherited the leadership of the Ni'matullahi Sufi order, a mystical brotherhood affiliated with Twelver Shi'i Islam. He was educated at Tehran University and Tehran Teachers' Training College and traveled widely in the Muslim world and also in Europe. He presented his commentary on human rights to the representatives of Muslim countries who attended the 1968 Tehran International Conference on Human Rights. His purpose was to advise them of the positions they should adopt vis-à-vis various provisions in the UDHR, which he had analyzed in terms of the requirements of Islamic law. In his comments, one sees the reactions of an Iranian Shi'i leader of a traditional religious order. He is much more outspoken in his criticisms of international human rights and his defenses of premodern doctrines than are many of his fellow conservatives.

A pamphlet entitled *Human Rights in Islam,* by the internationally prominent conservative Sunni religious leader from the subcontinent, Abu'l A'la Mawdudi, will also be covered. The centerpiece of the pamphlet, first published in 1976, is an English translation of a talk presented by Mawdudi in 1975 in Lahore, Pakistan. In 1941 Mawdudi founded a political group, Jama'at-i-Islami, whose members are committed to the reinstatement of Islamic law and the establishment of an Islamic state. The group has been active in politics in Pakistan. In addition to leading political campaigns on behalf of Islamization, Mawdudi wrote extensively on the application of Islam to contemporary problems, and his work was widely disseminated in translations, especially in the Arab world. He was honored in places like Saudi Arabia, where there is strong official support for the conservative line he promulgated. In recognition of what were said to be his outstanding services to Islam, he was accorded the King Faisal Prize. He died in 1979. Lacking a traditional religious education and standing among highly trained religious scholars, Mawdudi had nonetheless been able to present his ideas in a way that could reach a popular audience, which shared his bitter resentment of Western power and the West's dismissal of Islamic civilization as backward. He adopted a combative stance vis-à-vis the West, castigating Western society and culture for its decadence and materialism and arguing that Islamic civilization was far superior to its Western counterpart. His human rights pamphlet embodies the attitudes that informed his work generally.

The 1981 Universal Islamic Declaration of Human Rights (UIDHR) will be discussed as well. It was prepared by people from countries like Egypt, Pakistan, and Saudi Arabia under the auspices of the Islamic Council, a private, London-based organization affiliated with the Muslim World League, an international, nongovernmental organization that tends to represent the interests and views of conservative Muslims. The declaration was presented with great public fanfare to the United Nations Educational, Scientific and Cultural Organization (UNESCO) in Paris, in a ceremony attended by figures such as Ahmad Ben Bella and Mukhtar Ould Daddah, respectively the former leaders of Algeria and Mauritania, Prince Muhammad al-Faisal of Saudi Arabia, and an adviser of President Zia of Pakistan. In a casual reading, the English version of the UIDHR seems to be closely modeled after the UDHR, but upon closer examination many of the similarities turn out to be misleading. In addition, the English version diverges from the Arabic version at many points. Both versions of the UIDHR will be examined here. As I will show, many of the formulations in the UIDHR are obscure or ambiguous. Although the UIDHR is generally representative of conservative Muslim opinion, the inconsistencies and equivocation in the UIDHR suggest that its authors may not have been able to achieve a consensus among themselves about how Islamic human rights norms should be formulated.

There will be review of the rights provisions in the "Draft of the Islamic Constitution" devised by the Islamic Research Academy of Cairo, which is affiliated with al-Azhar University, the most internationally prestigious institution of higher education in Sunni Islam, and a center of conservative Islamic thought. This draft constitution, published in 1979 in Volume 51 of the Azhar journal, *Majallat al-Azhar,* appears to represent an official position of that institution as to what rights should be recognized in a political system based on Sunni Islamic principles. Published at the time that the Iranian Constitution was receiving much attention and Iran's Shi'i leadership was attracting a following in the Sunni world, the Azhar draft may be seen as a Sunni response to the political repercussions of the Iranian Revolution and an effort to demonstrate that Sunni Islam was not bereft of resources to fashion a constitution for a modern government.

The rights provisions in the 1979 Iranian Constitution, which, according to its Preamble, "is based upon Islamic principles," will be assessed. To date, Iran is the only country to have completely rewritten its constitution with the ostensible aim of bringing it into conformity with the requirements of Islamic law. The Iranian Constitution represents one attempt to resolve the question of what rights provisions should be included in a political system based on Twelver Shi'i Islam, and it may be usefully contrasted with the Azhar draft of an Islamic constitution.

The 1979 Iranian Constitution is a document that, unlike the other documents discussed here, has actual legal effect. It replaced Iran's first constitution, which was drawn up in 1906–1907. Iran's first constitution had emerged out of a struggle between secular and clerical forces, laypersons and clerics who supported the campaign to limit the powers of the shah by a constitution and laypersons and clerics who upheld a traditional autocratic system of government. The disagreements were not worked out, and the constitution that was adopted embodied compromises that left neither side satisfied.[3] The 1979 constitution did not signify a new beginning for constitutionalism but only an Islamic overlay resting on features of a constitutionalism that had become embedded in Iranian legal culture over many decades and that was heavily indebted to French and U.S. models.

Although there were many elements in Iran's first constitution that seemed to recognize the supremacy of Islamic law, in actual practice, Iran's legal culture became increasingly secularized over the decades following the adoption of the constitution. Objections by Iran's clerics to the displacement of *shari'a* law were largely ignored. After the Iranian Revolution of 1978–1979, a draft constitution was prepared in spring 1979. Like the 1906–1907 constitution, it contained both secular and Islamic principles, but it showed far less deference to the ideas and wishes of conservative clerics than the constitution that was subsequently adopted. The first draft was discarded, and in August 1979 a constituent assembly with a majority consisting of conservative Shi'i clerics was chosen to draft a new constitution in elections that were denounced as unfair by secular political groups. The new constitution, approved by a referendum in December 1979, retained some features of the earlier draft but gave much greater scope for the application of Islamic law and significantly enhanced the political power of the Shi'i clergy over the government and the legal system. Given the hostility of Ayatollah Khomeini to human rights, it is not surprising that the final text of the constitution, though referring to human rights in Article 20, did not include any endorsement of the UDHR. Secular groups had earlier called for the incorporation of the UDHR in the constitution.[4] The current Iranian constitution is, therefore, a product of a long history of struggle to define what role Islamic law and the clergy should play in the Iranian system of government. It perpetuates rather than resolves old tensions, and the revisions made in the July 1989 amendments are unlikely to resolve the quarrels about what the constitution should provide.

Aspects of a number of other publications dealing with how Islam relates to human rights will also be discussed for the purpose of comparison. It will be stressed throughout this study that the fact that the Islamic human rights schemes presented here are referred to as "Islamic" does not imply that the principles involved represent definitive statements of where Islamic doctrine stands on rights issues or that all or even a majority of the world's 1 billion Muslims would endorse them. Human rights and the question of how human rights protections relate to the Islamic tradition remain contested issues in the Muslim world; in contrast to the international documents that I cite here, there exist no Islamic human rights documents that enjoy a broad consensus.

The Islamic human rights documents have been selected for examination not because they are definitive but because they represent a middle ground between two sharply opposed positions that will also occasionally be referred to. At the extremes, there are Muslims who maintain that Islam embraces international human rights standards, and, opposed to them, there are Muslims who claim that these standards are completely alien to and incompatible with Islam and Islamic law. The Muslims in the middle tend to advocate compromise positions asserting that Islam does accept human rights—as long as the necessary Islamic rules and concepts are integrated in the rights to bring them in conformity with Islamic standards. The result is a melange—and often a very awkward one—of international law principles with rules and concepts that are taken from the Islamic legal heritage or that are presented as having Islamic pedigrees.

While it must be borne in mind that there are at the same time Muslims who see no conflicts between their faith and international human rights norms and others who believe that the two are irreconcilable, it is the literature corresponding to the compromise position that offers the most interesting material for comparison with international legal standards. It provides a fascinating illustration of what happens when two very dissimilar cultural legacies combine, producing a blend of legal principles that has no historic antecedent. As it happens, the compromise view that Islam tolerates rights in some form but imposes conditions and restrictions on international human rights is also one that has great current political significance. Regimes undertaking Islamization programs have utilized the notion that unfettered rights are incompatible with Islam to justify restrictions that they impose on rights and freedoms. Three Islamization programs will now be reviewed to demonstrate the contemporary political relevance of Islamic human rights schemes.

Islamization Programs and Human Rights: An Overview

Prior to a consideration of the way that the governments of Iran, Pakistan, and the Sudan have treated rights questions while they were pursuing Islamization programs, a brief review of some patterns of governmental responses to demands for Islamization and governmental initiatives to sponsor Islamization measures is in order. People outside the Muslim world tend to lose sight of the fact that measures to implement Islamic law and ideology in given countries cannot in the nature of things be severed from local political realities. A major concern of the regimes in Muslim countries, where adherence to democratic principles has been only sporadic, is justifying their staying in power and denying legitimacy to the programs of opponents and critics. When one reviews the situations in which Islamization policies have been contested, one is reminded of the variety of contexts in which Islamization campaigns can arise.

The autocratic and repressive regime of the late shah of Iran, a secular monarch who had little support outside military circles, belatedly discovered the political potency of Islam as a means of mobilizing political protest and was ultimately destroyed in Iran's Islamic Revolution. Subsequently Islamization was introduced in Iran under the auspices of the clerical faction that ultimately wrested control over the apparatus of government from secular elements and liberal Muslims in the revolutionary forces, whose views on law and justice were largely overridden and rejected. Iran's Islamization, coming in the wake of a major revolutionary upheaval and being controlled by conservative clerics, was naturally more far-reaching and more representative of clerical attitudes than the Islamization offered by basically secular governments. Although the Iranian model of Islamization is criticized and rejected by many Muslims, the Iranian experience of an originally popular Islamic Revolution being captured by conservative forces has implications for other countries.

Popular demands for Islamization in some countries have led to strong countermeasures by military dictators. Leaders like Saddam Hussain in Iraq and Hafez al-Asad in Syria have successfully crushed— by means of brutal repression and executions—opposition groups calling for Islamization. In Afghanistan the Marxist regimes in Kabul have been seriously threatened by *mujahidin* organizations in the resistance movement, which have fought for years a bitter civil war to drive out

Russian forces, overthrow a regime identified with atheism, and reimpose Islamic law.

Lacking legitimacy, some military dictators have been concerned about increasing their prestige and popularity by making concessions to the genuine popular sentiment favoring the idea of revival of Islamic law. This was the design of military governments of Pakistan in 1979 and the Sudan in 1983, which adopted ambitious Islamization programs that led to the official enactment of various Islamic laws as positive law.

For different reasons, relatively democratic regimes have felt that, in order to win the support of groups calling for reinstating Islam, it was politically expedient to enact laws that could placate them. The degree of movement toward Islamization in countries like Egypt and Kuwait has been uneven, but it has tended to be moderated by the relatively more democratic political processes in the societies. These piecemeal and inconclusive Islamization measures will not be treated here.

I shall analyze how in Iran, Pakistan, and the Sudan Islamization programs were used by the respective governments to justify denials of freedoms and to defend policies of either suspending or rewriting constitutional rights guarantees. After consideration of these examples, one can ask whether the dismantling of rights protections in the course of these programs is somehow attributable to factors inherent in the Islamic tradition or to other causes. The possibility must be borne in mind that Islamization is becoming associated with practices and policies shaped by political forces—quite separate from Islam as a religion—reflecting the mundane political interests of groups that have much to lose by the advance of freedom and democracy in the Muslim world. A skeptic could propose that official Islamization policy is no more than a strategy adopted by beleaguered elites in an attempt to trump growing Muslim demands for democratization and human rights. These elites may be making cynical appeals to divine authority as the rationale for oppressive, exploitative rule and a regime of inequality and discrimination.

A number of questions are necessarily raised that call for the comparison of Islamization schemes and Islamic teachings. Do the Islamic rationales for the curbs that governments have placed on rights have a real warrant in Islamic doctrine? Or do these official Islamization measures involve distortions of Islamic doctrines? Are there actual or potential rights protections in Islamic law, so that the rights abuses perpetrated under the rubric of Islamization could be said to constitute a betrayal of Islamic principles and values?

The burgeoning human rights movement in the Muslim world has already been mentioned. As the enthusiastic response to human rights

ideas at the grass-roots level has demonstrated, many Muslims are
convinced that Islam constitutes no barrier to their insisting on the
observance of international human rights norms. Muslims have also
offered schemes for harmonizing international human rights norms with
Islam, taking the position that Islam requires scrupulous respect for
rights, so that violations of international human rights standards also
violate Islamic law.[5] Muslims have been energetic in their public con-
demnations of the human rights abuses perpetrated in the name of
Islamization in Iran, Pakistan, and the Sudan. Even Muslims who do
not use the terminology of modern human rights in their protests over
rights denials often reveal that they believe that justice and respect for
human life and dignity are such central principles of Islamic law and
its attendant values that a legal system that fails to honor these cannot
be in conformity with Islamic requirements. Muslims who are appalled
by the rights violations perpetrated in the course of Islamization programs include prominent Islamic clerics who have denounced oppressive
governmental measures or curbs on rights undertaken in the name of
Islam.[6]

The denials of rights by the postrevolutionary Iranian government
in 1980 were vigorously condemned by the late Ayatollah Taleghani,
one of Iran's most distinguished clerics and a religious leader whose
ideas were particularly popular among younger, left-leaning Iranians.
He was obviously deeply troubled by the Khomeini regime's constantly
invoking Islam as it sought to cut down on freedoms, when, in his
view, the protection of freedom was a central concern of Islam. He
argued:

> The most dangerous of all forms of oppression are laws and restrictions
> forcibly imposed on people in the name of religion. This is what the
> Monks, through collaboration with the ruling classes, did with all the
> people in the name of religion. This is the most dangerous of all impo-
> sitions, because that which is not from God is thrust upon the people to
> enslave and suppress them and prevent them from evolving, depriving
> them of the right to protest, criticise and be free. These very chains and
> shackles are the ones which the Prophet [Muhammad] came to destroy.
> Islam is an invitation to peace and freedom. Let us keep aside oppor-
> tunism, group interests, forcible imposition of ideas and, God forbid,
> dictatorships under the cover of religion. [Let us] raise our voices with
> the toiling, oppressed, and deprived masses. Islam as we know it, the
> Islam which originates from the Quran and the traditions of Prophet,
> does not restrict freedom. Any group that wants to restrict people's
> freedom, [the freedom] to criticise, protest, discuss and debate, does not
> comprehend Islam.

Islam is the religion of freedom. Its goal is people's liberation. If a religion aims at liberating people from all forms of bondage, it cannot itself be made a chain for keeping people in bondage. . . . The reactionaries are trying to distort the concept of freedom by equating it with a decadent version [used by] the bourgeoisie in the West, in order to enslave the masses. In the name of religion [they wish to] further the interest of their own class by enslaving people in exploitative chains.[7]

From this one sees that skeptical, critical assessments of the Islamic warrants for rights violations perpetrated in the course of Islamization programs have not come only from Western observers but also from Muslims immersed in the Islamic tradition and committed to honoring it. The Ayatollah Taleghani saw Islam as a vehicle of liberation that is inherently inimical to restrictions on personal freedoms. He characterized the use of religion under the Khomeini regime to stifle freedoms as very dangerous, associating such use not with Islamic tradition but with the Christian church ("the Monks"). According to Taleghani, the mission of Islam is one of freeing people from the enslavement that results from the alliance of religion and the ruling classes. Far from concurring with the official view that the pursuit of Islamization justified curbs on freedom, Taleghani charged that the ruling classes in Iran were attempting to further their own interests by using a self-serving definition of "Islam" to justify enslaving and exploiting the poor. That is, in the view of this eminent Shi'i cleric, Iran's postrevolutionary ruling elite was distorting Islamic doctrine for its personal advantage by pretending that Islam denies people freedom, whereas, in reality, Islam should be recognized as the guarantor of freedoms. Although Taleghani did not use the language of human rights or appeal to international law in his denunciation of oppression, his understanding of Islam is one that could encompass guarantees of civil and political freedoms like those in international law. In appealing for observance of the values of Islam, he was effectively calling for respect for human rights and treating Islam and human rights as natural allies.

At the other end of the spectrum, particularly among Muslims whose political sympathies are conservative, one finds Muslims who defend Islamization programs in countries like Iran, Pakistan, and the Sudan. Such Muslims argue that the regimes deserve praise for seeking to implement Islamic law and that obedience to Islamic law must take precedence over all other considerations. Attacks on the human rights records of these countries are disparaged by these people as reflecting alien, Western values. In their view, the latter are incompatible with Islam, and Muslims must reject them in order to implement an Islamic system of law and government.

Thus, other Iranian clerics offer scornful denunciations of human rights. Ayatollah Khomeini asserted, "What they call human rights is nothing but a collection of corrupt rules worked out by Zionists to destroy all true religions"; and President Ali Khamene'i of Iran stated: "When we want to find out what is right and what is wrong, we do not go the United Nations; we go to the Holy Koran. . . . For us the Universal Declaration of Human Rights is nothing but a collection of mumbo-jumbo by disciples of Satan."[8]

In summary, contemporary Muslim opinion is far too divided to provide an outside observer with the basis for a conclusion about whether the denials of rights that are occurring due to Islamization programs rest on Islamic authority. It is not appropriate for an outsider to interfere in an internal doctrinal debate among Muslims. It is, however, legitimate for an observer to investigate what the range of opinion among contemporary Muslims is, to present critical appraisals of different positions that have been presented as deriving from Islamic tenets, and to evaluate the significance of various positions that have been taken on the relationship of Islam and human rights. I will attempt such examination here.

A Review of Islamization Programs in Pakistan, Iran, and the Sudan

In 1979, two years after he staged a coup and became president of Pakistan, Zia launched an official Islamization campaign, which he pursued until his death in 1988. After the Islamic Revolution of 1978–1979 Iran began Islamization, as did the Sudan in 1983–1985, during the last years of President Ja'far Nimeiri's rule, and again after the military coup of June 1989. In these countries Islamization was theoretically designed to bring the law and the administration of justice into conformity with the standards of the *shari'a,* or Islamic law. Many rules taken from the premodern *shari'a* or at least ostensibly inspired by *shari'a* principles were enacted into law, and the previous, Western standards were abandoned.

Not only substantive laws but also courts and enforcement practices were altered to reflect what were officially described as Islamic requirements. The Western-influenced bar and judiciary were regarded as roadblocks in the way of implementation of Islamic law. In all three countries there was a pattern of replacing judges with Western-style legal training by Islamic clerics or persons with traditional Islamic educations. Members of the bar in these countries, who had the outlook of highly trained professionals and who were generally influenced by liberal Western values, found it difficult, if not impossible, to fulfill their professional responsibilities in the changed circumstances, as respect for the rule of law dwindled and justice became politicized. Although modern legal institutions were under siege in all three countries, it was in Iran that Islamization had the most drastic impact on the legal profession. After sharply curtailing the powers of lawyers in reaction to their criticisms of mounting political repression and the increasingly arbitrary regime of justice, the Iranian authorities finally took measures in 1981–1982 to dismantle and altogether destroy Iran's bar association.

All in all, the systemic changes made under the rubric of Islamization in Pakistan, Iran, and the Sudan did much to eliminate due process, to erode the independence of the judiciary, to place legal proceedings under the control of political leaders, and to convert courts into instruments of repression and intimidation. Thus, in all three countries Islamization became associated with a decline in the quality of the administration of justice. The deterioration was particularly noticeable in Pakistan and the Sudan, where the legal systems had previously upheld a higher standard of justice than was common in developing societies.

The pursuit of Islamization in Iran, Pakistan, and the Sudan coincided with the emergence of distinctive patterns of human rights violations. Of course, there had been human rights violations in these countries prior to Islamization, but that program brought a new dimension to the violations. In Iran, for example, the human rights violations that followed the revolution were probably not more heinous than the abuses perpetrated under the late Shah Mohammed Reza Pahlavi, but often the new Islamic rationales for government conduct correlated with shifts in the patterns of violations, the targeting of new groups for persecution, and reorientation of repressive tactics. The seriousness of the patterns of human rights violations that accompanied the Islamization programs has been extensively documented by many reputable observers and by international organizations and institutions concerned with the protection of human rights.[9]

In general, the regimes reacted defensively when they were accused of violating human rights, and Iran has showed particular reluctance to allow international observers to monitor the operations of its system of justice, agreeing only after a decade of resistance to admit one group of UN observers in 1989.[10] This suggests that by and large the leaders, despite their assertions of confidence in the authority of the Islamization schemes even where these lead to human rights violations, regard international human rights as normative and fear criticism for violating them. In some cases, however, information establishing that government conduct constituting egregious human rights violations had taken place

was proudly disseminated by the governments involved as an indication
of the seriousness of their commitment to applying Islamic law. This
was, for example, the case in January 1985 when the Nimeiri regime
convicted Mahmud Muhammad Taha of heresy and chose to publicize
both the heresy trial and his subsequent execution by hanging, and in
February 1989 when Khomeini ordered death squads to murder Salman
Rushdie as a heretic. Such instances were exceptional.

The evidence indicates that the governments of Iran, Pakistan, and
the Sudan were conscious that the denials of rights under their Islamization programs would not only earn them criticism from outsiders
for violating international law but also could lead to embarrassing
charges by domestic critics that they were not even abiding by locally
applicable constitutional principles. Therefore, the governments involved
had to devise strategies for obviating constitutional challenges that could
undermine the authority of their Islamization measures. It is striking
that in all three countries, the constraints of Islamization were invoked
to justify the respective governments' tampering with constitutional
rights. While all three seem to have been anxious to avoid direct
challenges to their Islamization measures based on domestic constitutional rights provisions, they took different tacks in dealing with this
potential problem, either rewriting constitutional rights provisions or
suspending them.

In Iran, the basic approach was to discard the old constitution and
to rewrite constitutional rights provisions, inserting a number of vague
Islamic qualifications. Simply by invoking the latter, the government
was able to override rights protections at will. These Islamic qualifications will be discussed in greater detail in Chapters 4–8. Although
the addition of qualifications to rights provisions did not entirely eliminate problems of conflicts between the government's conduct and certain provisions of the Iranian Constitution, it provided sweeping constitutional justifications for infringing on rights and denying freedoms.
Article 4 of the Iranian Constitution, quoted here, illustrates what
Islamization meant for Iran's rights guarantees:

> All civil, penal, financial, economic, administrative, cultural, military,
> political laws and regulations, as well as any other laws or regulations,
> should be based on Islamic principles. This principle will in general
> prevail over all of the principles of the constitution, and other laws and
> regulations as well. Any judgment in regard to this will be made by the
> clerical members of the Council of Guardians.[11]

The article establishes that Islamic principles are to be considered not
only superior to ordinary laws but also as overriding provisions in the

constitution itself. As this article shows, it will be Islamic principles as determined by Islamic clerics (who, according to Article 110, are to be appointed by Iran's religious leader in his capacity as the leading jurist) that constitute the supreme law in Iran. In consequence, not even constitutional rights guarantees can have force should clerics, and in the Iranian context this inevitably means ones allied with the government, decide that those guarantees are not based on Islamic principles. In Iran, where in the wake of the revolution conservative Islamic clerics took control of the government with a professed mission to effectuate Islamic justice and where Islamic qualifications were formally placed on rights, the connection between the regime's Islamization policies and the denials of human rights that ensued was often a direct and very obvious one.

In the Sudan and Pakistan the approach taken was different. Constitutional rights provisions were suspended during the respective Islamization programs, although the suspension turned out to be in effect much longer in Pakistan than it was in the Sudan under Nimeiri, where a popular revolution in 1985 cut short the local Islamization experiment. The connection between Islamization and the human rights violations perpetrated by the Sudanese and Pakistani regimes is more complicated than in the case of Iran, and only a few aspects can be described here.

President Ja'far Nimeiri ruled the Sudan after seizing power in May 1969. Originally a leftist, he decided in 1983 to try to consolidate his increasingly unpopular regime by cementing an alliance with the Sudanese contingent of the conservative Muslim Brothers and inaugurated an ambitious but haphazard Islamization program. As he pressed in 1984 to overcome the widespread resistance to the program, Nimeiri sought to rewrite the Sudanese Constitution. He was at that time eager to have himself proclaimed "imam" of the Sudan, meaning in this context that he would have authority as the supreme political and religious leader in the country. All indications are that any modifications of the constitution that would have emerged under his auspices would have provided "Islamic" rationales for concentrating all power in his hands and eliminating any human rights protections that stood in the way of achieving his objectives. However, there was such determined political opposition to Nimeiri's constitutional project that he was unable to carry it out. Instead, in order to press ahead with his Islamization program while avoiding charges that government measures were in violation of the constitution, he had to rely on his declaration of a state of emergency on April 29, 1984, which allowed him to suspend all constitutional rights provisions and to grant extraordinary powers to the police and the military.[12]

The state of emergency in the Sudan was officially lifted in autumn 1984 after the United States exerted intense diplomatic pressure. Nimeiri, whose tottering government depended in its final years on U.S. aid, was ill equipped to resist demands for a formal end to the emergency. Thus, there was a period from late 1984 to early 1985 before Nimeiri's regime was finally toppled by a popular revolution in April 1985 when constitutional guarantees were theoretically again in force.

Despite the fact that one cannot say that the period of the formal state of emergency suspending constitutional rights provisions in the Sudan exactly coincided with the dates of the Islamization program, it is clear that in practice these rights were suspended from the date that the state of emergency was declared until Nimeiri's overthrow and that they were suspended to eliminate legal obstacles to carrying out the Islamization program. The state of emergency itself was declared by Nimeiri because of his frustration over the opposition to his Islamization policies and as part of an angry reaction to the Sudanese judges' and lawyers' opposition. As he pushed forward his Islamization program during the state of emergency, Nimeiri gave judicial appointments to many persons affiliated with conservative Islamic movements and with religious rather than secular legal training. This was designed to ensure that judges would henceforth be more amenable to serving the goals of his program and less concerned with respect for conventional legal constraints such as constitutional rights protections and due process.

It was Nimeiri himself who associated the state of emergency with the protection of Islam, insisting in his proclamation speech that it was needed to preserve Islam from its enemies and identifying his foes as "Satan and his supporters."[13] He claimed that the latter were "united to bring down the lofty banners of Islam," but that they would find in their path "very strong men who are determined to safeguard Islam and its laws . . . men who worship God day and night." He thus tried to portray himself as a deeply pious Muslim whose decision to declare the state of emergency had been motivated by a concern for protecting the Islamic religion from its enemies. He noted that there were corrupt persons who "exploited the situation by challenging the law and attacking the Islamic Shari'ah."[14] While Nimeiri expressed concern lest his "faithful sons" should be defeated by "pursuing Satan and his men," he offered the following assurance: "Plots have increased our faith. We shall be more determined and strong-willed. In view of this faith, in order to protect our faith and our homeland from the plotters and from the tampering of satan . . . and in view of my commitment to my constitutional responsibilities, I have issued Republican Decree No.

258 for the year of 1984 proclaiming a state of emergency in all parts of the country."[15]

Despite Nimeiri's invocation of his constitutional responsibilities in connection with the declaration of the state of emergency, he could not point to anything in the Sudanese Constitution that justified the suspension of rights protections to facilitate the imposition of a religious law on a resisting population. The reference to the constitution suggests, however, a residual concern on Nimeiri's part lest he be accused of acting in violation of constitutional tenets.

A few months later at a major international conference in Khartoum on the Sudan's Islamization program, Nimeiri again made statements associating the state of emergency with the program. He asserted that the state of emergency had been declared "not to fight an incoming enemy or to resist an external military attack but to protect a believing society against those who infiltrate it and transgress against its values, morals and security."[16]

A systematic account of the consequences of Nimeiri's Islamization program for human rights in the Sudan has yet to be produced. The evidence available so far suggests that the harshest consequences of the suspension of rights provisions were in the area of criminal justice, where the regime implemented its version of Islamic criminal law with particular zeal, but human rights in the area of criminal justice lie outside the scope of this study. However, there were also consequences in the areas of civil and political rights, some of which will be considered in what follows. The critical point here is that Sudanese Islamization was directly associated with the suspension of human rights protections guaranteed in the Sudanese Constitution.

After Nimeiri's overthrow and a period of interim rule by a benevolent caretaker military regime, during which the 1973 Sudanese Constitution was replaced by an interim constitution,[17] the Sudan reverted to a free, democratic system in April 1986. As moves were afoot in spring 1989 to abrogate Nimeiri's Islamic laws, military leaders allied with the Islamic fundamentalists in the National Islamic Front staged a coup on June 30, which resulted in the installation in July 1989 of a military dictatorship committed to Islamization. This regime promptly abrogated the interim constitution and suspended all the rights and freedoms that the Sudanese had enjoyed in the brief period of democracy. Mass arrests of politically active Sudanese ensued, human rights activists were jailed, political parties were suppressed, harsh censorship was imposed, and critics of Islamic fundamentalism in government employment found themselves dismissed from their jobs. Again, oppressive military government and systematic denials of rights and freedoms were associated with governmental support for Islamization.

There are intriguing similarities between the legal situation in the Sudan under Nimeiri and in Pakistan in the period 1977–1988. President Mohammad Zia ul-Haq, after overthrowing the elected government of President Zulfikar Ali Bhutto in a coup in July 1977, ruled Pakistan as a military dictator until his death in a plane crash in August 1988. President Zia declared martial law after seizing power, and it remained in force until December 1985. One may speculate that U.S. pressures forced Zia to announce a formal end to martial law. U.S. military and financial support were important props for his regime, and it was embarrassing for the United States to be supplying aid to a leader whose lack of sympathy for democratic ideals was evidenced by the protracted regime of martial law. However, the formal termination of martial law in 1985 did not mean an end to the dominance of the military over Pakistan's political life, nor did it mean in practice a full restoration of constitutional guarantees of fundamental rights, even though these were officially revived when martial law ended.

In Pakistan, as in the Sudan, one sees a coincidence of suspension of constitutional rights and pursuit of Islamization. The relationship between the imposition of martial law, the suspension of fundamental rights, and the implementation of the Islamization program has been documented.[18]

President Zia's reliance on a suspension of constitutional rights may be connected to the fact that in Pakistan, as in the Sudan, a project for drafting an Islamic constitution eventually came to naught. Although Zia's government encouraged proposals for rewriting the existing 1973 constitution to make it more Islamic, it appears Zia found the question of what constitutes an Islamic constitution to be so contentious and divisive that he decided to abandon the project. Had it been pursued, given President Zia's dictatorial style, it is probable that Islamic qualifications would have been placed on constitutional rights provisions, substantially reducing the protections that they afforded. It would then have ceased to be necessary to suspend constitutional rights, since the rights themselves would have become eviscerated, as they were in the rewritten Iranian Constitution.

Lacking any political base of his own, Zia was in great need of something to legitimize his power. He used his commitment to pursue Islamization as the justification for his retention of dictatorial powers and the suspension of constitutional rights. In a major address given in 1983, while all fundamental constitutional rights were formally suspended, Zia analogized his position as chief martial law administrator to that of a traditional prince, or *amir.*[19] Like Nimeiri, in assuming the role of the pious leader who was seeking to apply Islamic law, Zia indicated that opposition would not be tolerated:

One basic point that emerges from a study of the Quranic verses and the Prophet's sayings . . . is that as long as the Amir or the head of State . . . abides by the injunctions of Allah and his Prophet (PBUH) ["peace and blessings upon him"] his obedience becomes mandatory for his subjects or the people, irrespective of the personal dislike that someone may harbour for the Amir or any of his actions. . . . Not only in my opinion but also in the opinion of legal experts and scholars, my Government, too, is a constitutional Government, which has been acting upon the tenets of Islam. . . . We are . . . devout Muslims. I concede, and I am proud of it, that the present Government is a military Government.[20]

Here one sees Zia's dedication to Islam offered as the rationale for a one-man dictatorship. In fact, Zia's position goes back to premodern Islamic thought, in which there was considerable support for the proposition that Muslims should obey persons in authority as long as they were not being commanded to engage in conduct that was sinful. One also finds support among contemporary Muslims who are politically conservative for the idea that a government that follows and applies Islamic law must be obeyed. Still, for all his appeals to Islamic loyalties, Zia seems to have been concerned about possible charges that his overthrowing the previous, elected government and his rule by martial law violated the Pakistani Constitution—hence his surprising assertion that his was a "constitutional" government. In this assertion, Zia relied on the fact that his government was acting "upon the tenets of Islam," which, apparently, justified in his mind a military seizure of power and a subsequent military dictatorship. Notwithstanding this claim, "legal experts and scholars" would be hard-pressed to cite a constitutional provision that supported Zia's position. In fact later events proved that Zia was apprehensive that if he ever lost political control, he and his associates would be prosecuted for rules that they had made and acts that they had committed during the period of martial law. In 1985 he had the constitution amended to validate and affirm all the acts and rules of the martial law regime. The fact that he felt the need for a constitutional amendment to shield himself from prosecutions and lawsuits certainly suggests that he himself had serious doubts whether acts under martial law could withstand court challenges and that he thought he would need special immunity to escape civil and criminal liability once martial law had ended.

Islamization had a great impact on the legal system, as Zia tried to consolidate his alliance with Islamic clerics who supported his program by giving them the chance to serve as judges. As a result of his policy, many persons deficient in the conventional professional qualifications but with religious educations were appointed to the judiciary, leading to changes that compromised the integrity and independence of Pakistan's formerly distinguished judiciary.

During his years as Pakistan's military strongman, President Zia cowed his political enemies into submission, using the powers that he enjoyed under martial law to stave off challenges to his unpopular military dictatorship. Despite the execution of Zulfikar Ali Bhutto, the latter's political party, the Pakistan People's party, retained such a wide following that it would have won an overwhelming mandate if it had ever been allowed to contest a completely free election—which Zia repeatedly denied it an opportunity to do. The fact that in the elections held after Zia's death, Benazir Bhutto, Zia's most prominent political foe, was able to do well enough to become prime minister, indicated that Zia's fear of democracy was well founded. Despite the very advantageous circumstances of the elections for the candidate pledged to continue Zia's policies, Nawaz Sharif, the latter was unable to win enough votes to block Bhutto's ambitions to succeed her late father.

The consequences of Islamization programs for human rights in these countries deserve to be carefully considered. To date one cannot point out a single government purporting to be applying Islamic law that has shown any real solicitude for protecting human rights embodied in the local constitution, much less human rights established in international law. On the contrary, the Islamization programs in these countries have meant patterns of disregard for human rights and also the adoption of policies designed to undermine the autonomy of legal institutions that could afford people the opportunity to vindicate these rights. Although only the Iranian government was able to reduce the scope of rights protections by formally subjecting constitutional rights provisions to restrictive Islamic criteria, in all three countries there were patterns of denials of freedoms and serious rights abuses connected to the legal changes effected in the course of official Islamization.

CHAPTER 3

International Human Rights: The Historical Background

The Contribution of Western Civilization

To understand the contemporary problems of accommodating human rights within an Islamic framework, it is necessary to review the development of international human rights concepts. The human rights principles utilized in international law came from the West and are of relatively recent vintage. Although one can find ideas that anticipate human rights concepts in Ancient Greek thought, the articulation of human rights principles—though not labeled as such—came much later. Certainly, the development of the intellectual foundations of human rights was given an impetus by the Renaissance in Europe and by the associated growth of rationalist and humanistic thought, which led to an important turning point in Western intellectual history. This was the abandonment of premodern doctrines of the duties of man and the adoption of the view that the rights of man should be central in political theory.[1] It was during the European Enlightenment that the rights of man became a preoccupation of political philosophy, and it was then that the intellectual groundwork for modern human rights theory was laid.

Eighteenth-century British and French thinkers put forward the precursors of modern human rights ideas and had great influence on the rights provisions in the American Declaration of Independence of 1776, the Virginia Declaration of Rights of 1776, and on the Bill of Rights that was added to the U.S. Constitution in 1791. These, along with the Fourteenth Amendment, of 1868, have in turn had great influence on subsequent rights formulations, as have the concepts of the 1789 *Déclaration des droits de l'homme et du citoyen,* developed at the time of the French Revolution.

Common to the British and French philosophies that contributed to the production of rights doctrines was the idea that the rights of the individual should be of paramount importance in a political system. In a survey of the historical evolution of rights concepts, one scholar has said that the significance of the shift from concern for law to the concern for rights "derives from the fact that the concept of rights is individualistic in the sense that it is a from-the-bottom-up view of morality rather than one from the top down, and from the related fact that it generally expresses claims of a part against the whole."[2]

Long before international human rights law emerged, constitutionalism had been viewed as a means of placing legal limitations on the powers of governments, and the U.S. Constitution and later European constitutions became models that were widely copied elsewhere. Reflecting the fear that state intrusions would harm individuals' rights, constitutional statements of rights were frequently formulated as negative rights: The provisions sought to protect the individual's freedoms from restrictions that states might impose. Thus, for example, the First Amendment to the U.S. Constitution says, "Congress shall make no law . . . ," the Second enjoins that "the right of the people to keep and bear arms, shall not be infringed," the Fourth commands that "the right of the people to be secure . . . shall not be violated," and so on.

Recognizing that individual rights would sometimes need to be curtailed in the public interest or because of extraordinary circumstances, the constitution makers sought to define and restrict the justifications that states could invoke to deprive people of freedoms. The desire to restrict the ability of the state to intervene in the area of freedom afforded the individual was due to an awareness that if excessive qualifications were placed on these freedoms, they could render them nugatory, as the state would no longer be effectively restrained from infringing on individual freedoms.

It was on these Western traditions of individualism, humanism, and rationalism and on legal principles protecting individual rights that twentieth-century international law of human rights ultimately rested. Because of the linkage among individualism, humanism, and rationalism, a rejection of these values would make it difficult to accept human rights.

The Role of the United Nations

Proponents of international human rights espoused the idea that rights should be guaranteed not just in constitutional rights provisions but also by an international law, binding on all nations. After World War II, the United Nations, as the preeminent international organization, took a leading role in formulating rights that had previously been left to domestic legislation. The UN Charter (1945) called for respect for human rights and fundamental freedoms but did not undertake the difficult task of specifying what these entailed. The UDHR, adopted by the General Assembly in 1948, specified the centrality of human rights issues in the mission of the United Nations. Its Preamble called on members to seek to construct a new world order on a sounder basis, one in which "recognition of the inherent dignity and of the equal and inalienable rights of all members of the human family is the foundation of freedom, justice, and peace in the world."

In the decades since its foundation, a major mission of the United Nations has been to secure protection for what came to be known universally as "human rights." Many rights instruments and conventions codifying international human rights norms were subsequently produced under the auspices of the United Nations.[3] A study of the very numerous instruments on international human rights norms reveals that doctrines have developed well beyond the negative rights referred to earlier, now encompassing many affirmative rights that require governments to take measures to meet people's needs, especially in the social and economic spheres. Although the patterns of ratification of international human rights conventions have been uneven and there is much that remains controversial about international law in the area of human rights, on many human rights principles there is a consensus great enough to justify saying that since World War II an international human rights law has come to be part of public international law.

The Role of Islamic Law

Islamic law and Islamic thought have been treated as irrelevant by people involved in the development of international human rights law. A study of serious treatises by recognized specialists on the development of international human rights law will not reveal claims on behalf of the possibility of Islamic inspiration for international human rights law or its historical antecedents.

One person who has written extensively on Islam but is not a specialist in international law has suggested that there may have been indirect Islamic influences on the early stages of the development of international law itself.[4] If this had been so, there might have been some indirect Islamic influence on the concepts relevant for international human rights law, but the case for an Islamic influence has not yet been documented in a convincing fashion.

In the case of the learned literature on international human rights by academic specialists, there is an indifference to the Islamic tradition: The idea of consulting Islamic law has clearly been dismissed by specialists in the field. This is hardly surprising, because international human rights law is closely linked with the Western legal heritage, within which Islamic law has no normative value and little prestige. Questions of Islamic law are only occasionally mentioned in scholarly writing on international human rights—for the sake of comparison with the international norms or to illustrate the problems of introducing international norms in areas of the developing world. Islamic law is treated, if at all, as a marginal, exotic phenomenon. The critiques offered by Muslims who object to international human rights norms on religious grounds do not seem to have provoked much consternation or interest on the part of Western scholars of the theory of international law, for the latter do not feel that the legitimacy of international law is in any way jeopardized by assertions that it fails to conform to Islamic norms. Underlying all of this is definitely a presumption in favor of the superiority of international law and its associated institutions and a belief in the relative backwardness or inappropriateness of any Islamic models with which they may conflict.

These perspectives of legal scholarship in the area of international law are connected to the relative positions of the West and the Muslim world today. One should recall that Islam is overwhelmingly the religion of Third World countries and that it has been associated with traditional societies and premodern legal institutions. Centuries ago it was Islamic civilization that was more advanced than Western civilization, and Europe borrowed extensively from Islamic culture, but now it is the Western world that has attained the model of civilization that other societies generally seek to emulate. Islamic culture no longer beckons as something to be studied and learned from; it seems at the moment to have little to teach the economically more highly developed and technologically much more advanced societies of the West.

To note that today the West has a legal tradition that is more advanced, more modern, than the Islamic one is not to say that Western law is by its nature superior and that Islamic law is by its nature inferior. Similarly, to indicate the historical lag in the development of human rights concepts in Islamic thought is also not the same thing as ascribing inadequacy to Islam. The lag in Islamic legal development vis-à-vis that of the West, including Muslims' belated attempts to construct Islamic human rights schemes, is the result of a complex interplay of political, economic, and cultural factors in which Islamic doctrines often were as much shaped by their environment as they were forces shaping that environment. Thus, to point out that there are anachronistic features that persist in some versions of Islamic law is not to blame Islam for the relatively underdeveloped state of contemporary Muslim countries.

While this study in no way aims to establish that human rights could not have developed in an Islamic milieu, it relies on the evidence showing that, as a matter of comparative legal history, Islamic human rights concepts developed after Western and international human rights models had been produced. I emphasize this point here in the belief that the reasons for this lag must be taken into account. Without paying adequate attention to the historical circumstances that delayed the production of human rights in Islamic milieus, one cannot account for many of the peculiar features of Islamic human rights schemes. To understand what shaped the Islamic human rights schemes discussed here, it is essential to remember that aspects of Western rights concepts associated with a different level of political and legal development have been superficially imitated without their underlying tenets being fully examined or accepted and that these rights concepts have been combined with features of a legal culture that tends to express the very different values and experience of premodern traditional societies.

The Premodern Islamic Heritage

As we have seen, the individualism characteristic of Western civilization was a fundamental ingredient in the development of human rights concepts. Individualism, however, is not an established feature of Muslim societies or of Islamic culture,[5] nor can one find a historical example of an Islamic school of thought that celebrated individualism as a virtue. Islamic civilization did not create an intellectual climate that was conducive to according priority to the protection of individual rights and freedoms.

Islamic doctrines were historically produced in traditional societies, where one would not expect individualism to be prized, irrespective of the formal religious affiliation of the members of such societies. Non-individualistic and even anti-individualistic attitudes are common in traditional societies, where individuals are situated in a given position in a social context and are seen as components of family or community structures, rather than as autonomous, separate persons. Premodern Islamic thought naturally reflects these traditional values and priorities. When one says that Islamic doctrines formulated by premodern Muslim thinkers tend to be anti-individualistic, one is making an observation that relates more to the historical context in which these ideas were produced than to Islam as a religion. To describe such doctrines is not to say that Islam is inherently incapable of accommodating principles of individualism.[6] But the absence of any heritage of individualism cannot have been helpful for the development of human rights concepts on an Islamic foundation.

The connection of Islamic thought with the values of traditional societies has not, however, meant that Islamic culture lacks features that in the West contributed to the development of human rights. While a philosophy of individualism is absent, the Islamic heritage offers many other philosophical concepts, humanistic values, and moral principles that are well adapted for use in constructing human rights principles. Such values and principles abound even in the premodern Islamic intellectual heritage. However, a variety of historical factors as well as the political ascendancy of an orthodox philosophy and theology that were hostile to humanism and rationalism—and, ultimately, hostile also to the liberal ideals associated with human rights—kept the exponents of such values and principles in a generally weak and defensive position over much of the history of Islamic civilization. If the adherents of rationalist and humanistic currents had had greater political power and influence, such thinkers might have directed Islamic currents in intellectual development in ways that would have created a much more propitious climate for the early emergence of human rights ideas. As it is, despite their minority position, the views of rationalist and humanistic Muslim thinkers are definitely anchored in the Islamic tradition.

One of the most important rationalist currents in Islamic thought was that of the group known as the *mu'tazila,* whose members' influence in the Sunni world reached its zenith in the ninth century, after which they were largely suppressed.[7] Although since the crushing of the *mu'tazila* rationalist thinkers have generally been on the defensive in Muslim milieus, rationalist currents were never entirely extirpated, and in Twelver Shi'i Islam such currents have remained influential. There was an ongoing tension between the rationalist inclinations of Islamic philosophers, many of whom were influenced by Greek philosophy, and the tenets of the dominant philosophy of ethical voluntarism, which strongly deprecated the value of human reason. According to ethical voluntarism, whatever God willed had to be accepted as just and believers were not entitled to use criteria based on the exercise of human reason to make independent judgments about what constituted justice. Some eminent Islamic philosophers, such as al-Farabi (d. 950) and Ibn Rushd (d. 1198) ["Averroës"], came close to saying that it is reason that determines what is right and true and that religion must conform to its dictates.[8] However, Islamic thinkers who too openly espoused the idea of the supremacy of reason over Revelation and called for laws to conform to human notions of justice have always risked being branded heretical by staunch adherents of the view that both Islam and its divine law cannot be evaluated by reference to the tenets of human reason.

Orthodox theologians in Sunni Islam were generally suspicious of human reason, fearing that it would lead Muslims to stray from the truth of Revelation. The prevailing view in the Sunni world, one that the *mu'tazila* unsuccessfully combatted, has been that because of their divine inspiration, *shari'a* laws supercede reason. They embodied God's will and were necessarily just. Human reason, in the orthodox Sunni view, was incapable of ascertaining what was just, and human reason could not be relied on as a guide in fashioning just laws. Instead, the orthodox view was that Muslims should unquestioningly defer to the wisdom of God as expressed in divine Revelation and the example of the Prophet of God, the truth having been set forth in the texts of the religious sources.[9] Given the dominance of this mainstream Islamic view, it naturally became difficult to realize an Islamic version of the Age of Reason. Still today one finds this emphasis on duties. For example, Ayatollah Khomeini insisted that man had no natural rights and that believers were to submit to God's commands.[10]

The ascendancy of ethical voluntarism and the relative weakness of rationalist currents in Sunni Islam had important consequences for Islamic thinkers' view of the relationship of ruler and ruled. Islamic thought tended to stress not the rights of human beings but, rather, their duties to obey God's perfect law, which, by its nature, would achieve the ideal balance in society. Since whatever God willed was ipso facto just, according to the orthodox Islamic view, perfect justice could be achieved if all God's creatures, both ruler and ruled, were obedient to his commands as expressed in Islamic law.

Since the pious Muslim was only supposed to understand and obey the divine law, which entailed abiding by the limits that God had decreed, demands for individual freedoms could sound distinctly subversive to the orthodox mind. Such demands might be taken to suggest that individuals did not consider themselves strictly bound to submit to the dictates of Islamic law and the commands of the authorities charged with its execution or that they were presuming to use their own fallible human reasoning powers to challenge the supremacy of religious teachings.[11]

The aim of Islamic law was to ensure the well-being of the Islamic community, or *umma,* as a whole, in a situation where both the ruler and the ruled were presumed to be motivated to follow the law in order to win divine favor and avoid punishment in Hell. In consequence, *shari'a* doctrines remained highly idealistic and were not developed to provide institutional mechanisms to deal with actual situations where governments disregarded Islamic law and oppressed and exploited their subjects.[12] Scholars of Islamic law did not traditionally address issues like how to curb abuses by the ruler or how to restrict oppressive government practices; rather, they tended to think of the relationship between ruler and ruled solely in terms of this idealized scheme, in which rulers were conceived of as pious Muslims eager to follow God's mandate.[13] No need was perceived to protect the rights of the individual vis-à-vis society or the government—with the single exception of the area of property rights, where the *shari'a* did provide remedies for the individual wrongfully deprived of property by official action.[14]

These features of Islamic orthodoxy inhibited the growth of concepts of individual rights that could be asserted against infringements by governments, while never totally eclipsing other currents in Islamic thought that were hospitable to rights ideals. The rationalist current, though placed on the defensive, survived—notably in the minority Shi'i tradition. One can identify humanistic currents beginning in the early stages of Islamic thought and continuing to the present.[15] In addition, early Islamic thought includes precursors of the idea of political freedom.[16] Concepts of democracy very much like those in modern political systems can be found in the earliest period in Islamic history in the ideas of the Kharijite sect, which broke off from mainstream Islam in the seventh century over the latter's refusal to agree to the Kharijite tenet that the successors to the Prophet Muhammad had to be elected by the community.[17] Adherents of the Kharijite sect have been castigated for their unorthodox views and their literature is not familiar to most other Muslims; if their doctrines became better known and more widely accepted by Muslims than they presently are, it might be said that the Islamic tradition from the earliest stages has included ideas that anticipated some of the democratic principles that underlie modern human rights norms.[18]

One thus sees that the premodern Islamic heritage was rich in ideas. The dominant currents were ones that did not provide a congenial setting for the early development of human rights concepts, but there were from the earliest stages features of the Islamic tradition that offered the potential for successful integration of the premises of modern human rights theory.

Western Ideas of Constitutionalism

Just as there is no unitary Islamic position on the merits of rationalism and humanism, so there is no unanimity on where Islam stands vis-à-vis constitutionalism, an institution closely tied to the development of legal protections for rights. The modern system of human rights, though formulated in international law, must be translated into rights provisions of national constitutions in order to afford individuals effective legal guarantees for the rights involved. The reactions of Muslims to constitutionalism, which clearly came to the Middle East from the West, have historically run the gamut from enthusiastic endorsement to hostile rejection.

The hold of traditional Islamic doctrines, which tended to support the maintenance of the existing order and to stress the duties of the individual rather than individual rights, started to weaken as Muslim elites became familiar with Western ideas of law and governance in the nineteenth century. When Muslims began seeking legal means for curbing despotic and oppressive rulers, they turned not to the Islamic tradition but to Europe for models. Constitutionalist movements, typically inaugurated in the Middle East by adherents of secular nationalist movements—led by Westernized elites and often by Western-trained lawyers—were formed.[19] These people perceived traditional Islamic institutions as unsuitable for Middle Eastern societies that were launching programs of modernization to remedy their military and economic weakness. New ideas about the proper relationship between government and citizens were borrowed from Europe, and establishing the political freedoms of citizens vis-à-vis the state became a major goal. Early constitutionalists moved in the direction of dismantling legally imposed inequalities among citizens, and the nation rather than the religious community became the focus of political loyalty.[20] New concepts of freedom percolated through Muslim societies in the nineteenth and twentieth centuries as Middle Eastern governments began to accede to mounting pressures for adopting constitutional forms of government borrowed from the West.

Muslims who advocated constitutionalism often found that conservative *'ulama,* or learned men of religion, were among their most determined foes. Often the *'ulama* fought constitutionalism in the name of preserving Islam because they were convinced that constitutional principles conflicted with *shari'a* law.[21] The historical pattern of *'ulama* resistance to constitutionalism still persists in Saudi Arabia, the Muslim country where conservative *'ulama* have retained the greatest political influence. Because of their opposition, in Saudi Arabia there still is no constitution, despite decades of efforts by liberal members of the Saudi elite to win acceptance for the notion of constitutionalism.

However, there is no necessary opposition between Islam and constitutionalism, and there were many *'ulama* who worked closely with liberal and reformist movements and who favored the adoption of Western-style constitutions. The famous and extremely influential Islamic reformer Muhammad 'Abduh (d. 1905), who served as grand mufti of Egypt, was one of the latter. An Azhar graduate and Islamic legal scholar, 'Abduh was a strong supporter of Egyptian nationalism and constitutionalism. He and other like-minded clerics saw no fatal conflict between constitutionalism and fidelity to Islam or between political freedoms and the *shari'a.*

In sum, one can say that Islamic clerics were divided and have remained so on the merits of constitutionalism and whether the *shari'a* permits the adoption of constitutional safeguards for individual rights and freedoms like those in the West. As the record of current events shows, Muslims continue to dispute whether constitutionalism is compatible with the *shari'a;* thus there is no unanimity of Islamic opinion on an institution that is of central importance for the protection of human rights.

Muslim Ambivalence on Rights

As has been noted, there is demonstrable support among Muslims for international human rights. Obviously, these supporters find the values and priorities of international human rights congenial. One can presume that the majority of Muslims who embrace human rights have attitudes that are influenced by Islamic teachings and Islamic culture. The phenomenon suggests that currents of Islamic thought must provide conditioning that is favorable for the reception of human rights. But what of those Muslims who accept human rights only warily and with substantial modifications and restrictions? What influences from the Islamic tradition or the associated value system account for their attitudes?

The best evidence of the attitudes of the Muslim conservatives who wrote the Islamic human rights schemes examined here lies in the texts of the schemes and in comments that they and other persons associated with the production of Islamic human rights documents have made. These sources will be analyzed in detail in Chapters 4–8. However, here I will anticipate some of the conclusions of this study and offer some general characterizations of the attitudes that have shaped the distinctive features of Islamic human rights schemes. As will be argued here, the perspectives of these Muslim conservatives vis-à-vis human rights issues are fundamentally at variance with the perspectives of Western scholars writing on international law. An attempt will be made to explain how these perspectives evolved and how the lack of awareness of the significance of these differences in perspectives has in turn affected some features of Islamic human rights schemes.

The indifference of Western scholars of human rights to Islamic law and to criticisms of human rights that are based on Islamic criteria has been mentioned. Unlike those scholars, who regard the international rights model as normative, the authors of Islamic human rights think in terms of two conflicting models simultaneously. Even while promoting Islamic versions of human rights, they seem to regard international human rights as the ultimate norm against which all rights schemes are inevitably measured and from which they fear to be caught deviating. It is important to bear in mind how great Muslim sensitivity is regarding criticisms leveled against the Islamic tradition by Westerners. This accounts for the defensive or apologetic tone that pervades much of the literature that defends distinctive Islamic human rights. On the evidence of the schemes analyzed here, the authors of Islamic human rights principles must feel torn between a desire to protect and perpetuate principles associated with their own tradition—in many respects a premodern one—and anxieties lest that tradition be assessed as backward and deficient if Islam is not shown to possess the kind of "advanced" institutions that have been developed in the West. They thus seek to accentuate the formal resemblance between their schemes and the international ones even where that resemblance is misleading in terms of the actual level of rights protections that they envisage.

The authors' apparent sense of cultural inferiority vis-à-vis Western legal culture is reflected in strained attempts to blur distinctions between Islamic rules and their Western counterparts. They make special efforts to disguise features of the schemes that are most likely to provoke the opprobrium of the West. As the following analysis of Islamic human rights schemes will show, the discussion of rights protections is often kept at a level of idealistic abstraction, and the individual provisions become vague, equivocal, and evasive when the authors address areas where the premodern *shari'a* rules deviate sharply from modern human rights norms.

The desire to produce human rights schemes that appear to correspond to internationally accepted norms leads to a lack of coherence in the thinking behind Islamic human rights schemes. This lack of coherence would not have arisen if the authors were deriving their rights schemes from Islamic models and were using an explicit methodology. One would expect that Islamic rights schemes would be offered only after the authors had first identified the philosophical premises on which an Islamic approach to rights issues should be based and the methodology appropriate for developing coherent interpretations of the Islamic sources. Creating a human rights scheme in this fashion would entail real confidence in the appeal and viability of the Islamic tradition on rights questions and the suitability of the Islamic sources. These authors do not in fact possess that confidence.

As will be illustrated by the analyses of the Islamic human rights schemes, the authors lack any clear theory of what rights should mean in an Islamic context or how to derive their content from the Islamic sources in a consistent and principled fashion. Instead, they merely assemble pastiches of ideas and terminology drawn from two very different cultures without determining a rationale for these combinations or a way to reconcile the conflicting premises underlying them. That is, the deficiencies in the substantive human rights principles are the inevitable by-products of methodological confusion and weaknesses.

It must be emphasized that neither these methodological inadequacies nor the problematical results are necessary consequences of resorting to the Islamic tradition for inspiration. One can see, for example, in the work of Abdullahi an-Na'im the recognition that methodological questions are central to resolving the problem of where Islamic law stands on human rights. Offering a methodology that allows a fresh approach to the Islamic sources, an-Na'im has been able to develop a coherent scheme of human rights principles that is, for those who accept the validity of the proposed methodology, also one that emanates from Islamic values and principles.[22]

The methodological failings that have so affected the quality of the Islamic human rights literature are just another manifestation of problems that afflict contemporary Islamic thought generally and that have seriously hampered its ability to keep pace with modern intellectual and scientific developments. Especially valuable critiques of the unscientific quality of contemporary Islamic thought have been provided by Mohammed Arkoun, a professor at the Sorbonne,[23] and also from a very different angle, by Sadiq Jalal al-'Azm, formerly a professor at the University of Damascus.[24] It is impossible here to do justice to these critiques, but it is necessary to note that the methodological defects decried here reflect a much bigger problem that presently preoccupies some of the most outstanding Muslim intellectuals.

Authors also seem to worry that their Islamic human rights schemes, which emerged after those of international law were firmly established, will be perceived as basically derivative, as the schemes examined here obviously are. When they address the issue of what came first, the authors insist, against the weight of historical evidence, that Islam invented human rights and that the international standards are at best belated attempts to codify rules that Islam introduced in the seventh century. Examples of such assertions can be found in the literature under consideration here and will be discussed also in Chapter 9.[25]

In their attempts to support the contention that human rights originated in the Islamic tradition, the authors cite the very earliest sources. Because they have not worked out an adequate methodology for developing rights from the sources, they rely on strained readings of the Qur'an or the accounts of the custom, or *sunna,* of the Prophet Muhammad to establish the Islamic pedigrees of rights.[26] They cite passages that in their opinion mean that the Islamic sources had established the equivalents of modern human rights. But in the Qur'an and *sunna,* there are only a small number of rules that have any bearing on human rights. By concentrating on the era of the Prophet and projecting human rights principles back to the start of Islamic history, and then jumping more than a millennium to the present, they largely avoid referring to the actual record of Islamic political and intellectual history. However, if one is arguing that the Islamic tradition has a much older set of human rights principles than those developed in the West, it is important to show how Muslims have historically interpreted these sources.

Traditionally, the learned expositions of *shari'a* rules in the juristic treatises have been consulted as the definitive statements of how the Islamic sources should be interpreted to apply to various problems. To answer the question of whether and when human rights concepts were produced in Islamic culture and to discover what Islamic authorities have traditionally believed Islam provided in the area of rights and freedoms, a legal historian would turn first to the great legal treatises and possibly also the writings on theology and philosophy that were produced in the premodern period of Islamic civilization—very approximately, from the ninth century to the fourteenth—and that are still widely consulted as the most prestigious statements of premodern Islamic doctrine. Barring the discovery of a previously unknown document, the search for an authoritative text dealing specifically with the problems that modern Muslims face in the rights area would be in vain. There is really no documented Islamic authority dating from the premodern period that squarely addresses human rights issues or that anticipates the interpretations of the sources that are being advanced by authors of Islamic human rights schemes.

By ignoring many centuries of juristic elaborations of the Qur'an and *sunna,* authors of Islamic human rights schemes are in effect rejecting the bulk of the Islamic legal tradition, which one would expect them to examine and assess before asserting that Islam has a longer tradition of human rights than does Western culture. Even if the principles of Islamic human rights did inhere in the original sources, for purposes of legal history, one would want to know when Muslims first started perceiving the human rights implications of the sources. This, the record shows, did not happen until very recently. Thus, Islamic human rights principles are newly coined ones, much newer than rights principles in the West, which can be traced to the Enlightenment and to a certain extent even before that.

When one abandons the search for express treatments of human rights issues and looks instead in the writings of the premodern jurists, theologians, and philosophers for the elaboration of ideas that would either tend to accommodate human rights principles or to create obstacles to their reception in the Islamic tradition, one finds voluminous relevant material. The problem then becomes that there is too much authority and that it is conflicting in its implications for rights. After one surveys premodern Islamic intellectual history, one realizes that there was no settled Islamic doctrine on rights or protorights in that period, only currents of thought that would create either a more or a less propitious foundation for the assimilation of modern human rights concepts within an Islamic framework.

Exacerbating the dilemma of authors of Islamic human rights schemes as they confront the history of the development of human rights is the motivation for the production of these Islamic human rights schemes. That motivation is connected to the overall pressures for Islamization, entailing the extirpation of Western cultural influences and returning to Islamic models in the area of government, law, social organization, and culture. A prominent feature of Islamization programs has been demands for decolonization in the legal sphere—a rejection of Western legal models that were imposed or borrowed in a period when Muslims were ruled or dominated by Western powers. This legal decolonization in theory should mean the reinstatement of indigenous Islamic models. However, the Islamization programs rest on a false premise: that there exist in all areas Islamic legal countermodels of the Western models that are being repudiated. It is an article of faith to proponents of Islamization that Islam is a comprehensive ideology and scheme of life; they do not acknowledge that there were major gaps in the *shari'a*.[27] But, as noted, there was just such a gap with regard to human rights, whence the dilemma.

Under these circumstances, provisions of Islamic human rights schemes, to serve the ends of Islamization programs, must be given enough distinctively Islamic characteristics to satisfy the demands for Islamic versions of rights. Simultaneously the schemes must stick close enough to Western models to cover essentially the same terrain as the Western schemes that are being rejected.

In general, in areas where the theory of Islamization requires the abandonment of Western law but where there are no juristically elaborated Islamic models to be resuscitated from the premodern tradition, gaps are filled with newly minted Islamic rules. It is inevitable that the latter be in some respects modeled after the Western rules that they are intended to supplant, even if they are given Islamic features and attributed to the Qur'an and *sunna*. The pressures to avoid acknowledging a debt to the Western human rights tradition entails expansive and even strained interpretations of the Islamic sources, which, in reality, provide little express guidance for drafting specific rights provisions except in matters of personal status law.

It is natural, therefore, that some authors of Islamic human rights schemes who have not actually developed an adequate methodology for relating Islam to human rights should feel tempted to rewrite the historical record of the development of human rights in an attempt to cancel out in advance the intellectual debt that they owe to Western culture and to defend their schemes against charges that they are merely imitations of Western human rights concepts. The failure to examine honestly the historical evolution of human rights concepts in the West and to study their philosophical antecedents, combined with the neglect of rights issues in Islamic civilization until recently, often seems to prevent the authors of Islamic human rights from understanding the philosophical underpinnings of international human rights and the meaning of "rights" in modern legal systems. This disregard for preliminary methodological questions accounts, one presumes, for some of the incoherence in the way that the term *rights* is used in these schemes.[28]

The Persistence of Traditional Priorities and Values

For reasons already treated, proponents of Islamic human rights schemes often do not comprehend the philosophical and logical problems involved in integrating schemes of individual rights and freedoms, which are inextricably bound to values emanating from Western civilization, in a matrix of values found in traditional societies and premodern Islamic thought, values that the proponents of Islamic human rights schemes are trying to preserve. Although there are currents in premodern Islamic thought that would mesh readily with modern human rights theories, the authors of the Islamic human rights literature tend to be influenced by the ideas and attitudes of traditional orthodoxy, such as ethical voluntarism, the supremacy of divine Revelation, and hostility toward rationalism and humanism. They have thus elected to adhere to the same intellectual framework within which the precepts of the premodern *shari'a* were elaborated. Historically, this framework proved to be an inhospitable setting for the development of human rights concepts. The consequences of grafting certain Western rights concepts and terminology on a system that is imbued with precepts and values of Islamic tradition will be shown in subsequent analyses of specific individual Islamic human rights provisions (Chapters 4–8).

Ideally, one would want complete expositions of the authors' philosophies of human rights appended to each of the schemes. Then the analysis of those philosophies could be correlated with a critical appraisal of the provisions of each scheme. Unfortunately, the authors have not provided such essays. In default of them, I shall present segments of rights philosophies that these authors and other Muslim conservatives who write on Islamic human rights have offered in order to show that traditional antihumanistic, antirationalist, and anti-individualistic ideas are still influencing some Muslim conservatives' perceptions of human rights. Ultimately, the persistence of these orthodox perspectives will be obvious in the features of the Islamic human rights schemes that they have shaped. The analysis will show how Islamic human rights schemes express and confirm the premodern values and priorities that have predominated in orthodox Islamic thought for more than a millennium. Meanwhile, Muslims who have been won over to international human rights have implicitly discarded these premodern perspectives as outmoded.

Insofar as the schemes expressly indicate their priorities, they uphold the primacy of Revelation over reason and none endorse reason as a source of law. For example, when one examines the Preamble to the English version of the UIDHR, one sees that it takes the position that divine Revelation has given the "legal and moral framework within which to establish and regulate human institutions and relationships." This idea is implicit throughout the text of the Arabic version, as texts of the Qur'an, God's Revelation, and the *sunna* of the Prophet, the practice of the divinely inspired messenger, are extensively quoted. It is thus clear that for the authors of the UIDHR divinely inspired texts enjoy primacy as the source of law. The status of reason is correspondingly demoted. In a later passage in the Preamble of the UIDHR, the authors proclaim in the Arabic version that they believe that human reason (*al-'aql al-bashari*) is insufficient to provide the best plan for human life, independent of God's guidance and inspiration. In the corresponding part of the English version, after stating that "rationality by itself" cannot be "a sure guide in the affairs of mankind," they express their conviction that "the teachings of Islam represent the quintessence of Divine guidance in its final and perfect form."

In such a scheme any challenges that might be made to Islamic law on the grounds that it denies basic rights guaranteed under constitutions or international law are ruled out ab initio; human reason is deemed inadequate to criticize what are treated as divine edicts. This affirms the traditional orthodox view, that the tenets of the *shari'a* are perfect and just, because they represent the will of the Creator, being derived from divinely inspired sources. In the Islamic human rights schemes proffered by Mawdudi and Tabandeh, there is heavy reliance on extensive quotes from the Islamic sources, which is an indication that they follow the traditional view that the texts of Revelation are the definitive guides for what law should be, not human reason.

The supremacy of Islamic law in Iran is confirmed in various provisions of the Iranian Constitution in addition to Article 4, which has already been quoted. The primacy of Revelation is confirmed in Article 1, which calls for a government based on truth and Qur'anic justice, and in Article 2, which states that the Iranian Republic is based on belief in the acceptance of God's rule and the necessity of obeying his commands, affirming belief in "divine Revelation and its fundamental role in expressing his law" and the "justice of God in creation and in divine law." Also according to Article 2, these aims are to be achieved by "judgment made on a continuous basis by the eminent clergy, based on the Book [the Qur'an] and traditions of the saints," the last-named meaning the divinely inspired imams of Twelver Shi'ism. The Iranian Constitution thus professes to be anchored in principles derived from divine Revelation.

In the Azhar draft Islamic constitution the evidence is less clear. One can, however, infer a similar emphasis on divine Revelation and conclude that a command of religious texts is deemed central to knowledge from individual provisions that incorporate Qur'anic language and concepts, the requirements in Articles 12 and 13 that call for the memorization of the Qur'an in schools and teaching the prophetic traditions, and the provision in Article 11 that religious instruction should be a main subject in education.

In addition to according Revelation a central role in their Islamic human rights schemes, the authors do not show the shift from an emphasis on human duties to an emphasis on human rights that characterizes modern thought on rights. In a passage in the English version of the Preamble to the UIDHR that has no obvious counterpart in the Arabic version, the authors indicate "that by the terms of our primeval covenant with God our duties and obligations have priority over our rights," thereby coming close to reaffirming the traditional idea that Islam provides a scheme of duties, not a scheme of individual rights. It is therefore obvious from the outset that the UIDHR will have the effect of denying rights, including ones that are guaranteed under international human rights law, in the guise of establishing Islamic duties. Should there be complaints that this Islamic scheme strips away protections afforded the individual under international human rights norms, the ready-made defense will be that the Islamic sources must be deferred to because they represent God's plan and that the purpose of Islam is not so much to secure rights as to ensure obedience to divine commands.

In the Azhar draft constitution one sees a similar concern for the fulfillment of Islamic duties. In Article 12 the government is required to teach Muslims their duties (*al-fara'id*). In contrast, in Chapter 4, which deals with the individual's rights and freedoms (and these turn out to be highly circumscribed), there is no mention of the existence of need to teach Muslims about freedoms.

A. K. Brohi, a former minister of law and religious affairs in Pakistan, has written a number of pieces on human rights in Islam and exhibits a rights philosophy similar to the ones embodied in the schemes under discussion here. Brohi has been prominent enough in this field to be selected to give the keynote address at a major international conference on human rights in Islam held in Kuwait in 1980 under the sponsorship of the International Commission of Jurists, Kuwait University, and the Union of Arab Lawyers.[29] Brohi's speech recapitulated points made in an earlier piece on Islam and human rights, published in the official Pakistani case law reporter in 1976[30]—while Zulfikar Ali Bhutto, the prime minister whom Zia executed after his coup, was still in power. It is significant that the same points were incorporated in an article in the official Pakistani case law reporter in 1983, when President Zia's martial law regime and Islamization programs were in full force. Apparently the Zia government did not find anything in the article that would tend to undermine its position that military dictatorship and suspension of rights were compatible with Islamization.[31] Excerpts from the seminar and the article offered here show how Brohi rejects the philosophical underpinnings of Western human rights:

Human duties and rights have been vigorously defined and their orderly enforcement is the duty of the whole of organized communities and the task is specifically entrusted to the law enforcement organs of the state. The individual if necessary has to be sacrificed in order that the life of the organism be saved. Collectivity has a special sanctity attached to it in Islam.[32]

The Western man's perspective may by and large be called anthropocentric in the sense that there man is regarded as constituting the measure of everything since he is to be regarded as the starting point of all thinking and action. The perspective of Islam, on the other hand, is theocentric, that is, God-consciousness, the Absolute here is paramount; man is here only to serve His Maker. . . . [In the West] rights of man are seen in a setting which has no reference to his relationship with God—they are somehow supposed to be his inalienable birthrights. . . . Each time the assertion of human rights is made, it is done only to secure their recognition from some secular authority such as the state or some such regal power.[33]

[In Islam] there are no "human rights" or "freedoms" admissible to man in the sense in which modern man's thought, belief, and practice understand them: in essence, the believer owes obligation or duties to God if only because he is called upon to obey the Divine Law and such Human Rights as he is made to acknowledge seem to stem from his primary duty to obey God.[34]

Thus, it would appear, there is a sense in which Man has no rights within a theocentric perspective; he has only duties to His Maker. But these duties in their turn, give rise to all the rights, Human Rights in the modern sense included. . . . There can, in the strict theory of the Islamic law, be no conflict between the State Authority and the individual—since both have to obey the Divine Law.[35]

Human Rights conceived from the anthropocentric perspective are treated by Western thinkers as though they were no more than an expedient mode of protecting the individual from the assaults that are likely to be made upon him by the authority of the State's coercive power—by the unjust law that may be imposed by that authority to deny man the possibility of self-development through the law-making power of the brute majorities. Islam, on the other hand, formulates, defines and protects these very rights by inducing in the believers the disposition to obey the law of God . . . and showing obedience to those "constituted authorities": within the realm who themselves are bound to obey the law of God. . . . Furthermore, affirmation of these rights is to enable man not only to secure the establishment of those conditions in terms of which the development of man as an individual on earth may be possible, but also to enable man so to conduct himself, inwardly as well as outwardly, as to be able to obey the Divine Law. . . . By accepting to live in Bondage to this Divine Law, man learns to be free.[36]

The tenets of Western individualism are unacceptable in Brohi's scheme, in which man is clearly not meant to be the measure of all things. The idea that individuals enjoy certain inalienable rights is dismissed with scorn. In Brohi's comments one sees again the emphasis on duties; it is the perspective of the authority at the apex of the pyramid of power from which the question of rights is examined. The individual is expected to obey the duly constituted authorities, who, in their turn, should obey God. The idea that human rights standards would need to be fashioned to deal with tensions between the rights of the individual and the policies and actions of the government is rejected, as it was in the idealistic visions of the structure of society that were presented by premodern Islamic thinkers and that precluded the development of modern concepts of individual rights. The need to protect the rights of the individual against the state, which is a central concern of Western human rights provisions, is treated as irrelevant in a system that is based on Islamic law. Like the premodern theorists of Islamic government, Brohi assumes that when Islamic law is in force, the government will be obedient to the dictates of the *shari'a,* so the individual will have no cause to complain of government misconduct.

In Brohi's treatment of rights one sees both a strong affirmation of the idea that the individual is bound by the duty of obedience and, withal, a carelessness regarding the issue of to whom or to what the individual owes obedience. One notes that Brohi is sometimes speaking of subordination to God and Islamic law, which is clearly required in the Islamic tradition, but that at other times he means the subordination of the individual to organized communities, a collectivity, political authorities, or the state. Regarding the latter, there is much less in the way of unequivocal Islamic authority justifying claims of obedience. Brohi does not seem to perceive that the Islamic warrant establishing the duty of a believer to obey the commands of God cannot necessarily be extended to cover the obligations of a citizen of a contemporary country to obey the commands of its political leadership.

Like many other Muslim conservatives who write on rights, Brohi fails to appreciate that the model of communal solidarity that one finds in traditional societies in the Muslim world is in no way distinctively Islamic but reflects the features commonly found in societies before the intrusions of industrialization and urbanization. Brohi does not analyze the significance of the original linkage between the lack of support for individualism in premodern Islamic thought and the situation of the individual in traditional societies, where the lack of individual rights and freedoms did not have the same nefarious consequences that the lack of protection for individual rights has had in the modern nation-state. From the fact that premodern Islamic thought was not anthropocentric, he leaps to the conclusion that in the twentieth century, the anthropocentric perspective should be treated as unacceptable by Islamic criteria. Brohi goes from a description of the subordination of the individual that was widely accepted in traditional societies—regardless of whether Islam was or was not the dominant religion—to the unwarranted conclusion that Islamic doctrine calls for such subordination even in the drastically changed circumstances of contemporary states, where the power of the central government is immeasurably enhanced over what it was in the medieval era.

Brohi's perspective is echoed by many others who write on this subject. A Muslim academic of Syrian origin who has written a number of pieces on human rights in Islam characterized the difference between Western and Islamic approaches to human rights as follows:

> The Western liberal emphasis upon freedom from restraint is alien to Islam. . . . Personal freedom [in Islam] lies in surrendering to the Divine

Will. . . . It cannot be realized through liberation from external sources of restraint . . . individual freedom ends where the freedom of the community begins. . . . Human rights exist only in relation to human obligations. Individuals possess certain obligations towards God, fellow humans, and nature, all of which are defined by Shariah.[37]

Those individuals who do not accept these obligations have no rights. . . . Much of Muslim theology tends toward a totalitarian voluntarism. . . . [In the West there is] a strong tradition that sees the elimination of repression and want as the goal of society and of humankind. There has thus emerged a false dichotomy between the individual and society, with the former seen constantly as the victim of the latter.[38]

The West places more emphasis on rights while Islam values obligations. The Western tradition posits freedom in order to avoid the outcome of a despotic system, while Islam emphasizes virtue as a goal to perpetuate traditions of society which often support a coercive system. The West emphasizes individual interests while Islam values collective good.[39]

Like premodern natural law theorists in the West, the author spoke primarily in terms of the duties of the individual, according little importance to the idea of rights. While recognizing that modern rights provisions in the West have the goal of curbing repression and despotism, the author expressed no disapproval of the use of "a coercive system" in an Islamic setting to perpetuate traditions. Not only does the downgrading of the importance of individual freedoms that one sees here correspond to the priorities of Islamic orthodoxy, but it also reflects the ongoing links of Islamic doctrine to the values of traditional societies, where communal solidarity and the rights of the majority are accorded primacy over the rights of the individual who might suffer under or rebel against societal constraints.

The same attitude was expressed in a magazine published by the Kuwaiti Ministry of Education, in an article that advocated the setting up of a learned academy to codify *shari'a* law as part of a project for Islamization of law. The author condemned the systems of imported Western law that are currently in place in Arab countries, saying that they are incompatible with the social and religious attitudes of the citizens of these countries. The article listed the following as the first of the basic principles that needed be kept in mind in interpreting how the *shari'a* applies to contemporary problems:

Understanding of the texts in the context of collective interests: this principle is uncontested in the Islamic *Shari'a,* and expresses *shar'i* [legal] aims of fulfilling social needs and interests. Indeed, one of the most important established foundations of the *Shari'a* is the circumscribing of individual rights by the interests of society. This fundamental concept of the special importance of the interests of society must be respected.[40]

One sees in these comments how the reapplication of the *shari'a* and the abandonment of Western law are associated with adopting a system in which the rights that the individual enjoys in Western law are downgraded and circumscribed and the interests of society are accorded paramountcy.

A similar anti-individualistic stance was reflected in comments by a member of Egypt's Conseil d'Etat on the differences regarding rights in the West and in Islam in a book defending Islamic rights norms in the area of criminal justice: "Unlike Western law, Islamic jurisprudence has not lost sight of the value of the community in a headlong rush to protect the individual. Its principle of legality stems from its concept of community, and ultimately protects the individual because he is a member of the community. Islamic jurisprudence steadfastly refuses to elevate the human above the divine."[41] Individual freedom is clearly not a prime concern in the Islamic rights scheme envisaged by this lawyer; instead there would seem to be a bias against any claims for protection of individual rights where these might undermine the interests or the values of the community.

In the same work a law professor of Arab origin in a discussion of the relationship of the individual and the state in Islam revealed a similar philosophy:

Unlike other sources of the law, the Qur'an emphasizes duties rather than rights. It insists upon the fulfillment of individual obligations before the individual can claim his privileges. The individual is neither apart nor separate from society, and his rights are neither different from nor conflicting with those of the community. He is part and parcel of society, and the fulfillment of his obligations and those of the other members of the society constitutes the reservoir of social rights which are then shared by all.[42]

Unlike western philosophical and political perceptions on the separability of the individual and the state, Islamic social concepts do not make such a distinction. The individual does not stand in an adversary position vis-à-vis the state but is an integral part thereof. The consequence of this relationship which flows from the concept of Islam . . . is that there is no apparent need to delineate individual rights in contraposition to the state.[43]

Again one sees a confusion of the traditional pattern of communal solidarity in premodern society and normative Islamic prescriptions, which are not viewed in relation to their original historical context.

One sees the rejection of the idea that in the modern state there will naturally be conflicts between the competing interests of individual citizens and the government. The author's notion that in an Islamic system one cannot separate the individual and the government reflects adherence to the premodern jurists' views that the ruler and ruled stood together, united in their duties of obedience to the *shari'a*.[44] When one relies on such anachronistic views, it is not surprising that denials of individual rights and freedoms by governments are seen as a nonexistent problem. It is conclusively presumed that in an Islamic setting individual-state tensions do not arise.

Mawdudi's main political concern seemed to be how to preserve the power of the state and how to enhance the ruler's right to demand obedience. In his book *The Islamic Law and Constitution,* Mawdudi, who inaccurately quoted the Prophet as saying that "the state" (not referred to in the original) "shall have to be obeyed, in adversity and in prosperity, and whether it is pleasant or unpleasant to do so," opined:

> In other words, the order of the State, be it palatable or unpalatable, easy or arduous, shall have to be obeyed under all circumstances [save when this means disobedience to God] . . . a person should, truly and faithfully and with all his heart, wish and work for the good, prosperity and the betterment of the State, and should not tolerate anything likely to harm its interests. . . . It is also obligatory on the citizens of the Islamic State to cooperate wholeheartedly with the government and to make sacrifices of life and property for it, so much so that if any danger threatens the State, he who willfully refrains from making a sacrifice of his life and property to ward off that danger has been called a hypocrite in the Qur'an.[45]

This is obviously an attempt to provide an Islamic rationale for total subjugation of the individual to the state—although assuming that the Prophet was referring to the modern state involves a definite anachronism. One can see how similar Mawdudi's formulation of the individual's obligations to obey the government is to that offered by President Zia in justifying his military dictatorship in Pakistan (Chapter 2). The only excuse for disobeying the government is in cases where obeying the government would entail violating Islamic law, thereby constituting disobedience to a command of God. Of course, a government that purports to follow Islamic law, as President Zia's did, would not concede that it was giving the citizenry any grounds whatsoever for disobedience, so it is unlikely that such a government would deem legitimate the believer's excuse for disobedience. In fact, many members of the political group that Mawdudi founded as well as others who shared his outlook were among the mainstays of support for President Zia's program of Islamization in Pakistan. They were clearly at ease with the loss of rights and freedoms attendant on the coming to power of Zia's military dictatorship, since the latter meant the resuscitation of the values they associated with Islamic tradition.

Persons like the authors just cited may take the position that there exist such things as Islamic human rights; their comments, however, reveal that they are philosophically at odds with the ideas that the rights of the individual should be accorded central importance and deserve legal protection from interference by governments. The authors are hostile to individualism and well disposed toward the anti-individualistic currents of premodern Islamic orthodoxy. These currents are incompatible with the idea that individual rights and freedoms deserve strong protections against government infringement. Given their position, one would expect these authors to say that modern human rights concepts according primacy to individual rights and freedoms cannot be accommodated within an Islamic framework. Instead, many Muslims writing in this area have been inclined to try to preserve traditional anti-individualistic, communitarian values and priorities while paradoxically trying to insert human rights provisions in that unsuitable matrix. But rights in the context of a value system so inimical to individual freedom will not mean rights as commonly understood in international law.

In contrast, the international human rights standards rest on the assumption that the rights of the individual are the primary concern of human rights theory and that they must be afforded legal protections that will secure them against infringements, particularly by governments, but also by society.[46] If one accepts Ronald Dworkin's definition of a "right" as a claim that it would be wrong for the government to deny an individual even though it would be in the general interest to do so, one could say that it would be impossible for authors with such attitudes to conceive of rights in the Western sense, since they consistently accord priority to the interests of the community and the government at the expense of the rights of the individual.

A person unfamiliar with Islamic history might assume that special circumstances or unique institutions in Islamic civilization may have compensated for the lack of formal legal safeguards for individual rights and freedoms and that this lack had less nefarious consequences in the Muslim world than it had in Western societies prior to the imposition of legal restraints on governments' ability to infringe on human rights. One might speculate that special forms of social solidarity within the community meant that the relationship of the state and the individual was less adversarial than it was in the West, so that the authors of

Islamic human rights were justified in downgrading the significance of protections for individual rights in terms of their own cultural experience.

In fact, in the Middle East the absence of legal protections for human rights has correlated with patterns of misrule, oppression, and denials of rights by despotic rulers that are very similar to those historically experienced in the West. The idealized schemes of Muslim ruler and Muslim ruled both acting in concert and in common obedience to the divine law that are invoked in the cited passages were not realized in practice. Although some Muslims would say that the Islamic ideal was illustrated by the harmonious collaboration of ruler and ruled in the era of the Prophet and under some of his immediate successors—to which the Shi'is would add the era in which they were ruled by divinely inspired imams—these reports of saintly rulers in the earliest period of Islamic history by no means signify that the dictates of Islamic piety have normally proved to constrain the behavior of the despotic regimes that have dominated most societies in the Muslim world. The historical record shows that religious scruples rarely deterred governments in Muslim countries from indulging in cruel mistreatment and oppression of their subjects. Although Muslim rulers had at their disposal the mechanisms to impose obedience on their subjects, individual subjects had few ways other than the risky course of overt rebellion to challenge cruel and tyrannical rulers.

In reality, the individual and the state in the Muslim world have had conflicting interests that have most often been resolved at the expense of individual rights and freedoms. The authors of these Islamic human rights schemes must be aware that this pattern has continued in the Muslim world today and now has more serious consequences, given the enormous increase in the powers wielded by central governments. Nonetheless, such writers are disposed to ignore the significance of the enormous disparity in power between the individual and the modern nation-state.

Since most current theorists of Islamic human rights persist in talking exclusively in terms of an idealized vision of Islamic social harmony, even though the historical record and the acts of current governments have manifestly demonstrated the inadequacy of the very scheme that they propose, one may doubt that their Islamic human rights schemes were actually devised to deal with contemporary political problems or to improve protections for human rights in contemporary Middle Eastern societies. Because of their otherworldly, idealistic focus and their failure to come to grips with the philosophical premises underlying modern human rights theories, it is not surprising that the authors of Islamic human rights schemes produce rights provisions that seem grossly inadequate by the standards of international human rights. In terms of the practical consequences that these schemes may have, it is even more disturbing that they fail to call for human rights protections that could address and remedy the real problems of human rights deprivations in contemporary Middle Eastern societies.

It is entirely consonant with their mistrust of the ability of human reason to ascertain what is right and just and their inclination to rely on Revelation as the true source of law that these authors of Islamic human rights schemes decided not to bother with the philosophical exercise of working out a coherent theory of what rights mean. Instead, they have in some instances simply appropriated ideas from texts on Islamic law and ethics, treating them as if they offered authoritative statements of rights, irrespective of whether these involve principles deserving of the status of rights according to the international criteria or whether they would even be susceptible of legal enforcement. The consequence is the inclusion of many trivial or meaningless "rights" that in international law would not rise to the level of human rights. The authors have apparently neglected to examine systematically what freedoms are fundamental and important in terms of the contribution that they make to the happiness and well-being of the individual—and what freedoms most need protection in light of the patterns of governmental human rights abuses prevalent in modern political systems in general and in contemporary Middle Eastern societies in particular.

In consequence, the priorities implicit in these schemes are not those of international law. The Islamic schemes do not offer protection for what international law deems fundamental rights, but they do cover issues unrelated to conventional rights principles. The Iranian Constitution is a noteworthy exception in this respect. It appears that Iran's established tradition of constitutionalism inhibited its drafters from abandoning the familiar categories that are normally used in formulations of rights.

Examples of the inadequate rights formulations will be offered to show frivolous notions of entitlements. Some inadequate formulations seem to have resulted from an author gleaning from the Islamic sources the idea that certain conduct is censured and drawing the conclusion that human beings have "rights" not to be affected by such conduct. Thus, Islamic human rights include the "right" not to be made fun of or insulted by nicknames,[47] which is obviously taken from the Qur'an 44:11, "Let not a folk deride a folk who may be better than they . . . neither defame one another, nor insult one another by nicknames." Other "rights" that have been derived from Islamic texts include the right of the women of the household not to be surprised by a male family member coming in suddenly and unannounced,[48] and the "right" not to be tied up before being killed.[49] There is a prohibition against public indecency and a command to observe standards of modesty, which, in context, could be taken to mean that there exists a male "right" not to be titillated or offended by women wearing provocative or vulgar clothes and makeup.[50] In addition, one encounters a "right" not to have one's corpse mutilated,[51] which seems to envisage that human rights protections should be extended to corpses, even though human rights concerns ordinarily presuppose that the rights claimant be living, not dead.[52]

Indeed, when one thinks about the rights provisions involving women, one realizes that, far from affording protection for freedoms, they contain implicit restrictions on women's rights. There is an assumption that the world is sexually segregated and that women stay at home in seclusion from men. So strict is this segregation meant to be that even male family members should not ever intrude on women's quarters without giving women warning so that they can cover themselves in a suitably modest manner. Thus, the provision implies that even in the home there will be female seclusion and veiling, which in turn is connected with the woman's duty to avoid indecency. There is really nothing connecting this supposed right of women not to be surprised by men of the family coming in unannounced with any principle of international human rights, only with traditional notions that women's obligations under the *shari'a* include the duties to stay segregated, secluded, and veiled.

As a kind of corollary to the development of "rights" not to be subjected to behavior censured in the Islamic sources, something that is treated as good or proper in those sources may be considered a human right. "Rights" that fall within this category include "the obligation of believers to see that a deceased person's body is treated with due solemnity"[53] and the "right" to safety of life—meaning that people should come to the aid of a person in distress or danger.[54] Ordinarily, one thinks of human rights as rights that guarantee freedom to the beneficiary or right holder and that involve the ability of that person freely to exercise his or her choice about a potential course of action. In the cases just mentioned, it is hard to see how any "right" in this sense can be involved, since the beneficiaries are either dead or in a state of peril where they are helpless to vindicate the "right" that is being afforded to them.

These frivolous rights concepts do not offer protection for any of the fundamental freedoms that are being abridged in the Muslim world, and they also fail to address the problem of government interference with individual rights, which is the main concern of international human rights. Here, the actors supposedly infringing rights are all private parties—such as the person who calls another a nickname or the man who does not announce his presence before he walks into a room in his family home that is occupied by women.

Another "right" stipulated is that of unbelievers to recover the corpses of their fellows who have fallen in battle against the Muslims without having to pay for the privilege.[55] The question of whether a fee could be assessed from unbelievers in these circumstances is hardly one that any serious advocate of enhanced human rights protections in the Middle East would choose to place on an agenda of important contemporary human rights problems.

This category of rights that have no international counterparts also includes the "right" to cooperate (in the cause of virtue—presumably, Islamic virtue) and not to cooperate (in the cause of vice and aggression—presumably, as defined by Islam)[56] and the "right" to propagate Islam and its message.[57] These "rights" are different from international norms, where religious freedoms are protected regardless of one's religion; here it appears it is only Muslims who would benefit from these "rights."

Other "rights" provisions that are included in these Islamic human rights schemes do not belong in compilations of human rights because they concern offenses dealt with by tort or criminal law, which involves the conduct of private actors. Generally, international human rights law, because it is concerned with governmental conduct, does not set rules for types of cases where injury or death is caused either due to negligence or as a result of criminal conduct by a private individual. Such cases are normally regulated through tort or criminal law, as most legal systems consider tort and criminal sanctions adequate for the purposes of compensation, retribution, and deterrence. In contrast, in Islamic human rights schemes, there are provisions that guarantee the "right" not to be burned alive,[58] the "right" to life—which turns out to be a right not to be murdered,[59] and a woman's "right" to have her chastity respected and protected at all times.[60] Although murder does violate international human rights law if it is practiced as a matter of state policy, if it is no more than a criminal act by a private actor, it is left to domestic criminal legislation to impose a penalty. The "right" set forth in the Islamic scheme does not appear to be directed against state policy, but only against the criminal. Furthermore, the woman's right to have her chastity respected is a very ambiguous one, since, in the context of the contemporary Middle East, protection of chastity is often associated with regimes of sexual segregation and seclusion and female veiling, all of which practices can be justified on the grounds that they are necessary to protect women's chastity. So, the "rights" just discussed do not offer meaningful protections for individual freedoms, and at least one could be utilized to deprive women of freedoms.

A similarly insignificant "right" is the right of ex-spouses to strict confidentiality on the part of their former spouses with regard to information that the latter have obtained that could be detrimental to them.[61] This belongs to the realm of evidentiary privilege or private tort claims, which are not normally the concern of human rights law.

After examining the vague and confused concepts that the authors of Islamic human rights include in their lists of Islamic human rights, one sees that they have no sure grasp of what the concerns of human rights are. Their efforts to incorporate elements from the Islamic sources, relying on Revelation rather than reason to find rights principles, lead them to include provisions that would be totally out of place in a scheme that shared common philosophical premises with those of international human rights.

Other consequences of the failure by Islamic human rights schemes authors to adopt a concept of what a right means that is philosophically coherent and truly comparable to the way that "right" is used in international law will be illustrated in the discussions of specific problems in subsequent chapters. In summary, the distinctive features of the Islamic human rights schemes do correlate in a general way with the authors' decisions to try to graft rights terminology on a body of concepts and values derived from the premodern Islamic tradition without first rethinking that tradition in terms of its compatibility with modern human rights norms.

CHAPTER 4

Islamic Restrictions on Human Rights

One of the most striking features in all the Islamic human rights schemes is the use of Islamic criteria to qualify human rights principles. The consistency of the pattern of restrictions shows that the authors of Islamic rights schemes are aware of the scope of the freedoms offered under international human rights and that they share the view that these freedoms are excessive. They have decided that these excessive freedoms should be cut down to their appropriate size by the imposition of limits—ones that they present as being inherent in Islam and Islamic law. Provisions in the Islamic human rights schemes reflect the thesis that only when Islamic restrictions are used to circumscribe international human rights do human rights have a proper scope. There is, however, no explicit articulation of this idea.

Reducing the scope of rights according to Islamic criteria opens the door to many questions. Since there was no human rights tradition in Islamic civilization, there are no historical antecedents that establish exactly what limits—if any—Islamic criteria impose on the range of civil and political rights afforded by international human rights law. The Islamic human rights schemes avoid clarifying exactly what these restrictions on rights would entail. The ambiguity in these rights formulations, in which rights are qualified by reference to vague "Islamic" limitations that are not specifically described and that are not fixed in Islamic jurisprudence, turns out to be one of their distinguishing characteristics. The significance of these Islamic criteria circumscribing the otherwise applicable international human rights norms is evaluated in this chapter.

Permissible Qualifications of Rights and Freedoms

International law recognizes that many rights protections are not absolute and may be suspended or qualified in exceptional circumstances such as wars or public emergencies or even in normal circumstances in the interests of certain overriding considerations.[1] In international law, one expects these overriding considerations to fall within one of several settled categories. Qualifications may be placed on human rights in the aggregate common interest and to serve particular, specified policies.[2] The latter include qualifications for reasons of preserving national security, public safety, public order, morals, the rights and freedom of others, the interests of justice, and the public interest in a democratic society.[3] To ensure that accommodations and derogations are made within structures of authority and to prevent arbitrariness in decisions, the measures imposing these limitations must be taken in accordance with or in conformity with the law.[4]

International law therefore tries to balance the need to protect human rights against other needs with which rights protections may occasionally come in conflict. It recognizes that unless the circumstances in which curbs can be placed on human rights are strictly limited, the rights protections would dwindle to the point that they would become illusory. However, the degree to which it is permissible to curb human rights and exactly what grounds justify restricting rights remain contested questions in international law.

Despite the unsettled nature of international law in this area, in documents that make up the International Bill of Human Rights there are some guidelines regarding the qualifications that may be imposed on civil and political rights. I shall first review the guidelines that are relevant for evaluating the restrictions in Islamic rights provisions.

A number of rights are treated in the "international bill" as absolute, meaning that there could be no justification for curbing them. Among these are the right to freedom and equality in dignity and rights; the right to equality before the law and to equal protection of the law; the right in full equality to a fair and public hearing by an independent and impartial tribunal; the right to marry and the right to equal rights in marriage and divorce;[5] freedom of thought, conscience, and religion, including the freedom to change one's religion;[6] and the right to work and to free choice of employment.[7]

The UDHR includes a separate clause that defines the limits that may in general be placed on the human rights set forth in the Declaration. In Article 29.2 one sees the following provision: "In the exercise of his rights and freedoms, everyone shall be subject only to such limitations as are determined by law solely for the purpose of securing due recognition and respect for the rights and freedoms of others and of meeting the just requirements of morality, public order and the general welfare in a democratic society." It is clear that the absolute rights just mentioned are not intended to be subject to limits. That is, there are no indications that the UDHR philosophy would accept any criteria that would deny people the right to equality before the law, to a fair hearing, to equal rights in marriage and divorce, to freedom of conscience, to free choice of employment, and the like. The category of unqualified rights includes those rights whose exercise does not infringe on the rights of others or interfere with the requirements of morality, public order, and the general welfare.

One can see that the recognition of the absolute character accorded to rights such as these correlates with the values and priorities of societies at an advanced state of development. In contrast, in traditional cultures, hierarchy and inequality and systems of control over individual behavior and choices are often important elements of the social structure. In legal systems based on traditional values, considerations analogous to ones of morality, public order, and the general welfare invoked in Article 29.2 might be precisely the ones that would be used to justify blanket denials of rights of the kinds just mentioned.

Since they do not apply to the absolute rights, the qualifications permitted in the general provision in Article 29.2 of the UDHR should be taken to apply to other rights, rights that were not among the absolute rights. They might apply to UDHR provisions regarding freedom of opinion and expression; freedom of peaceful assembly and association; and the right to take part in government and the right to equal access to public service.[8] The exact limitations that could be applied to the various provisions were clarified in subsequent international human rights documents, as specific qualifications were inserted in the texts of individual rights provisions. With the added qualifications, the new provisions guarantee rights as follows:

1. Freedom of expression: subject only to qualifications provided by law and necessary for respect of the rights and reputations of others and for the protection of national security or of public order (*ordre public*), or of public health and morals;
2. The right of peaceful assembly: subject only to restrictions "imposed in conformity with the law and which are necessary in a democratic society in the interests of national security or public safety, public order (*ordre public*), the protection of public health or morals or the protection of the rights and freedoms of others";
3. Freedom of association: subject to the same qualifications as the right of peaceful assembly, above;
4. The right to take part in the conduct of public affairs, to vote and be elected, and to have access, on general terms of equality, to public service "without unreasonable conditions."[9]

A number of other fundamental rights are qualified, including the right to life, which is qualified by the state's ability to impose a death penalty, but only for the most serious crimes and subject to a number of other conditions, and the right to liberty and security of person, which is qualified by the state's ability to deprive the person of these "on such grounds and in accordance with such procedure as are established by law."[10]

The ICESCR has a general provision on how rights may be qualified, providing in Article 4 that states "may subject such rights only to such limitations as are determined by law only insofar as this may be compatible with the nature of these rights and solely for the purpose of promoting the general welfare in a democratic society."

Thus, one sees in the "international bill" definite standards regarding what constitutes permissible reasons for curbing human rights protections. The standards may not have been perfectly drafted, and the formulations of the qualifications are not so airtight that they completely preclude efforts by states to manipulate them at the expense of the rights of the individual. However, one perceives that the bill strives for formulations that carefully circumscribe the circumstances in which states will have justifications for cutting back on the rights set forth in it. As will be indicated in the following examinations of Islamic human rights schemes, one of the most important ways in which the Islamic human rights differ from those in the "international bill" is that the qualifications on rights in the former are so vague and so broad that they allow states vast leeway in circumscribing rights.

Islamic Formulas Limiting Rights

With the exception of the creation of novel "rights," which do not correspond to what are recognized as rights under international law, the substantive rights in Islamic human rights schemes are rarely distinctive. Instead, what is distinctive is the implicit theory of how limitations should be placed on human rights by Islamic criteria. A review of the protections offered in schemes of Islamic human rights shows a pattern of borrowing substantive rights from international human rights documents while reducing the protections that they actually afford. This is accomplished by restricting them so that the rights can only be enjoyed within the limits of the *shari'a,* which are unspecified. These emendations leave virtually unlimited discretion to states in deciding what the scope of the affected rights should be.

There is no theory in international law that supports the notion that fundamental human rights may be curtailed—much less permanently curtailed—by reference to the requirements of a particular religion.

Under international law non-Muslims cannot legally be deprived of their rights by the use of Islamic standards. There is also no warrant under international law for Muslims being deprived of their rights due to governmental application of restrictions taken from Islamic law. Thus, relying on the *shari'a* to limit and water down human rights means that the rights that are established under international law are being qualified by standards that are not recognized in international law as legitimate bases for curtailing rights. Not only does the use of the *shari'a* to restrict human rights have no justification in international law, but given the vagueness of the formulations of the qualifications, it ultimately means that the rights involved become illusory.

In general, limitations on rights implied by using terms like "the *shari'a*," "Islamic precepts," or "the limits of Islam" to qualify human rights cannot be unambiguously defined by consulting the work of the premodern jurists, because this work is far too diverse. Premodern Islamic law included the doctrines of several sects and many law schools. Divergence of opinion among major law schools was historically tolerated in Islam, a situation acknowledged in the *shari'a* concept of *ikhtilaf al-madhahib,* or difference of law schools. In fact, even within one law school, doctrines and opinions could differ significantly as to what the interpretations of the Islamic sources should be.[11] Furthermore, there were many jurists whose opinions differed from the views of the major schools, but whose works, nonetheless, are part of the premodern *shari'a* legacy.

In some areas, one might make tentative projections regarding what *shari'a* limitations would entail. Despite the great diversity in Islamic doctrine, on certain points of premodern jurisprudence there is sufficient consensus to allow surmises as to how the application of Islamic principles would affect rights. Reliance on rules of the premodern *shari'a* to determine the permissible scope of modern human rights could open the way to nullification of rights in areas where the *shari'a* calls for restrictions on rights and freedoms, such as the rules relegating women and non-Muslims to subordinate status or prohibiting conversions from Islam. Even on these topics, where there are extensive rules in the *shari'a,* there is enough diversity and nuance in the relevant legal doctrines to give the state considerable leeway in deciding what rules should be chosen as embodying the official Islamic norms.

On other topics relevant for civil rights and political freedoms, where the premodern jurisprudence is very underdeveloped and the *shari'a* standards are often uncertain and fraught with controversy, the reliance on the *shari'a* to qualify rights is also incompatible with the protection of the rights involved. Where there is no settled doctrine in the premodern jurisprudence and no established Islamic authority on a point, states naturally are left free to invent what curbs on rights should be imposed in the name of "Islam."

Just as there is no definitive guidance in the premodern *shari'a* on the proper scope of human rights, there is no settled doctrine in contemporary Islamic thought. Whatever ambiguities existed in the premodern tradition have been enormously augmented by the growth of diverging interpretations of the requirements of Islamic law in this century. This occurred as Islamic law was reinterpreted in the light of changed conditions and new intellectual currents. Reformist movements led to substantial departures from premodern models of Islamic thought around the turn of the century.[12] More recently, these changes have been augmented by the addition of new ideologized approaches to *shari'a* interpretation.[13] The differences in approaches to understanding Islam have been compounded by the absence of any generally recognized central authority for resolving disputed points of *shari'a* doctrine. Since vague "Islamic" qualifications that are used in Islamic human rights schemes do not specifically refer to the premodern *shari'a,* widely diverging contemporary versions of Islamic requirements could also be read into the qualifications.

It is natural that in the circumstances that prevail in the contemporary Middle East, all such ambiguities in rights formulations will be exploited by the state and resolved at the expense of individual rights and freedoms that are qualified by these Islamic limits. Thus, vague and unspecified "Islamic" limitations on human rights have ominous significance.

Restrictions in the Iranian Constitution

Before examining the 1979 Iranian Constitution to see how the provisions qualified by Islamic principles laid the legal groundwork for the denial of basic freedoms, earlier Iranian formulations of civil and political rights provisions should be considered. Iranian constitutional history illustrates the tensions and conflicts involved in accommodating human rights within an Islamic framework.

Many of Iran's *'ulama* were violently opposed to the adoption of Iran's 1906–1907 constitution, and one of the grounds for their objections was their opposition to the whole idea of freedom, which they considered dangerous and inimical to Islamic principles and values.[14] Clerical denunciations of freedom and constitutionalism as heretical were often vehement and uncompromising.[15] Clerics in fact interpreted "Islam" in ways that opposed the programs of early advocates of constitutionalism.

However, the popular desire for a mechanism to place constraints on the tyranny and misrule of Iran's Qajar shahs and to realize the aspirations of Iranian nationalism was ultimately strong enough to overcome clerical opposition to the proposed constitution. In addition, one should remember that there were clerics who believed that constitutionalism was compatible with Islam and who were supportive of constitutionalism. However, their support was in part attributable to the fact that they did not fully grasp the significance of constitutionalism and often interpreted its concepts in ways that corresponded to *shari'a* categories and principles.[16] Thus, the first Iranian constitution emerged in an environment where the religious establishment was divided about the compatibility of constitutional freedoms and Islam.

The qualifications placed on civil and political rights provisions in the 1906–1907 constitution were largely secular. However, there were instances where religious criteria were invoked as justifications for restricting constitutional rights.[17] Article 20 qualified freedom of publication by saying that the freedom did not cover heretical books or materials hurtful to Islam. Article 21 qualified freedom of societies and gatherings by saying that it applied where they did not provoke religious disorder.

After the 1978–1979 Iranian Revolution the draft constitution of June 1979, devised in a period before the clergy had fully asserted its control over Iran's political life, likewise relied mostly on secular qualifications of civil and political rights, but there were exceptions. Article 25 of the proposed constitution limited press freedom by a number of secular criteria but also by excepting publications that would insult religious belief. In an ambiguous formulation, Article 26 denied freedom of association not just according to secular criteria, but also where it negated "the basis of the Islamic Republic," which might have allowed religious qualifications on the freedom of association to be imposed. Article 28 qualified the freedom to choose a profession by saying that it should not be opposed to Islam or the public interest.

The draft constitution was subjected to criticism from many quarters. Among the proposals for rewriting it were ones emanating from a group that involved the Iranian Lawyers Association and the Iranian Committee for the Defense of Freedom and Human Rights. The concerns of this group included ensuring the independence of the judiciary and protecting individual rights and the rights of women. It proposed that the UDHR be incorporated in the constitution and that international human rights organizations and lawyers should be enabled to intervene in Iranian courts on behalf of Iranian nationals.[18] In other words, the proposals, had they been accepted, would have meant that international human rights law would have been treated as part of Iran's domestic law and that international human rights advocates would have had the capacity to defend Iranian nationals against their own government. A mistrust of the ability of Iran's domestic legal institutions to afford adequate protection for human rights is implicit in the suggestion about intervention.

However, the draft constitution was also subjected to critiques by a coalition of clerics and Islamic organizations that wanted it to be rewritten in a way that would give it a more Islamic character.[19] Ayatollah Khomeini said that he wanted the draft reviewed from an Islamic perspective, so that it would result in an Islamic constitution, not one made by foreign-influenced intellectuals who had no faith in Islam.[20] Ultimately, the rewriting of the draft was entrusted to an Assembly of Experts, in which clerics had a large majority; the assembly completed its task in December 1979. This was after the occupation of the U.S. Embassy in November 1979 and the taking of U.S. diplomats as hostages had signaled the onset of a shift in power from moderate elements and liberal nationalists to conservative clerics and their followers.

The revision of the draft reflected the political shift. The proposals to adopt the UDHR as part of Iran's law were not only rejected, but the rights provisions in the draft constitution were also rewritten with Islamic qualifications added to reduce the strength of the protections involved. Nonetheless, it is a significant token of the prestige that human rights enjoy that even with the ascendancy of a clerical faction opposed to human rights, references to human rights were not excised from the constitution. They appear in Article 3.14 and Article 20, both of which will be discussed. However, to make them palatable to conservative clerics, human rights had to be expressly subordinated to Islamic criteria. The most important provision in this connection was Article 4, quoted above, providing that Islamic principles should prevail over those in the constitution, and the text of Article 20, which provides: "All citizens of the nation, whether men or women, are equally protected by the law [*qanun,* or secular law]. They also enjoy human, political, economic and cultural rights *according to Islamic standards* [*mavazin-e eslam*]."

The equal protection clause will be discussed separately in greater detail, but here it should be noted that Article 20 constitutes a rejection of the position that it is international law that determines human rights standards. Instead, this article expressly states that Islamic criteria determine what human rights will be granted in Iran.

A brief clarification of the term *qanun* used in Article 20 and elsewhere needs to be offered at this point. In Islamic milieus, *qanun,* taken from the Greek *kanon,* is normally used to refer to secular laws, as opposed to laws based on Islamic sources in the *shari'a*. However, given the principles set forth in Article 4 and Article 20's provision that rights are enjoyed in Iran "according to Islamic standards," references to the *qanun* in articles of the constitution to qualify rights do not seem to mean that the qualifications used must be secular ones but only that the secular law will provide the legal framework for carrying out principles taken from the Islamic sources, which are ultimately controlling in this area.

Other rights provisions with similar qualifications, which in the following quotations are highlighted for emphasis, embody the same position on the relative superiority of Islamic over international norms.

Article 21

"The Government shall guarantee the rights of women in all areas *according to Islamic standards* [*mavazin-e eslami*]."

Like Article 20, this article indicates that in Iran Islamic criteria are controlling, and, therefore, it might be considered redundant. However, the specification that women's rights are determined by Islamic standards is meaningful in the particular cultural context of modern Iran, where the application of secular law has been associated with women's emancipation and the application of *shari'a* law with the relegation of women to a subordinate status. By including a separate provision stipulating that women's rights would be determined by reference to Islamic standards, the government was indicating its intention to reinstate discriminatory premodern *shari'a* rules to govern their status. The consequences of this for women's rights will be addressed in a later section of this study.

Article 24

"Publications and the press may express ideas freely, *except when they are contrary to Islamic principles* [*mabani-ye eslam*], or are detrimental to public rights. The law [*qanun*] will provide the details."

Article 26

"Parties, groups, political and professional associations, as well as Islamic or recognized minority religious associations are permitted, provided they do not violate principles of independence, freedom, and national unity, or which are *contrary to the principles of Islam* [*mavazin-e eslami*] *or the Islamic Republic*."

The status of minorities is discussed in greater detail in Chapters 7 and 8, but it is worth stating here that this provision not only waters down the protection of freedom of association by making it subject to

Islamic criteria, but it allows the government to deny minority religious groups even these fragile freedoms simply by refusing to accord them the status of "recognized" minority religious associations.

Article 27

"Unarmed assemblies and marches are permitted *provided they do not violate the principles of Islam [mabani-ye eslam].*"

Article 28

"Every person has the right to choose the profession he wishes, *provided it is not contrary to the principles of Islam [mokhalef-e eslam . . . nist]*, to the public interest or to the rights of others."

Article 168

"Investigations of political crimes and crimes of the press are to be held in the courts of the Ministry of Justice, openly and with judge and jury. . . . The definition of a political crime, the manner in which the jury will be selected, their qualifications and the limits of their authority shall be determined by law *[qanun] based upon Islamic principles [bar asas-e qavanin-e eslami].*"[21]

Under Article 168 of the Iranian Constitution, it is Islamic criteria that determine what constitutes a political crime, thereby placing religious restraints on political freedom.

One can see that in the above provisions concepts of fundamental rights have been taken from examples in Western constitutions and international law. Some of the provisions include secular qualifications in addition to the Islamic ones, but others have only Islamic qualifications. Islam, then, in the Iranian Constitution is conceived of, not as offering the basis for protecting rights, but solely as the basis for limiting or denying the rights that people could claim under secular constitutional principles or international human rights standards.

One might object to this conclusion by questioning the idea that the Islamic qualifications placed on these rights necessarily would restrict them more than secular qualifications would. Could it not be the case, one might ask, that the Islamic qualifications on rights might be narrower than the ones permitted under international law, that these clauses could be interpreted to mean that the government would have to produce much stronger justifications for curbing human rights than it would under secular criteria? That is, one might say that the assumption that broad Islamic qualifications on rights like those in cited articles imply the erosion of rights protections is only that—an assumption. Although in the abstract this question might seem justified, there are indications that warrant the assumption that these qualifications are designed to dilute rights. One can be assured of the validity of this conclusion by considering the historical and legal context in which the Islamic qualifications were introduced into the Iranian constitutional rights provisions. It then becomes reasonable to maintain that qualifications like these are designed to undermine rights protections.

First of all, there is the nature of the Iranian government itself. Liberal Muslims with strong commitments to human rights like Mehdi Bazargan and Muslim clerics like Taleghani, whose views were quoted earlier and who believe that Islam protects individual rights and freedoms, were quickly excluded from the circles of power. Liberal interpretations of Islamic requirements in the area of human rights were anathema to Khomeini, and proponents of such interpretations were quickly placed on the defensive by powerful clerics who supported the application of *shari'a* rules. Iran's ruling clerics have repeatedly lambasted liberal Iranians who resist their oppressive and antidemocratic policies as being necessarily "anti-Islamic," "enemies of God and the Prophet Muhammad," "Satanic," or "heretical." Both liberal secular politicians and liberal clerics who would have argued for the proposition that elements of the Islamic tradition should be utilized to enhance individual rights and freedoms were subject to censorship and punishment.

Iran's postrevolutionary ruling elite became dominated by conservative clerics, who were eager to exploit their newly won political power to realize their vision of clerical domination of society and whose lack of sympathy for human rights principles has been abundantly manifested by subsequent events. Both the conduct and the statements of the clerical members of Iran's ruling elite reveal that they see the official version of Islam as a tool of reverse social engineering for combatting the social changes that have accompanied Iran's modernization. In such circumstances, it is natural that Islamic qualifications of human rights embody retrograde interpretations of *shari'a* requirements and are used as instruments of repressive governmental policies.

Second, there is the general nature of the relationship of the individual and the state in contemporary Middle Eastern societies, a relationship that predisposes governments in the region to be hostile to claims on behalf of individual liberties and the rights of the citizen. It is characterized by deeply ingrained patterns of authoritarian, if not totalitarian, government. Suppression of opposition, censorship of dissenting opinion, and intolerance of any kind of political or intellectual pluralism are prevalent. Favoritism for members of the power elite and groups closely allied with it and corresponding discrimination against other groups are the rule. In a region where antidemocratic governments have the long-established habit of seeking to amass power at the expense of the rights of the individual and where the institutions that in other societies might protect the individual are weak or nonexistent, it is reasonable to expect that any vague qualifications of rights will tend to be exploited to enhance the power of the state, not to build up the freedoms enjoyed by the individual.

Third, one must recall a point that has already been made: There is no developed tradition of Islamic human rights protections. This means that none of the various formulas that are used to set the Islamic qualifications of rights in the Iranian Constitution has any settled legal content.

One might contrast the problem of Islamic restrictions on rights with the vast number of precedents that exist limiting the qualifications that may be placed on rights in the U.S. Bill of Rights. For example, legal precedents establish that there are very few limits that the government may impose on the right of free speech in the United States. In the United States, when individuals assert that the government has unconstitutionally infringed First Amendment guarantees of free speech, they can rely on an elaborate set of principles that has been developed by independent courts that sharply inhibits the ability of the government to curtail rights of free speech. The doctrinal constraints on the government's ability to curb speech are so firm that a heavy burden is placed on the government to justify conduct or laws in restraint of free speech. If the government does not abide by the limits that the courts have set, it will be deemed to have acted in violation of the Constitution and the speech in question will be protected by measures like injunctions or nullifications of relevant laws. U.S. free speech guarantees are strong in part because of the framework of legal rules that define narrowly and specifically the grounds on which this right can be restricted or denied, but also because of the respect for laws and legal institutions that characterizes U.S. society.

In contrast, in Iran there are no firmly ingrained precedents set by an independent judiciary that narrowly limit the circumstances in which Islamic principles can be invoked to justify restrictions or denials of rights. On the contrary, the Iranian judiciary is politicized and subservient to the government, and thus the Islamic qualifications on rights provisions will have the content that the government chooses to ascribe to them. Those qualifications leave the Iranian government and its agents such as the Revolutionary Guards free to engage in any repressive, arbitrary, and discriminatory conduct they choose without fear that the injured citizen can successfully invoke Islamic criteria to challenge the legality of the governmental actions. Of course, the ability of the government to rely on Islam to insulate its conduct from effective judicial review is linked to the fact that Iran's bar was destroyed after the revolution, that there is no regard for due process of law in the postrevolutionary legal system, and that courts simply endorse the positions taken by the regime. That is, Iranian courts cannot offer a neutral forum for review of constitutional claims by individuals harmed by government infringements of rights and Iranian judges cannot risk challenging government conduct or laws denying rights.

Furthermore, in considering how Islamic qualifications affect rights, one is entitled to regard the actual practice of the Iranian government since the revolution as a gloss on these qualifications. When one does so, one sees that the government, which, one should recall, has been led by an Islamic jurist and in which clerics play a prominent role, routinely violates international norms for the protection of rights. This violation, of course, corresponds to the contempt for international human rights that has been expressed by Iran's leaders and the conviction that Iran's adherence to Islamic values allows it to ignore the international standards. As we have seen, Iran's UN representative voiced this conviction.

The accumulated evidence shows that after the brief period of freedom immediately after the triumph of the revolution, the civil and political rights set forth in the constitutional provisions reviewed here have been denied in Iran on grounds of Islamic principles and the need to defend Islam against its enemies.[22] That is, the evidence is overwhelming that Islamic criteria qualifying rights as they are applied in Iran afford grounds for restricting and denying rights, rather than providing legal grounds for resisting such restrictions and denials.

A clarification seems in order at this point: Showing the correlation between the Islamic qualifications on rights in the Iranian Constitution and the subsequent pattern of government conduct restricting and denying human rights is not the same thing as asserting that, but for the Islamic qualifications that were placed on rights in the Iranian Constitution, the rights would have been protected or that the regime in each instance when rights were being overridden relied formally on the Islamic qualifications in the constitution to justify its conduct. That is, no attempt is being made to argue here that adding the Islamic qualifications to rights provisions in the constitution was a necessary precondition for the regime's undertaking measures that were incompatible with human rights norms or that the regime always felt compelled to show that its measures followed Islamic criteria before undertaking measures aimed at curbing or denying rights.

Instead, the connection appears to have been a more subtle one. The addition of the Islamic criteria qualifying rights signaled a general disposition not to be bound by the standards of the UDHR, which, as noted, its advocates had not been able to incorporate in the 1979 constitution. In addition, the Islamic qualifications were representative of the general philosophy of the associates of Ayatollah Khomeini, who eventually consolidated their hold over the country, and according to whom the norms of "Islam," as embodied in the views of the ruling elite of clerics, could override all secular legal norms. However, the subsequent conduct of the regime revealed that it did not lay great store by principles of legality, irrespective of whether these were religious or secular, and that it was even quite prepared to indulge in violations of basic tenets of Islamic law where the latter stood in the way of its political objectives.[23] Under Khomeini the government became both pragmatic and ruthless, acting out of its own notions of political expediency and resorting to whatever measures were deemed essential to defend its interests and the new hierarchy of power and privilege that it sought to preserve. In this, of course, it acted just like the many secular regimes in the Middle East that pay lip service to official ideologies of nationalism or socialism and also to trappings of legality that on closer inspection turn out to be mere window dressing for policies dictated by the desire to retain power and crush political opposition.

One must be careful to avoid creating the impression that somehow the Islamic qualifications in the articles that have been discussed created the human rights violations that ensued, but one should not underplay the correlation between the rights violations and the official position that rights could be restricted or denied in the name of Islam. Khomeini and his allies supported conservative interpretations of *shari'a* law, and the Islamic qualifications that were placed on constitutional rights actually had many parallels in the policies of the regime. During the Islamization programs in Pakistan and the Sudan, which have been carried out by military governments allied with conservative Islamic clerics and political groups, Islam has also been consistently invoked to justify the government's restricting or denying rights, not to afford greater protections for human rights. In the light of this experience, one may assume that vague, open-ended Islamic qualifications of human rights are likely to be interpreted in ways that will dilute or deny rights.

Restrictions in the UIDHR

The UIDHR relies more extensively and explicitly than the Iranian Constitution does on Islamic criteria to limit rights. It must be emphasized that this pattern of pervasive reliance on the *shari'a* to qualify rights is less readily apparent in the English version than it is in the

Arabic version of the UIDHR, which seems to be the authoritative text. The Explanatory Notes accompanying the English version of the UIDHR state that the Arabic text is "the original," which suggests that it should be treated as more definitive than the English translation. However, the relationship between the Arabic and English versions is a very problematic one, as there are inconsistencies between the two and vagueness and ambiguities in the Arabic.[24]

The Explanatory Notes include the assurance: "In the exercise and enjoyment of the rights referred to above every person shall be subject only to such limitations as are enjoined by the Law for the purpose of securing the due recognition of, and respect for, the rights and the freedom of others and of meeting the just requirements of morality, public order and the general welfare of the Community (Ummah)." Reading the English version, one could receive the impression that many of the UIDHR provisions are subject to qualifications imposed by secular laws, since the wording of the qualifications is consistently "according to the Law." The wording could leave the reader with the impression that secular standards are being used. However, in reality there is no similarity between the qualifications placed on rights in the UIDHR and those found in international law. In the UIDHR it is actually the *shari'a* that qualifies the rights involved when the term "according to the Law" is used in the English version to place conditions on rights, as will be illustrated in what follows.

It is difficult but not impossible for the reader of the English version to discover that by "the Law" the UIDHR means the *shari'a*. The Explanatory Notes accompanying the English version of the UIDHR state that the term *Law* in the text means the *shari'a*, which is defined as "the totality of ordinances derived from the Qur'an and Sunnah [the reports of what the Prophet Muhammad said and did] and any other laws that are deduced from these two sources by methods considered valid in Islamic jurisprudence."[25] This definition does not by any means settle how this term should be understood or what qualifications would thereby be placed on rights. At a minimum, "the *shari'a*" under this definition would seem to constitute the totality of premodern *shari'a* jurisprudence, which means that "*shari'a*" here is a term encompassing a vast range of diverging legal positions.[26] Depending on how the decision is made as to what methods are "considered valid in Islamic jurisprudence," this term might or might not also include many more recent interpretations as well. That is, given the enormous literature that this definition potentially covers, the standards that will be used are being left deliberately vague.

Some examples of how the *shari'a* is used in the UIDHR to qualify basic rights will now be considered. In the English version of the

UIDHR, Section 12 of the Preamble includes the guarantee that "no one shall be deprived of the rights assured to him by the Law except by its authority and to the extent permitted by it." Unless one bears in mind the fact that "Law" means the *shari'a,* one might not appreciate the implications of this provision, which are that *shari'a* requirements determine what rights people have. Essentially, this says that rights depend on the *shari'a;* the *shari'a* both assures them and takes them away. The wording of Section 12 of the Preamble in the Arabic version confirms this. It provides that "each person is guaranteed security, freedom, dignity, and justice according to the dictates of what the *shari'a* of God has decreed in the way of rights for people."

In the specific provisions of the UIDHR (English) one finds that the *shari'a* (the Law) determines the scope of the following rights:

1. The right to inflict injury or death, in Article 1.a.
2. The right to liberty, in Article 2.a.
3. The right to justice, in Article 4.a.
4. The right to assume public office, in Article 11.a.
5. The right of expression, in Article 12.a.
6. The right "to protest and strive," in Article 12.c.
7. The right to disseminate information (also qualified by considerations of the security of the society or the state), in Article 12.d.
8. The right to earn a living, in Article 15.b.
9. The right to pursue given economic activities (also qualified by considerations of the interests of the community), in Article 15.g.
10. The rights of spouses in marriage, in Article 19.a.
11. A wife's right to divorce, in Article 20.c, and her right to inherit, in Article 20.d.

Two other articles are problematic. The English Article 14 appears to guarantee a right to freedom of association, with distinctive Islamic qualifications, but as will be discussed, it has no counterpart in the Arabic original, so its status as part of the document is questionable.[27] Article 11 provides for a right to participate in public life, but the provision is qualified in a way that ensures that it will have discriminatory impact on non-Muslims, as will be explained.

To evaluate the strength of the human rights provisions in the UIDHR, one should put oneself in the position of a person being denied civil or political rights by the Iranian government in the name of Islam. Could one utilize the UIDHR to prove that the deprivations of rights that have occurred since the Islamic Revolution violated Islamic human rights norms? It seems not. The UIDHR accepts the idea that all rights may be qualified by the *shari'a,* but it effectively leaves it to the authorities to decide the Islamic qualifications of rights, because it defines the *shari'a* so broadly that governments are left free to choose what "Islamic" principles to apply. Thus, if the UIDHR standards were applicable in Iran, they would permit the Iranian government to do exactly as it has done, consistently interpreting Islamic law to legitimize government curbs on rights. In contrast, a person being denied civil or political rights in Iran could utilize the international human rights norms to establish that the Iranian government was violating human rights norms.

Restrictions in Other Islamic Human Rights Schemes

Just as the Iranian Constitution and the UIDHR provide for the use of vague Islamic criteria to restrict basic rights and freedoms, so other Islamic human rights schemes have restricted rights and freedoms. Some examples of these Islamic limitations on basic rights and freedoms are indicated in this section, while others that specifically affect women, minorities, and religious freedom will be treated in greater detail in later sections.

The Azhar draft Islamic constitution will be examined first. I shall refer to both the Arabic version, which one presumes was the original and the often awkward English translation that accompanies it.

The Azhar draft constitution uses a variety of Islamic formulas to qualify rights. Article 29 guarantees freedom of religious and intellectual belief, freedom to work, freedom of expression, freedom to form and join associations and unions, personal freedom (*al-hurriya al-shakhsiya*), freedom to travel,[28] and freedom to hold meetings, all within *shari'a* limits (*hudud al-shari'a al-islamiya*). Article 37 guarantees the right to work and gain a living within *shari'a* precepts (*ahkam al-shari'a al-islamiya*). Article 43 says that rights are enjoyed according to the objectives of the *shari'a* (*wafqan li maqasid al-shari'a*). With the exception of Article 42, which places secular conditions as well on rights, Islamic law is treated as the sole basis for restricting or denying rights.

Although all of these qualifications are left very indefinite, one might be particularly curious as to what Islamic restrictions on the freedom of travel would entail. Article 13 of the UDHR guarantees everyone the freedom of movement within the borders of each state and the right to leave and return to his to her own country without any qualifications, and it may not be immediately obvious why religious criteria would be relevant for the exercise of this freedom. However, Islamic conservatives tend to believe that women should not leave their homes save in case of necessity, and that if they do leave their homes, they should be chaperoned.[29] Some conservative Muslims believe that it is "un-Islamic" for women to be allowed to drive, which is why Islam is invoked as the reason for not allowing women to drive cars in Saudi Arabia. The general treatment of women in the Azhar constitution, which will be examined later, warrants the inference that the "*shari'a* limits" on freedom of travel would be used to justify restrictions on women's freedom of movement.

One sees in the Azhar draft constitution a rights philosophy that is very similar to the one in the Iranian Constitution and the UIDHR. In all of these, rights are subject to vague *shari'a* criteria. The Azhar draft constitution relies especially heavily on these Islamic restrictions.

In the work of the Iranian Sufi Sultanhussein Tabandeh, one finds similar religious qualifications placed on human rights. However, he coupled Islamic qualifications with others that indicate a bias in favor of preserving social order and harmony and enforcing respect for authority. Thus, he associated obedience to Islamic law with deference to the will of the majority and the dictates of the government. The UDHR in Article 3 guarantees the general right to life, liberty, and security of person without qualification, but according to Tabandeh, those rights should be qualified by the requirement that it not be "contrary to the regulations of Islam nor molest the peace of others."[30] It is striking to see that in Tabandeh's view, even the right to life itself is qualified by Islamic criteria, meaning that religious rules suffice in his mind as justifications for taking life. Apparently, life could also be taken under his scheme where a person's continuing to live was disturbing to other people, which would allow the subjective reactions of persons who felt their peace had been molested to deny someone the right to live.[31] These standards deviate sharply from the international norms, such as the principle in Article 6 of the ICCPR that the right to life should be protected by law and that no one should be arbitrarily deprived of life. With regard to freedom of opinion and expression, Tabandeh said that freedom in these areas ceases to be a right where "it threatens public order or grows contumacious against government and religion."[32]

As has already been noted, Mawdudi's discussion of Islamic human rights is very sketchy and uneven and leaves the impression that he was avoiding a number of difficult problems. His presentation of Islamic qualifications on human rights is correspondingly short and incomplete. In his scheme he did limit freedom of expression and association by imposing the condition that such freedom must conform to the Islamic command to order what is good and forbid that which is evil.[33] This indicates that Islamic standards of virtue would be used to determine what could be expressed and what associations would be allowed, but the exact meaning of this qualification was not explained. On the basis of this example, one can say that he showed in his Islamic human rights pamphlet a disposition to think of Islam as a curb on rights. However, as we shall see, there is much more evidence that he supported the use of rules of premodern Islamic law to deny rights of women and non-Muslims.

Summary

As the foregoing illustrates, the authors of these Islamic human rights schemes do not see the relationship of the individual and the state as being an adversarial one in which the weaker party, the individual, needs iron-clad guarantees of civil and political rights to offset the tendencies of modern governments to assert their powers at the expense of the freedoms of the individual. Furthermore, they seem to believe that where the freedom of the individual and the religious values of the traditional culture are in conflict, it is the former that should give way. There seems to be concern lest the individual attempt to assert excessive rights that could harm the authority of the state or undermine social cohesion. Islam is viewed in these schemes as a device for restricting individual freedoms and keeping the individual in a subordinate place vis-à-vis the government and society. However, the *shari'a* criteria that are employed to restrict rights are left so uncertain and general that they do not define any line beyond which the demands of the government and society for obedience and submission could be said to constitute an impermissible infringement of individual rights. That is, they afford no means for protecting the individual against deprivations of the rights that are guaranteed by international law. Thereby the stage is set not just for the diminution of these rights but potentially for denying them altogether.

CHAPTER 5

Discrimination Against Women and Non-Muslims

Equality in the Islamic Legal Tradition

Accommodating the principle of equality in an Islamic human rights scheme involves dealing with two aspects in the Islamic tradition, one egalitarian and the other mandating sexual and religious discrimination, as well as the mixed reactions of contemporary Muslims to these two aspects. The degree of difficulty of reconciling the two depends on which aspect is taken to be more truly representative of Islamic values.

There is much in the sources of Islamic law that bespeaks a fundamentally egalitarian philosophy. For example, it is an important tenet of Islam that the best person is the person who is most pious. The accounts of the earliest rulers of the community, including stories of the life of the Prophet, are full of incidents indicating the rulers' humility, their egalitarian spirit, and their humane concern for the rights and welfare of all of their subjects. However, the Islamic sources do distinguish in a number of areas between the rights of Muslims and non-Muslims, men and women, and free persons and slaves. The jurists of the premodern period tended to deemphasize the egalitarian features of Islam and to interpret *shari'a* requirements in ways that reinforced the hierarchical features of the Islamic social order, in which the free male Muslim possessed the most rights and the female non-Muslim slave, the fewest.[1]

In modern times, Muslims have generally agreed that slavery is a retrograde institution that is now unacceptable, and the large body of premodern *shari'a* law on slavery has been effectively discarded. At present Muslims are deeply divided on the question of whether legal distinctions based on sex and religion have become similarly superseded, so that the premodern *shari'a* rules in this area should be discarded as well. For this reason, Muslims today disagree about whether a legal system in which women and non-Muslims were given equal rights with Muslim men would be compatible with the requirements of Islam.

When it comes to deciding whether the principle of equality is compatible with Islam, one can distinguish between two different approaches on the part of those Muslims who wish to retain the premodern *shari'a* rules affecting women and non-Muslims. One is to affirm that the principle of equality violates *shari'a* law. Conservative Muslim clerics in the past have been outspoken in their condemnation of the principle of equality on the grounds that it makes equal those who under the *shari'a* must be treated differently.[2] The other approach is to offer reasons why the principle of equality is not violated by the retention of the discriminatory rules of the premodern *shari'a* and to justify according subordinate status to women and non-Muslims. Today it is rare for spokespersons of Islam to take the former position, and it is the second approach that one commonly encounters.

In seeking to understand the position of Muslims who assert that the retention of discriminatory rules of the premodern *shari'a* does not violate the principle of equality, one should bear in mind that "equality" may have a different connotation for many Muslims than it has for people in the contemporary West who have grown up with the idea of the absolute equality of all human beings. Social conditioning plays a crucial role in how people think about the principle of equality, as is clear from the history of the principle of equality in the United States. Although egalitarianism was a fundamental tenet of the political and legal order envisaged by the Declaration of Independence and the Constitution, almost no white males in the era of the Founding Fathers thought that the principle of equality extended to women and to black slaves, who were assumed to be inherently different and unequal. Thus, it was possible to affirm equality while at the same time supporting a regime of laws that discriminated based on sex and race. Only in the 1960s was the contradiction between the principle of equality and legal discrimination finally eliminated by civil rights legislation that prohibited discrimination based on sex and race.

Because of the cultural conditioning that prevails in the Middle East, it is easy for conservative Muslims to think that the distinctions made between different groups of persons in Islamic law are part of the natural order of things and to believe that the retention of premodern Islamic rules does not in any way contravene the principle of equality. Thus, one finds Muslims who argue that Islam recognizes the principle of equality even while they maintain that women and non-Muslims must be accorded an inferior status.

From the perspective of Muslims who have been conditioned by their culture and traditions to think such distinctions are natural and essential, Islam treats as equal all those who should be so treated. From this perspective, *shari'a*-based discrimination is compatible with the principle of equality. However, those Muslims have a problem when they try to deal with international human rights standards, which clearly rule out the notion that the principle of equality is compatible with a regime of discrimination against women and non-Muslims.

Equality in Islamic Human Rights Schemes

In the case of the Islamic human rights schemes examined here, there is no real attempt to abide by the principle of equality set out in international human rights law. Nevertheless, the authors appear reluctant to acknowledge their unwillingness to respect this principle. Perhaps conscious that by perpetuating a regime of discriminatory *shari'a* rules they are breaking with a widely respected tenet of modern political and legal thought, the authors of Islamic human rights schemes attempt to disguise the extent to which they are repudiating the notion that all people should enjoy equal rights.

They may attempt simply to avoid the issues involved. For example, Mawdudi included "the equality of human beings" in his list of Islamic human rights.[3] In his discussion of this principle, he asserted that Islam outlaws discrimination between "men"—not between "men and women"—based on color, race, nationality, or place of birth.[4] In his comments on the principle of equality before the law in Islam, he stated that Islam also outlaws discrimination based on class.[5] (As will be seen, this formulation resembles the provision on equality in Article 3.a of the UIDHR.) This formulation is disturbingly evasive, since in Muslim societies it is de jure discrimination based on sex and religion that constitutes the problematic area.

In any social context, the measure of the human rights protections that are afforded by the law is the extent to which the laws aim at redressing ingrained patterns of discrimination. Where local laws have traditionally deprived certain classes of persons of their rights, it is essential that provisions on equality mandate an end to those classes' second-class status. Therefore, it would have been hypocritical for the United States to have outlawed discrimination based, say, on caste while ignoring discrimination based on race, just as it would be meaningless in a Hindu environment to outlaw discrimination based on race while ignoring discrimination based on caste. In each case, the actual patterns of discrimination in the local culture would have been ignored.

It is obvious that Mawdudi was endeavoring to avoid dealing with the real problems that are posed by trying to integrate the international norm of equality before the law in a rights scheme that retains discriminatory rules taken from the premodern *shari'a*. In a scheme like Mawdudi's—designed to be implemented in the Muslim world—it is disingenuous to talk about equality before the law without addressing the problems posed by discriminatory *shari'a* rules denying women and non-Muslims the rights and freedoms enjoyed by Muslim men. Mawdudi, because he failed to prohibit discrimination based on sex or religion, was effectively condoning the perpetuation of discrimination against these groups.

Article 19 of the Iranian Constitution uses a similar, evasive formula to deal with the principle of equality: "The people of Iran, regardless of their ethnic, family and tribal origins shall enjoy equal rights. Color, race, language and the like shall not be a cause for privilege." It is noteworthy that Article 19 does not address the issue of whether equality can be denied on the grounds of sex or religion. The extensive discrimination practiced in postrevolutionary Iran against women and non-Muslims indicates that the omission of these categories was not accidental but was designed to accommodate patterns of discrimination that are widely supported by the government and the more traditional segments of Iranian society.

The gaps in the equality guarantee of Article 19 are significant, since they correlate with the practice of the government. However, the Iranian Constitution also has a provision that echoes one in the draft constitution. The draft constitution had provided in Article 22, the very first principle in the chapter on rights, that "all members of the people, both women and men, are equal before the law." In the section of the 1979 constitution setting forth the aims of the Islamic Republic, one finds in Article 3.14 that these aims include: "securing every human right for both men and women, and establishing judicial security for all based on justice and the equality of all before the law [*qanun*]."

The conservatives who participated in the revising of the draft constitution and who were able to impose so many Islamic features on the final version of the constitution were apparently unable to excise this particular provision from the constitution. The fact that this provision was retained, even though it expressed a philosophy of equality that was radically at odds both with the actual policies of the regime and with other provisions in the constitution, is highly significant, because it shows how much normative force international human rights concepts still had in Iran despite the attempts by conservative clerics to discredit them.

Equal Protection in U.S. and International Law

The principle of equality before the law is closely related to the principle of equal protection of the law, which merits consideration at this juncture. The most influential formulation of the principle of equal protection of the law was set forth in the 1868 Fourteenth Amendment to the U.S. Constitution, which stipulates that "no State shall . . . deny to any person within its jurisdiction the equal protection of the laws."

The purpose of the U.S. equal protection clause in the aftermath of the Civil War was to end slavery and the legal regime of discrimination against blacks in the South.[6] Its original reach has been extended by judicial interpretation to provide protection against discrimination on a number of bases other than race. In general, one could say that classifications of people for the purpose of placing minorities at a disadvantage and ones based on the idea that one group is inherently inferior to another group or based on stereotypical views of traditional victims of societal discrimination violate the equal protection clause. That is, the principle of equal protection is understood to afford remedies in cases where one can identify laws that reinforce actual patterns of discrimination and inequality in U.S. society.

Although many features of U.S. equal protection jurisprudence necessarily reflect the peculiarities of U.S. history and environment, the basic concept has been emulated in other laws, and the idea of equal protection of the law is endorsed in international law. Article 7 of the UDHR stipulates: "All are equal before the law and are entitled without any discrimination to equal protection of the law. All are entitled to equal protection against any discrimination in violation of this Declaration and against any incitement to such discrimination."

One sees in Article 7 of the UDHR unequivocal endorsement of the idea that equal, nondiscriminatory treatment under the law is due all persons. Just as U.S. law has classifications on the basis of which it is impermissible to discriminate, so Article 7 of the UDHR outlaws discrimination on the basis of what are stipulated as impermissible grounds. According to Article 2 of the UDHR, it is impermissible to discriminate based on sex and religion, race, color, language, political or other opinion, national or social origin, property, and birth or other status. Any legal measures that discriminate between groups of people using these criteria violate the UDHR guarantee of equality and equal protection.[7]

Thus, both the U.S. constitutional principle and its UDHR counterpart envisage equal protection under a neutral law, a law that does not deny freedoms and rights to members of weaker or disfavored categories of society and that accords all people equal treatment. Therefore, under these concepts of equal protection, one could not say that a law like that of South Africa offers equal protection, because it mandates discrimination against the colored and black populations while granting privileges to members of the white population. The fact that South African law with its discriminatory features might be applied equally to persons within the separate categories would not save the laws from condemnation for violating the principle of equal protection.

Equal Protection in Islamic Human Rights Schemes

Although in Islamic law one can discern elements that in some ways anticipate modern notions of equality, one does not find any counterpart of the principle of equal protection under the law. For those trained in Islamic rather than in Western law, the meaning of equal protection may be obscure and confusing. In the past, when Muslims were first attempting to come to grips with the constitutional principles of equality, they tended to assume that the principle of equality was not violated as long as *shari'a* law, with its discriminatory features intact, was applied equally to persons within the separate categories that it established.[8] That is, they took the position that equality before the law meant that all Muslims should be treated equally under the *shari'a* and that all non-Muslims should also be treated equally under the *shari'a*[9]—not that Muslims and non-Muslims should be treated alike or accorded the same rights under the law. This original confusion about the meaning of the modern principle of equal protection of the law appears to persist among Muslims who are influenced by traditional culture.

Equal protection of the law in the Islamic human rights schemes does not have the same significance as it does in international law. As will be seen, the idea of equal protection is modified to accommodate forms of discrimination mandated by tradition and by premodern rules of Islamic law. In other words, according to the Islamic human rights schemes, it is possible to have equal protection under a law that itself mandates unequal treatment for the favored and disfavored groups in society.

In the English version of the UIDHR, Article 3.a provides that "all persons are equal before the Law and are entitled to equal opportunities and protection of the Law," which could leave the impression that the UIDHR has abolished the pattern of discrimination that *shari'a* law requires in the treatment of the rights of male Muslims versus those of women and non-Muslims. Although the uninitiated Western reader, having seen this formulation, might think that the authors espoused the principle of equal protection as known in international human rights law, this is not actually the case.

To understand the significance of the terminology, one needs to consult the Arabic version of Article 3.a of the UIDHR, which states that people are equal before the *shari'a,* and that no distinction is made in its application to them or in their protection under it. That is, people are not being guaranteed the equal protection of a neutral law but "equal protection" under a law that in its premodern formulations is inherently discriminatory and thereby in violation of international standards. The misleading formulation of the English version of Article 3.a, which tends to disguise this difference, is only one of many aspects of the UIDHR that suggest that the authors are aware that their philosophy is incompatible with international norms and are trying to hide from their Western audience the aspects of their schemes that conflict with international human rights norms.

Since the *shari'a,* at least in the traditional formulations that are acceptable to Islamic conservatives, requires legal discrimination against women and religious minorities, the claim in the Arabic version of Article 3.a that all people are equal before the *shari'a* seems self-contradictory. However, as will be shown in the discussion of the corresponding Arabic text, there are specifications in the Arabic version that reveal that the authors do not believe the principle of equality is violated where the discrimination is based on sex or religion. In other words, sex and religion are not included in the categories on the basis of which it is impermissible to discriminate. Thus, according to this approach, it becomes as legitimate to deny women and religious minorities the rights granted to Muslim males as it would be in Western legal systems to discriminate against noncitizens or convicted felons or to deny certain rights to children or to the mentally infirm. In consequence of this approach, women and religious minorities could not claim that their Islamic human right to equal protection had been violated if they encountered discrimination.

One finds the categories on the basis of which, according to the UIDHR, it is impermissible to discriminate in the Arabic version of Article 3.a. Following the statement that all persons are equal before the *shari'a,* there are in the Arabic text of Article 3.a quotations from the Prophet and the Caliph Abu Bakr, his first successor. These quotations support the notion that there should be no discrimination based on ethnic background, color, social standing, and political connections.[10] These are, in fact, categories on the basis of which *shari'a* rules do not ordinarily discriminate. It is noteworthy that the categories do not include sex or religion.

Some clarification of the real meaning of the UIDHR can be obtained by comparing provisions of various articles. Such internal comparisons reinforce the conclusion that the guarantee of equality in Article 3.a does not intend to abolish discrimination based on sex and religion, since such discrimination is endorsed in other provisions. Some of these will be treated in Chapters 6 and 7, but a few will be presented here to illustrate how the rights that women and minorities enjoy under international law fail to receive protection in the UIDHR.

Article 11 provides for a right to participate in public life. The Arabic version provides that all members of the *umma,* or Islamic community, who are possessed of the requisite *shari'a* qualifications are eligible to serve in public employment and public office. In the Arabic version it is specifically provided that race and class cannot be utilized as a basis for excluding people from such positions. Article 11 has, it appears, been drafted so as to accommodate discriminatory *shari'a* rules excluding women and non-Muslims from public office and employment as people lacking requisite qualifications. Islamic conservatives generally say that the *shari'a* excludes women and non-Muslims from most, if not all, governmental positions. Therefore, women and non-Muslims would probably be disqualified on grounds of sex, religion, or both from public employment and public office. By its terms the article seems to exclude non-Muslims from its protections since they are not members of the Islamic *umma,* which is a community of believers united by a common faith in Allah and the Prophet Muhammad as his final messenger.

The drafters of the Iranian Constitution, who, as noted (Chapter 4), included an equal protection clause in Article 20, were apparently aware that it was, at least from the standpoints of constitutional theory and international law, a contradiction in terms to guarantee equal protection under the *shari'a.* Thus, the first sentence in the article provides for equal protection under the *qanun,* or secular law. This makes the Iranian equal protection clause look more like the international standard set forth in Article 7 of the UDHR than Article 3.a of the UIDHR. The intent is not, however, to guarantee equality to all persons under the law; it is just that in the Iranian Constitution discrimination against women and non-Muslims is legitimated by other provisions. As we have seen, the second sentence of Article 20 provides that all human rights are determined by Islamic criteria, and Article 4 provides that Islamic principles in general prevail over constitutional principles. These provisions indicate that discriminatory *shari'a* principles would prevail over the secular equal protection principle.

The inclusion of an equal protection clause in Article 20 suggests the powerful influence that Western and international ideas of equal protection have had. Given the U.S. influences on Iran in the decades before the revolution, it is not surprising that the U.S. formula of equal protection had become familiar to Iranians. Today an equal protection clause seems to have become part of the necessary apparatus of a modern constitution, so that it is included even where the philosophical

premises on which the concept of equal protection rests are rejected—
as they are in the case of the Iranian Constitution.

In any event, the incongruous inclusion of an equal protection clause
in the context of the Iranian Constitution is perfectly emblematic of
the awkward blend of Islamic principles and dissimilar and imperfectly
integrated international norms that is presented in the treatment of
equality in Islamic human rights schemes. It shows that even when
they are determined to apply discriminatory *shari'a* rules in ways that
violate international human rights norms, the authors of Islamic human
rights schemes find the internationally recognized formulations of the
principle of equality so prestigious that they cannot refrain from including them in their schemes.

The question remains: How do the authors of the Iranian Constitution rationalize the conflicting norms they have placed in the text?
It is interesting to consider the treatment of equality in an article by
a Shi'i cleric and strong supporter of Ayatollah Khomeini, Ayatollah
Yahya Nuri, who has played a prominent and active role in the postrevolutionary regime.[11] Nuri attempted to adjust the idea of equality
so that it could fit within a framework of premodern *shari'a* rules
mandating inequality. He argued that the principle of equality is the
basis of Islam and that Islam shuns the violation of human rights and
grants freedom to all under the law.[12] However, in listing impermissible
bases for discrimination, he enumerated only the categories of race,
color, social class, "weakness," and poverty.[13] Nuri's omission of the
critical categories, sex and religion, categories on the basis of which
discrimination is mandated by the premodern *shari'a*, is already familiar. Obviously, this leaves the door open for the application of all
the discriminatory *shari'a* rules that relegate women and non-Muslims
to an inferior status in Iran.

Ayatollah Nuri elaborated his philosophy of equality. He said that
Islam supports the idea that all men (here the omission of women is
probably not accidental) should have equal political and social rights,
but this is with the qualification that "equality must be established by
the law and it must not transgress the law."[14] In other words, in his
view, equality, correctly understood, does not challenge the hierarchy
of privilege established by the *shari'a*, where male Muslims are meant
to possess rights that are denied to others.

One sees that to Nuri, the *shari'a* serves as a necessary corrective
to the principle of equality, which, if not adequately curbed, would
have undesirable effects on society, whence his formula "equality must
be established by the law" but "must not transgress the law." By holding
that equality should be confined within legal limits so that excessive
equality can be avoided, Nuri is effectively saying that some inequalities

should be imposed by law. Ultimately, he is appropriating the ideal of equality while at the same time calling for upholding laws that favor some at the expense of others.

A comparison of Nuri's formula and the treatment of equality in the Islamic human rights schemes shows that they share a common assumption—that the right to equality should be incorporated in Islamic rights schemes and is acceptable as long as people who should not be made equal are kept in their proper place by the retention of the rules of Islamic law. In contrast, in international law, as embodied in the UDHR Articles 1 and 3, the rights to equality and equal protection of the law are absolute and not subject to any legal qualifications. Because they are unqualified rights, there can be no legitimate societal or governmental interest in mandating inequality. Indeed, the right to equality and equal protection becomes illusory unless one takes this absolutist position that there may be no denying rights and privileges on the basis of sex, religion, or other impermissible category of discrimination.

Nuri's formula, which is designed to enforce legal inequality, although he purported to support the ideal of equality, is in the final analysis a cousin of the conceit of the elite pigs in George Orwell's *Animal Farm,* according to which all animals were equal but some were more equal than others.[15]

Tabandeh expressed approval of Article 1 of the UDHR, which says that all human beings are born free and equal in dignity and rights, and declared that it reflects ideas in the Qur'an.[16] In discussing equality, however, he talked of prohibiting class-based or racially based discrimination only, omitting any mention of sex discrimination. He explicitly said that differences are recognized based on "religion, faith, or conviction," seemingly in the belief—unfounded—that the UDHR Article 1 provision on equality allows such religious discrimination.[17]

In his discussion of Article 2, the general provision of the UDHR prohibiting discrimination, Tabandeh also avoided addressing the issue of sex but did indicate his approval of Islamic rules according Muslims a higher status than non-Muslims and free persons a higher status than slaves.[18] He therefore concluded that Islam cannot accept certain parts of Article 2, "for it cannot deny the difference between Muslim and non-Muslim."[19] One gathers from Tabandeh's failure to mention the status of women in connection with these articles that the idea of female equality struck him as so far-fetched that he did not need to bother explaining that it was unacceptable under the *shari'a.*

The Azhar draft constitution circumvents the issue of equality by avoiding any specific discussion of categories on the basis of which it is impermissible to discriminate. Article 28 does say that justice and equality are the basis of rule, but this vague provision is far from a stipulation that all persons are equal before the law. One can speculate that the authors of the Azhar draft constitution may have been less comfortable than authors of some of the other Islamic human rights schemes with stipulating an equality that was incompatible with the tenets of the premodern Islamic law. They intended to adhere to those tenets and were thus prompted to try to avoid the issue.

One sees in contrasting treatment of equality in the Azhar draft constitution and the Iranian Constitution the impact of the very different circumstances in which the two were produced. The Iranian model is an actual constitution, unlike the Azhar draft, which was no more than a hypothetical agenda of rights formulations produced by Islamic conservatives, who did not have to deal with the arguments of more liberal Muslims who demanded rights protections. In Iran, the forces of Islamic conservatism had to engage in a dialogue with a real political opposition, since, at the time of the drafting, Iran's liberal opposition had not yet been quelled and held fast to the constitutionalist ideals that had been percolating through Iranian legal and political culture since the late nineteenth century. Iran's Islamic conservatives also had to deal with a political reality in which spelling out their rejection of human rights concepts would have been unpopular and could have undermined the prospects for clerical domination of the government. It is significant that in this real-world conflict between differing Muslim attitudes on human rights issues, Islamic conservatives backed away from the more extreme positions they had traditionally advocated and agreed to accommodate—at least at the formal level— a number of fundamental human rights principles like equality and equal protection.

The contrast with other rights schemes, which lack an endorsement of equality or equal protection, highlights the fact their authors did not have to respond either to popular pressures for such provisions or to the arguments of liberal jurists on behalf of fundamental norms of constitutionalism. This is yet another ground for questioning whether these Islamic human rights schemes are at all representative of where Muslim opinion stands in practice on rights issues. They may merely reflect the ideas of a very conservative element that is philosophically aligned with repressive governments.

Dealing with specifics of equality seems to have presented great problems for the authors of the UIDHR, who offer treatments of equality that are extremely convoluted and ambiguous. Since it is very easy, if one actually endorses full equality, to provide for it using the international standards, the obscurity of the UIDHR provisions on equality suggests that the authors had great difficulty in finding for-

mulations that would offer token recognition of the principle while
restricting equality to domains where the principle would not threaten
entrenched patterns of discrimination or the advantages enjoyed by
Muslim males.

Turning to Article 3.c of the UIDHR, one finds that in the English
version under the rubric "Right to Equality and Prohibition Against
Impermissible Discrimination" there is the following guarantee: "No
person shall be denied the opportunity to work or be discriminated
against in any manner or exposed to greater physical risk by reason of
religious belief, color, race, origin, sex or language."

This differs significantly from the wording of the corresponding
Arabic provision. In the Arabic version under the rubric of the "Right
of Equality," the corresponding section, in Article 3.b, says that all
people are equal in terms of their human value (*al-qaima al-insaniya*),
that they are distinguished in merit (in the afterlife by God) according
to their works (*bi hasab 'amalihim*), that no one is to be exposed to
greater danger or harm than others are, and that any thought, law, or
rule (*wad'*) that permits discrimination between people on the basis of
jins (which can mean nation, race, or sex), *'irq* (race or descent), color,
language, or religion is in direct violation of this general Islamic principle (*hadha 'l-mabda al-islami al-'amm*).

As a result of the difference between the English and Arabic texts
and the ambiguity in the Arabic, one cannot tell whether the intent
was to abolish discrimination based on sex with regard to the areas
covered.[20] In light of the pattern of evasiveness that one finds in the
provisions in the UIDHR, one would be justified in assuming that the
wording here may be deliberately opaque and ambiguous because it
was the authors' intent to hide the purport of the provision.

The problem of construing the meaning of the wording in this
provision may not actually be as significant as it first appears, because
on closer examination one sees that the range of discriminatory laws
and practices is so narrow that no important guarantees of protection
against discrimination are being afforded for any categories of persons.
The English version in Article 3.b does seem to bar discrimination in
work opportunities, but there is no corresponding provision in the
Arabic version of Article 3. The Arabic version does not say that no
one should be discriminated against "in any manner" based on the
categories mentioned. Instead, it appears merely to endorse the notion
that people should not be discriminated against in the sense of being
exposed to greater danger or harm by reason of those categories. It is
not clear what kind of discrimination this greater exposure to danger
or harm would involve, but regardless of the construction placed on

these terms, it seems certain that it would cover an area much smaller than is indicated in the English version.

Although the Arabic version of Article 3.b does not correspond to any tenet of international human rights law, it could herald a concern for advancing rights protections if it addressed an actual pattern of rights deprivations in Muslim countries. However, the principle that groups of people should not be exposed to greater danger or harm does not seem to deal with the actual problems of discrimination faced by women and non-Muslims in Muslim countries. Members of these groups complain that they are discriminated against in education, employment, and political life. To the extent that Islamic law is applied in the rules of evidence and in criminal law, members of those groups also object to being relegated to inferior status. Feminists condemn discrimination in personal status law and in the area of personal freedoms, while non-Muslims protest the favored status accorded to Islam and the denials of religious freedoms.

Therefore, in context, the protections offered in Article 3.b seem quite trivial. There is every reason to assume that the kinds of discriminatory rules that the premodern *shari'a* employs to relegate women and non-Muslims to a subordinate status could coexist with this provision. In fact, other provisions of the UIDHR indicate that such discriminatory rules are being retained. Furthermore, the lack of protection against discrimination afforded in the Arabic version of Article 3 is not mitigated by the initial stipulation that all persons have the same human value. In context, this seems to be an abstract moral proposition, not a principle designed to establish full equality before the law.

The great disparity between the English and the Arabic versions of Article 3 of the UIDHR has been shown. It is noteworthy that the English, not the Arabic, version of Article 3 was invoked in a recent case in Pakistan.[21] In the case, the petitioner charged that the appointment of women as judges in Pakistan was un-Islamic. Although the petitioner was unable to adduce any support from the Qur'an and *sunna* for his argument, he did manage to cite prestigious medieval jurists who had ruled that women could not be judges. The attorney general of Pakistan in turn found a medieval jurist who held the contrary view and also argued that the other jurists had drawn an overly broad conclusion from a statement by the Prophet on women's capacity to rule. The court found that the petitioner had been mistaken in his interpretations of many of the requirements of Islamic law as they would affect the ability of women to serve as judges. Although the decision did not turn on the UIDHR, the court did refer to Article 3 of the English version to support its decision that Islamic law did not prohibit women from serving as judges. It characterized the article as follows:

> [It] deals with the equality before Law, entitlement to equal opportunities and protection of the Law [and] also provides firstly that all persons shall be entitled to equal wage for equal work and secondly that no person shall be denied the opportunity to work or be discriminated against in any manner or exposed to greater physical risk by reason of religious belief, color, race, origin, sex, or language.[22]

Obviously, had the court examined the Arabic version of the same article, it would have had much greater difficulty finding support for the proposition that under Islamic law women should not be discriminated against in employment or excluded from serving as judges. Women aspirants to the bench were fortunate that in Pakistan competence in Arabic was not more widespread.[23]

It is not just in the provisions of Islamic human rights that deal expressly with equality or discrimination that one finds instances of concepts of premodern Islamic law being applied to restrict the rights of persons in disfavored categories. Careful scrutiny may be needed to identify discriminatory biases in measures dealing with other rights issues. Frequently, attempts are made to obscure or disguise these discriminatory features, and in a superficial reading of Islamic human rights schemes they may entirely escape notice. A number of such instances of hidden biases in seemingly neutral provisions will be discussed in the next two chapters, but one example will be given here, where the objective is to deny to non-Muslims rights that are accorded to Muslims.

One might get the impression from a reading of the English version of Article 14 of the UIDHR that there was a right of free association. In fact, on closer reading, the provision is one that mandates inequality between Muslims and non-Muslims in terms of their rights of association and expression. The "Right of Free Association" in the heading of Article 14 of the English version of the UIDHR seems to be qualified by the requirement in Article 14.a that such associations enjoin the good and prohibit the evil. The UIDHR provision states:

> Every person is entitled to participate individually and collectively in the religious, social, cultural and political life of his community and to establish institutions and agencies meant to enjoin what is right (*ma'ruf*) and to prevent what is wrong (*munkar*).

This relates to the Qur'anic command in 4:104 to Muslims to enjoin the good and prohibit the evil. There is no protection for institutions or agencies with other purposes. The right of free association as understood today was unknown in premodern Islamic law. Given the absence of Islamic precedent for interpreting the Qur'anic command in 4:104 as a principle limiting the entities protected by the principle of freedom of association, it is unclear what limits this provision would mean for the right involved.[24]

When one looks at the heading of the Arabic version of the same provision, one sees that one is not even dealing with what would be considered a right to free association in the sense current in international law. Instead, according to the Arabic heading of Article 14, it deals with *haqq ad-da'wa wa'l-balagh,* or the right to propagate Islam and to disseminate the Islamic message. Among the Qur'anic passages cited in the Arabic version of Article 14 is part of 12:108, "Say, this is my way. I call on Allah with sure knowledge, I and whosoever follows me."

From this one understands that the only freedom of association that is being guaranteed is one that protects activities connected with spreading Islam. It is possible to interpret the provision of this restricted freedom as an indication that there is no intent to recognize a broader freedom of association. It is highly unlikely that the right to spread religions other than Islam or to disseminate works associated with philosophies of secularism or atheism could be accommodated within the scope of this wording. The Arabic Article 14 therefore actually seems to amount to a curb on the association rights of non-Muslims.[25]

Summary

On the basis of these examinations one can say that Mawdudi, Tabandeh's commentary, and the Azhar draft constitution, which never fully and unequivocally endorse the notion that all persons are equal and that no discrimination based on religion and sex is permissible, are less internally inconsistent than the Iranian Constitution, which is a remarkable admixture of international human rights principles regarding equality and assertions of the supremacy of Islamic law that directly contravene them. It is more difficult to characterize the treatment of equality in the UIDHR because of the numerous ambiguities and inconsistencies in the provision regarding equality, discussed above. However, in general the UIDHR treatment of equality resembles that in the models of Mawdudi, Tabandeh, and the Azhar draft constitution more closely than it does that in the Iranian Constitution.

Taken together, these schemes reveal the ambivalence that conservative Muslims feel about the principle of equality, a principle that they are in general reluctant to condemn openly but seek to circumvent in practice. In these circumstances, reference to Islamic criteria on rights is not likely to result in respect for the principles of equality and equal protection of the law as mandated in international human rights law; instead, such reference tends to undermine the rights involved and to afford legal rationales for discrimination.

CHAPTER 6

Restrictions on the Rights and Freedoms of Women

In this section I will examine the significance of Islamic human rights schemes for the status of women. I will first consider some of the important facets of Islamic law affecting that status and also the problem, which by now has become acute, of determining what constitutes "Islamic law" on this topic. Next, specific tenets of Islamic human rights schemes will be analyzed to ascertain how they would affect the status of women in the contemporary Middle East. In this connection, I will discuss aspects of actual state practice in the area of women's rights. The relationship of the tenets of Islamic human rights schemes and the principles of international human rights law affecting the status of women is complex; therefore, a separate section covers international human rights provisions relevant for judging Islamic human rights provisions. Because sex stereotyping is an important, though often only implicit, feature in Islamic human rights schemes, the connection between it and international human rights law will also be examined.

Islamic Law and Women's Rights

The basic features of premodern Islamic law affecting the status of women will be outlined to set the stage for discussion of issues of women's rights. To avoid endless and repetitive qualifications, I will refer to "Islamic law" and "Islamic principles" without detailing the diversity in the positions of the various schools of law and Islamic sects regarding various facets of women's status. Although this oversimplification is necessary to avoid converting this background discussion into a treatise on the Islamic law of personal status, it should be borne in mind that generalizations about where "Islam" stands on questions of women's status can often be misleading, since even within the law schools of Sunni Islam one finds a variety of opinions on the status of women.

What Islamic sources one cites on questions of women's status is of critical importance because there is a cleavage between the early sources and the later juristic tradition. Increasingly, feminists and modernists seem to believe that the Qur'an and the example of the Prophet provide material favorable for feminist and modernist positions, whereas the juristic tradition and the associated cultural norms, which developed in the context of traditional societies in the Muslim world, provide material for the opponents of feminism and modernism.

The Qur'an, as divine Revelation, is obviously a central source of guidance. It is also a source that devotes considerable attention to the status of women, and it is noteworthy that the Qur'anic changes in women's status are in the direction of enhancing their rights and elevating their status and dignity. In an environment where women were so devalued that female infanticide was a common and tolerated practice, the Qur'an introduced reforms that prohibited female infanticide, permitted women for the first time to inherit, restricted the practice of polygamy, curbed abuses of divorce by husbands, and gave women the ownership of the dower, which had previously been paid to the bride's father.[1] As the thrust of the Qur'anic reforms in women's status is an ameliorative one, it is reasonable to conclude, as one leading Islamic modernist did, that "the principal aim of the Qur'an was the removal of certain abuses to which women were subjected."[2]

Not only did the Qur'an attack institutions of pre-Islamic Arabia that contributed to women's degraded and vulnerable status, but Islam also conferred rights on women in the seventh century that women in the West were unable to obtain until quite recently. Muslim women, for example, enjoyed full legal personality, could own and manage property, and, according to some interpretations of the Qur'an, enjoyed the right to divorce on very liberal grounds. The historical accounts regarding the status of women in the first decades of the Islamic community under the Prophet Muhammad suggest that women were originally accorded considerable freedom, that within the family the rights given them by Islam enabled them to protect their interests, and that they participated in public and religious affairs on a footing of approximate equality with men.[3]

It is natural that contemporary Muslim feminists, when they look at the history of their religion, are very skeptical when assured that Islam, initially aimed at removing the disabilities women had suffered in pre-Islamic Arabia, provides the rationale for keeping women in a subjugated, inferior status. They have tended to place the blame for what they see as distortions of the original, authentic Islam on male interpreters of the Islamic sources who had vested interests in the preservation of the patriarchal system. This position was stated forcefully by one Muslim feminist: "Through an historical process of cooptation, Patriarchy was able to devour Islam and quickly make it its own after the death of the Prophet Muhammad."[4] A distinguished Islamic modernist has argued that as a result of social conditions and the interpenetration of many diverse cultural traditions, the inferior status of women was written into Islamic law.[5] A person disposed to agree that the thrust of the original Islamic message was in the direction of improving the status of women and bringing women up to what was in the context of the existing culture approximate parity with men would be naturally inclined to dispute the authority of the later juristic tradition, which seems full of male biases and influences from patriarchal culture that can be distinguished from Islam.[6]

In traditional Islam, it is not the original sources that one consults to find the law. Islamic law had traditionally been a jurists' law. The *shari‘a* is viewed as being stated in the works of authoritative jurists. Depending on their allegiances to various sects and schools of law, Muslims at a given time or place referred to a particular jurist for authoritative guidance.

The juristic elaborations of the *shari‘a,* like so many laws formulated in the premodern era and associated with societies where traditional patriarchal family structures prevailed, treated women as needing male tutelage and control, imposing many disabilities on women, putting them in a distinctly subordinate role vis-à-vis men within the family, and keeping them in a secluded domestic role. In the premodern *shari‘a,* child marriages are allowed, which in practice means that women can be married off at early ages and against their will by male marriage guardians. Women are required to be monogamous, while men may have up to four wives at a time. Wives owe obedience to their husbands, who are entitled to keep them at home and to beat them and withhold maintenance for disobedience. Husbands can terminate marriages at their discretion simply by uttering a divorce formula, whereas wives under the doctrines of many jurists face considerable obstacles to getting a divorce over their husbands' objections. Men enjoy great power as the guardians of minors, and after a divorce, men get custody of children once they have passed the stage of infancy. In the scheme of succession, women get one-half the share of males who inherit in a similar capacity.[7]

When one leaves the area of personal status, one finds other tensions and ambiguities in the Islamic legal heritage affecting women. As has been noted, Muslims were rarely unanimous on points of family law and inheritance affecting women—areas where the rules in the Qur'an and *sunna,* although subject to diverging interpretations among the various schools and sects, were very elaborate. In areas like education, employment, and participation in public life, relevant textual authority was vague or wanting. The gaps in the sources left many questions of how women were meant to function in the society at large very difficult to resolve by references to textual authority. Naturally, there was great dissension on what the Islamic rules should be regarding the rights of women in these areas where the Qur'an and *sunna* offered scant guidance. Furthermore, there was an unresolved question of how to reconcile the rights that women were granted by the *shari'a,* such as managing their own property and conducting business, with *shari'a* rules that seemed to be in direct conflict with them, such as the rules allowing the husband to control his wife's activities and to keep her at home in seclusion from all but close family members. Thus, in all discussions of women's status in Islam, it is essential to bear in mind these observations about the diversity and complexity of the Islamic heritage.

Since the late nineteenth century, members of the elites in Muslim societies have been gradually won over to the idea that the premodern *shari'a* rules need to be reformed. Except for Saudi Arabia, Middle Eastern countries have introduced reforms to improve women's status and remove many, if not all, of the disabilities formerly imposed under the *shari'a.*[8] Until the forces of Islamization became so powerful that they were able to reverse the legal trend in favor of granting women greater rights, it seemed that changes in the legal status of women were moving in the direction of their achieving greater equality.

Secular political forces have generally been supportive of the expanded opportunities that political, economic, and social changes have meant for women, but Islamic clerics and Islamic institutions have by and large manifested strong opposition to allowing women to escape from their cloistered, subordinate, domestic roles. Muslim conservatives in recent decades have been speaking out on the status of women in Islam, purporting to demonstrate that fidelity to Islam requires rejection of the tenets of feminism.[9] New issues regarding women's status that have arisen in the wake of modernization have prompted conservatives to undertake the expansion of Islamic rules to cover problems that had no exact counterparts in the past. As salaried employment outside the home has become common and even necessary for many urban women, Muslim conservatives have asserted that "Islam" requires that women should not work outside the home, that they should not be allowed in jobs where they will have contact with men, or that they should only take jobs dealing with women and children—which typically means work in fields like obstetrics and gynecology, elementary school teaching, and home economics. With the growth of public education, questions have arisen about the degree to which women should have equal opportunities for study with men. Muslim conservatives argue that Islam calls for sexual segregation in education and that women should only be allowed to study subjects suitable for females—which tend to be ones that prepare women for a life oriented toward the home and family.

With the modernization of political institutions, new questions about women's political role have been raised. Muslim conservatives tend to believe that women should not participate in politics and many argue that women should not be permitted to vote. As other issues have come up, "Islamic" rationales for forbidding women to drive, banning women from participating in sports, and excluding them from working in television and radio programs have been proffered. New contraceptive techniques and expanded medical care have increased the ability of women to control their fertility, but Muslim conservatives, ignoring Islamic doctrine, have argued that Islam forbids abortion and limits the use of contraceptives.[10]

Arrayed against the conservatives are Muslims—generally among the better educated classes of society—who have reappraised and discarded many traditional interpretations of the Islamic sources and concluded that authentic Islamic doctrine actually supports reforms in the premodern *shari'a* rules, reforms designed to ensure the equality of the sexes. Professor Abdullahi an-Na'im, formerly of Khartoum University Law School, has been a prominent spokesperson for the view that Islam, properly understood, calls for equal rights for men and women.[11] Just as feminist perspectives have challenged the gender biases in Christian and Jewish theology, so Muslim feminists are reappraising the theological justifications that have been offered for restricting women's rights.[12] The kinds of restrictions that conservative Muslims wish to impose on women's rights tend to be dismissed by Muslim feminists as representing nothing more than patriarchal attitudes and cultural traditions disguised as religious norms.

Conservative Muslims routinely attack Muslims who advocate equality for women as being servile imitators of the West who lack loyalty to and pride in the Islamic tradition. Feminists are condemned as agents of Western cultural imperialism who aim to destroy sound customs and *shari'a* principles in the name of promoting enlightened interpretations of Islamic requirements.[13] Mawdudi complained that in the works of Muslims who support feminist interpretations of the Islamic sources "the limited and conditional freedom that women had been allowed by Islam in matters other than home science is being used as argument to encourage the Muslim women to abandon home life and its responsibilities like the European women and make their lives miserable by running after political, economic, social and other activities shoulder to shoulder with men."[14]

The postrevolutionary Iranian regime has been vociferous in denouncing women who object to its policies of cloistering women in the home, labeling them "foreign dolls," whereas Mawdudi labeled Muslim feminists "Oriental Occidentals," who espouse the philosophy, moral concepts, and social principles of the West, which they try to propagate in the Muslim world.[15] Therefore, Muslims who endorse feminist interpretations of the Islamic sources are often put on the defensive, as they try to rebut charges that they are disloyal to their own tradition and that they have been intellectually colonized by the West.

One also encounters Muslims who may not believe that full equality of the sexes is compatible with Islamic doctrine but who are nonetheless unsympathetic to the arguments of conservatives that Islam requires that women be kept enshrouded, subordinated, and secluded. A substantial portion of the Muslim community seems to espouse views on women's status that constitute a middle ground between the opinions of Muslim feminists and those of conservatives.[16]

Because of all these competing trends in Islamic thought, one cannot predict from the fact that someone is a believing Muslim what that person's position on issues of women's status will be. Given the intense controversies that have developed regarding the status of women in Islam, Muslims can no longer rely on settled doctrine in this area but must decide which of the great variety of diverging views on the rights that Islam accords women they find persuasive.

The authors of the Islamic human rights schemes that are being examined here adopt relatively conservative positions regarding women's rights, which means that under their schemes women are denied many rights to which they are entitled under international law. However, just as the authors were loath to concede that *shari'a* norms conflicted with the principle of equality, so, with the exception of Tabandeh, they go out of their way to avoid expressly stating that in Islam women are assigned inferior status and therefore not entitled to the same rights as men. Since the details of their rights schemes and applications—or, in Mawdudi's case, principles set forth in his other writings—amply demonstrate that they believe in denying women equality and keeping women in a subordinate role, it is noteworthy that they seek to avoid formally acknowledging that the de jure status of women in their schemes is a subordinate, inferior one. It suggests that they have been profoundly impressed by international norms that teach that modern rights schemes afford men and women equal rights, and that they fear that any frank admission that women cannot be equal with men in Islam will lead to their schemes being branded "backward" or "reactionary," or unacceptable under international law. They are therefore responding to the challenge posed by the prestige of international law in their formulations of principles even as they advocate substantive rules that are in conflict with international human rights norms.

Tabandeh's Ideas

Tabandeh is exceptional in his forthright assertion that Islam opposes the idea of male-female equality. His candor on this point may be a by-product of his general lack of political sophistication, which is much in evidence in his commentary. He himself conceded: "I have never taken part in politics, and know nothing of any political aspects or implications which the Declaration [the UDHR] may have. It is only from the religious angle, and in particular the relation to the sacred theology of Islam and of Shi'a beliefs, that I shall discuss the matter."[17]

Tabandeh seems to have been less afraid of being branded a reactionary than the others because his major concern is defending tenets set forth in the medieval juristic tradition of Islam—as opposed to being concerned about the reaction that his ideas might provoke if presented in an international forum like the United Nations. He not only considered that the Islamic sources are the authoritative criteria for how society should be ordered, but he even proposed that where there are discrepancies, it is the UDHR that should be rewritten to make it conform to Islam.[18] That is, he had much more real confidence in the definitive and binding character of Islamic law than did the others, who often seem genuinely confused and uncertain in their own minds about whether Islamic law can still be deemed viable if its rules fly in the face of international legal norms.

Thus, Tabandeh was unusually candid in his reaction to Article 16 of the UIDHR, which provides for equal rights for men and women in matters of marriage and divorce and guarantees the right to marry without any limitations due to race, nationality, and religion. He flatly stated that it contains several points that are contrary to Islam.[19] He roundly castigated the representatives of Muslim countries who were involved in the drafting of the UDHR for not rejecting this article and explaining at the United Nations what Islamic teachings were regarding the status of women.[20]

The Islamic rules that in his view are violated by Article 16 include the *shari'a* ban on Muslim women marrying non-Muslims[21] and the right of initiating a divorce being reserved to men.[22] Tabandeh also professed his opposition to the notion of male-female equality embodied in Article 16 if it means "that a natural equality exists between men and women, fitting them to undertake identical tasks and to make equal decisions."[23] He said that a wife must obey her husband, consult his wishes, not go out of the house without his permission, take due care of the property, look after the household equipment, invite a guest only with the husband's agreement, uphold the family's good name, and maintain her husband's good standing when he is present or absent.[24] In addition, Tabandeh stated that Islam forbids women from "interference in politics."[25] He also made much of women's obligation not to stir up male lust, charging that "liberty granted to women, contrary to all reason and religion, results in libertinism, licence, lust, lechery, and libidinousness."[26] He supported the Islamic curbs on women's freedom that conservative interpreters of the *shari'a* call for as part of a woman's duty not to provoke male lust, asserting:

> Islam has taken measures to prohibit practices which would lead to stimulating of sensual passion or to deviation from chastity. Women are therefore ordered not to do what would titillate men's feelings of lust. She must therefore cover her body, and not show her adornments of beauty or of jewelry or make-up to the outside world or to strangers. She must not frequent, more than absolutely essential, public gatherings attended by men. She must spend much time at home.[27]

In Tabandeh's exposition of the status of women in Islam, one sees themes that are characteristic of the ideas that are set forth by Muslim conservatives generally. It is assumed that all women will marry, so the primary determinant of an adult woman's life will be her relationship with her husband. In this relationship, she is required to submit to her husband's authority and follow his wishes. It is expected that her life will be passed at home fulfilling domestic duties, and women's involvement in politics is seen as inappropriate. There is no concern for protecting women's rights to develop as individual persons with distinct identities and abilities, to become educated in ways that fit their specific talents and interests or that enable them to become productive members of society, or to ensure that they play a part in the social, economic, or political institutions that shape their destinies. Women are seen not as actors but as passive, dependent beings—all of whom are basically fungible, as they are not recognized to possess the same variety in personality and capacity as males do. Furthermore, women are assigned the burden of preserving morality: It is their responsibility to stay secluded and enshrouded so that they do not provoke sexual excitement in men. Sexual importunings or advances on the part of men are attributed to the flouting of norms of modesty by women, not to any lack of morality or to any blameworthy, lascivious attitudes among the male population. As will be indicated in the following discussion, while other authors are less frank than Tabandeh, when one scratches the surface, one finds that they have similar philosophies about women's proper role.

Mawdudi's Ideas

Mawdudi in his human rights pamphlet stayed away from the subject of women's rights. Unlike Tabandeh, Mawdudi was a canny politician who seems to have appreciated the damage that it would do to the credibility of his human rights scheme if he admitted that it aimed at denying fundamental rights to one-half of the population. However, Mawdudi's views on women are on record in his other writings; thus one knows that they were similar to Tabandeh's, with the exception that Mawdudi believed that women should be able to sue for divorce on liberal grounds.[28]

Some aspects of his ideas on the question of female equality are detailed here because they are typical of the arguments made by Muslim conservatives in opposing granting women equality. In his book defending the status of women under premodern *shari'a* rules, Mawdudi listed as doctrines of Western society the principles of male-female equality, economic independence of women, and "free intermingling of the sexes"[29] and went to considerable lengths to document his abhorrence of these ideas and to argue that they lead to undermining the family, declining natality, immorality, promiscuity, perversion, and social decay.[30] The result of these principles is that in the West people "perpetually remain in a feverish condition on account of nude pictures, cheap literature, exciting songs, emotionally erotic dances, romantic films, highly disturbing scenes of obscenity and ever-present chances of encountering members of the opposite sex."[31] He accused Muslims who advocate the kind of rights for women that he associates with the West of abandoning the concepts of "the sense of honour, chastity, moral purity, matrimonial loyalty, undefiled lineage, and the like virtues."[32]

Perhaps realizing that it would seem strange if he failed to provide any rights for women in his human rights pamphlet, Mawdudi did list as one of his "basic human rights" respect for the chastity of women.[33] However, as has been amply demonstrated in practice in many Middle Eastern countries and, particularly, in the treatment of women in Iran in the wake of the Islamic Revolution, the need to shield women's chastity has been exploited by Muslim conservatives like Mawdudi as a justification for denying women a broad spectrum of rights and for keeping them largely restricted to the home. Mawdudi himself has indicated that he associates preserving chastity with maintaining women housebound and in purdah. Thus, the only "right" Mawdudi stipulated for women, respect for the chastity of women, does not really qualify as a human right but is a principle that is, in context, being used to deny women freedoms that they are entitled to enjoy under international standards.

Furthermore, as has already been discussed, protection of chastity is not actually a human right in the international sense, one designed to protect individual liberties against infringements by the state. In the average cases, persons who violate a woman's right to chastity will be criminal offenders committing acts of sexual molestation or rape, persons who by virtue of their criminal conduct indicate their unwillingness to be bound by the laws of society. International human rights law is no more designed to protect the principle of respect for chastity against violation than it is to deter other criminal conduct such as robbery, murder, or arson. International human rights standards are addressed to presumptively law-abiding officials and governmental institutions and are ineffectual in protecting individuals from criminals, a task that is left to the police forces and criminal justice systems of states. The deterrent to the criminal activity would lie in sanctions provided under domestic criminal laws. Thus, Mawdudi's chastity right is not a human right as understood in international law any more than a right not to be robbed would be.

Mawdudi tried to implicate Western governments in patterns of crimes against women's chastity by linking the issue of respect for chastity to military policies and practices. As has previously been indicated, Mawdudi was inclined to take the offensive against the West as a way of responding to the arrogant and critical stance that he thinks that the West takes vis-à-vis Islam. In connection with his Islamic "right" to respect for chastity, he made an interesting observation, one that at first blush would seem entirely out of place in a discussion of human rights in Islam:

> This concept of the sanctity of chastity and the protection of women can be found nowhere else except in Islam. The armies of the Western powers need the daughters of their own nations to satisfy their carnal appetites even in their own countries, and if they happen to occupy another country, the fate of its womenfolk can be better imagined than described.
>
> But the history of the Muslims, apart from individual lapses, has been free from this crime against womanhood. It has never happened that after the conquest of a foreign country the Muslim army has gone about raping the women of the conquered people, or, in their own country, the government has arranged to provide prostitutes for them.[34]

Mawdudi's resentment of and hostility toward the West seems to have impelled him to make the patently false charge that no legal systems other than the *shari'a* protect a women from sexual molestation and assault or rape.[35] In addition, there is no evidence that Muslim armies have historically conducted themselves any better in their treatment of women than their counterparts in other societies or that camp followers and prostitutes have not served the sexual needs of soldiers in Muslim armies over the centuries. One is prompted to inquire why this curious, contrary-to-fact assertion was included in Mawdudi's human rights pamphlet.

It seems relevant that Mawdudi was making his remarks on this subject in Pakistan after a notorious mass rape, one that was carried out by the Pakistani army in the course of the 1971 civil war fought in East Pakistan, which culminated in the independence of Bangladesh.[36] Mawdudi and his followers strongly supported the efforts of the Pakistani government to combat the Bengali independence movement, and Mawdudi must have been aware of the Bengali outrage in November 1975 when he made the speech in Lahore that became the basis of his human rights pamphlet.[37] Similarly, his audience in the capital of the Punjab, the province that has traditionally been a main source of Pakistan's military manpower, must have been aware of this infamous incident and also of the bad light in which it had placed Pakistan's armed forces.

In this political context, Mawdudi's insistence that a Muslim army had never raped women was a deliberate misstatement that served at least two functions. It was designed to give comfort to members of the audience who were still smarting from the embarrassment of the international condemnation of the Bengali mass rapes by denying that rape by Muslim armies was possible. It was also designed to place the West on the defensive by charging it with being guilty of systematic sexual exploitation and mistreatment of women in wartime. This correlates with Mawdudi's general approach to Islamic law, which is infused with a polemical spirit and serves as a vehicle for anti-Western propaganda. Mawdudi's reaction to Western imperialism and the bitter experience of the difficulties in catching up to the Western level of development was a cultural nationalism that was strongly anti-Western in tone and that sought to denigrate Western models and achievements even as it was expressive of a preoccupation with Western models and achievements.

It is therefore not surprising that Mawdudi included his claims that Muslims had a superior level of respect for women's chastity in the context of his discussion of human rights in Islam. Being aware that his model of women's status was defective by international standards, he was prompted to take the offensive and to concoct arguments purporting to show that the West was guilty of condoning sexual violence against women. Mawdudi's treatment of female chastity shows how Islamic human rights schemes wind up with features that are designed to deflect attention from actual human rights issues and also to obscure the real disparities between international human rights norms and the principles espoused by Islamic conservatives. As in Mawdudi's characterizations of the conduct of Muslim and Western armies, the goal of this whole exercise is not accurate comparison or even truthful representation of the local culture but a picture of local institutions and those in the West that discredits the latter.

The UIDHR

In order to present Islamic human rights in a diplomatic fashion that would deflect criticisms from an international audience, the UIDHR treatment of the status of women is deliberately obscure. There is no admission that women are to be accorded second-class status under the scheme. Nonetheless, from a careful reading of the UIDHR one can glean that, under the guise of applying Islamic principles, it denies women a number of rights and freedoms. However, many of the provisions assigning women to a subordinate role do so only indirectly and are written in such a convoluted style that their significance may not be obvious to readers—and especially not to readers of the English version.

For example, in the UIDHR one sees in the English version of Article 19.a, a provision beginning with the following tenet: "Every person is entitled to marry, to found a family, and to bring up children in conformity with his religion, tradition and culture." This should be compared carefully with the wording of its international counterpart in the UDHR Article 16.1: "Men and women of full age, without any limitation due to race, nationality or religion, have the right to marry and to found a family."

In international law the freedom to marry is unqualified. In contrast, the UIDHR Article 19.a qualifies the entitlement to marry: The qualification "in conformity with his religion" means that rules of the *shari'a* will impose restrictions.[38] For example, under this provision, Muslim women are not allowed to marry non-Muslim men because Islam does not allow it. Furthermore, a Muslim man is not allowed to marry a woman who is neither a follower of Islam nor a member of one of the religions of the "people of the book." In addition, other Islamic rules such as the prohibition of marriages between persons related by suckling or the requirement of civil death for any person who abandons Islam act to bar or terminate marriages.[39] Therefore, the impact of this UIDHR provision is directly contrary to the principle in the UDHR that men and women should be allowed without any religious restrictions to choose their own spouses. The UIDHR provision is not designed to protect the right of the individual freely to choose a spouse but rather to deny that right according to Islamic criteria.

Article 19.a of the UIDHR continues in the English version: "Every spouse is entitled to such rights and privileges and carries such obligations as are stipulated by the Law." This language should be contrasted with the international norm in the UDHR Article 16.1: "They are entitled to equal rights as to marriage, during marriage and at its dissolution." In the international standards of the UDHR, there is unequivocal endorsement of equality of husband and wife. There is no talk of equal rights in the Islamic version in the UIDHR but only rights "stipulated by the Law." In the UIDHR "the Law" means the *shari'a;* thus all the gender-based disabilities of the premodern *shari'a* rules can be upheld under this provision. Therefore, this is a provision designed to deny women equal rights in marriage.

There are references to Qur'anic provisions in the English version of Article 19.a, but these have been relegated to the fine print of the references section in the back, where Islamic sources are noted.[40] The actual texts to which references are made are not, however, reproduced in the references section.

The implications of this provision regarding rights in marriage and divorce in the Arabic version are much clearer, since the Islamic sources are incorporated into the text of the Arabic version. A Qur'anic verse quoted on the status of women reveals that the inequality of the sexes is an underlying assumption of the UIDHR. The verse, 2:228, says that "[women] have rights similar to those [of men] over them in kindness, and men are a degree above them." This is one of the texts that is traditionally used by conservatives to establish male superiority in Islam and to justify keeping women in a subordinate position.[41]

It is also interesting to contrast the impressions created by the English and Arabic versions of Article 19.h. The English provision runs: "Within the family, men and women are to share in their obligations and responsibilities according to their sex, their natural endowments, talents and inclinations, bearing in mind their common responsibilities toward their progeny and their relatives." This English version suggests that men and women share family obligations and responsibilities, although it qualifies this sharing in ways that would prompt questions on the part of a reader who was alert to discrimination against women. Depending on what one might read into these qualifications, the English provision might or might not be taken to mean a fairly equal division of duties in the home between husband and wife was intended, particularly since factors other than sex are listed as determinants of the spouses' obligations and responsibilities.

The Arabic version of Article 19.h deals with quite a different subject. It says that the responsibility for the family is a partnership (*sharika*) among its members, each contributing according to his capacity and the nature of his character, and this is a responsibility that goes beyond the circle of parents and children and extends to close relatives and distant kinsmen (*al-aqarib wa dhawi 'l-arham*). In contrast to the English version of the article, the Arabic one establishes a right to collect support from members of one's extended family—not a right recognized in international law. The article calls for imposing the obligation on family members to support each other in a kind of informal, intrafamilial version of a social welfare program, one that potentially places support obligations on persons only distantly related to each other. Such support obligations among members of the extended family are imposed by premodern *shari'a* rules.[42] These rules in the past corresponded at least in a rough way to the customary patterns of mutual obligations among members of the extended family networks that were common in traditional societies of the Middle East.

The great disparity between the two versions raises the question of whether the English version was redrafted to make it correspond to something that was assumed would be more attractive to and meaningful for a Western audience than the idea of having to bear support obligations for distant relatives. That idea would have little appeal in environments where nuclear families are the norm and where the financial burden of maintaining distant relatives would typically be much greater and more inconvenient than it would be in traditional societies. In any case, it seems that the Arabic version of Article 19.h is the more authoritative one.

The UIDHR turns out to be largely unhelpful for women's rights. There appears to be little effort to propose reforms in the premodern *shari'a* rules that impose disabilities on women. However, there is one major exception, the provision in Article 19.i, providing that no one may be married against his or her will. Premodern *shari'a* rules on forced marriage allowed a girl's marriage guardian to marry her off at any age and without her consent.[43] Girls in traditional Muslim society were traditionally forced into marriages as soon as they reached puberty. Parents continue to compel their daughters to marry young in many parts of the Middle East today, causing much heartbreak for young women made to wed men they dislike—and who are often much older than they are—and to give up their hopes of pursuing studies and employment.[44] Many Muslims consider the premodern rules of *jabr* or *ijbar,* "forced marriage," outdated and incompatible with the ideal of marriage as a union freely consented to by both parties, and legal reforms in most Middle Eastern countries have officially eliminated the marriage guardian's traditional right to compel his ward to marry.[45] However, as the practice of forced marriage has not ceased, the UIDHR is performing a service by going on the record as supporting the idea that as a matter of Islamic principle no one should be compelled to enter a marriage. This stands out as an isolated instance in the literature under discussion, one where a real problem of human rights in the Middle East is confronted, the premodern jurisprudence is rejected, and an enlightened interpretation of Islamic requirements is offered.

The most extensive UIDHR provision dealing with women is Article 20. The rubric for Article 20 of the UIDHR in the English version is "Rights of Married Women." It is significant that in the UIDHR no provisions are made for the rights of unmarried women—just as there is no provision on the rights of married men or unmarried men. Given the nature of the document, one can hypothesize several reasons for this: All Muslim men are expected to marry, so the status of a single male is not significant. Married men will presumably all enjoy the husband's rights and privileges, which are counterparts of the wife's duty to obey and serve the husband. Given the apologetic nature of this exercise, it is understandable that the authors would not have wanted to include a separate article detailing the rights of the Muslim husband. To do so would make it all too obvious that they were endorsing a traditional, patriarchal system in which the law supports male control over females and a regime of male privilege in matters of marriage and divorce. For example, if they catalogued as rights of the husband under premodern Islamic law his entitlements to beat his disobedient wife, have four wives at a time, and to have sexual intercourse regardless of his wife's wishes unless she has a religiously acceptable grounds for her refusal, this would give their whole scheme the retrograde appearance that they were seeking to avoid.

It is often noted that in Muslim countries, there are no single women, since all women are expected to marry. It is natural for the authors of the UIDHR to assume that the contours of an adult woman's life are primarily shaped by her domestic obligations to her husband as his wife and as the mother of his children. The existence of autonomous adult women who are not answerable to male authority is not contemplated in this scheme, so there is no need to specify rights of unmarried women. By speaking exclusively of the rights of married women, the authors of the UIDHR reveal that they do not see women as autonomous individuals and do not envisage a system where women escape male tutelage. Instead, they share the perspective that is pervasive in traditional Muslim societies that a female child should be under the control of her father or other close male agnate until she marries, at which time she is to submit to the control of her husband.

It is important to note the significant disparity here. In the international human rights schemes, the focus is on the rights of individuals, irrespective of their marital status. Because the spouses enjoy equal rights in international law, although there are specific rights provisions dealing with marriage, marital status cannot be a prime determinant of status in the way it appears to be in the UIDHR.

What are the "Rights of Married Women" granted by the English version of the UIDHR? Article 20 provides:

Every married woman is entitled to:

a) live in the house in which her husband lives;

b) receive the means necessary for maintaining a standard of living which is not inferior to that of her spouse, and, in the event of divorce, receive during the statutory period of waiting (*Iddah*) means of maintenance commensurate with her husband's resources, for herself as well as for the children she nurses or keeps, irrespective of her own financial status, earnings, or property that she may hold in her own right;

c) seek and obtain dissolution of marriage (*Khul'a*) in accordance with the terms of the Law. This right is in addition to her right to seek divorce through the courts;

d) inherit from her husband, her parents, her children and other relatives according to the Law;

e) strict confidentiality from her spouse, or ex-spouse if divorced, with regard to any information that he may have obtained about her, the disclosure of which could prove detrimental to her interests. A similar responsibility rests upon her in respect of her spouse or ex-spouse.

Aspects of these provisions dealing with support and inheritance rights illustrate how this scheme reinforces the discriminatory treatment of women. The English Article 20.b, which gives a very different impression than does the Arabic version of the same provision, will be considered first. In the English version, Article 20.b seems to be concerned with assuring a wife's maintenance by her husband. Although the premodern jurists disagreed about exactly what the standards were for determining how much maintenance a husband owed his wife during marriage and in the 'idda, or waiting period, following divorce (either three months or if the divorcée turned out to be pregnant, till birth of the child), they agreed that this was a unilateral obligation on the part of the husband—as was to be expected in a system where it was assumed that the women would stay in the house and attend to the children and household matters. However, at the end of the *'idda,* the husband's obligation to support the wife ceases. There is no alimony in Islamic law, and the woman is expected to be supported after the *'idda* by her relations if she cannot support herself.

In a system where the husband enjoys a right of unilateral, discretionary divorce, this cutoff of support obligations can leave a woman destitute. The economic predicament of divorced women who are not wealthy or gainfully employed has worsened in modern times as urbanization and economic changes have undermined the extended family and reduced a divorced woman's ability to obtain her livelihood from relatives. Muslim reformers have tended to conclude that the husband's support obligation needs to be reconsidered. The tendency in family law reform in the Middle East has been to enable the judge presiding over a divorce to extend the husband's support obligations beyond what they were in the premodern *shari'a.* The judge acts out of concern for women who are divorced without any fault on their part and who are liable to fall into penury, particularly if they are divorced when they are no longer young and able to enter into another marriage.[46] It is therefore noteworthy that the UIDHR fails to address the financial hardships of the indigent divorced woman and limits the husband's financial obligations to the period of the *'idda.* In context, this constitutes a rejection of the reformist position and a reaffirmation of the premodern rules sharply limiting the husband's support obligation to a divorced wife, which in contemporary circumstances tends to mean economic hardship for many divorced wives.

The English version of 20.b makes no mention of the Qur'anic verse 4:34, which is mentioned in the Arabic version. The cited verse stipulates that God established male superiority and connects male control over women to the maintenance that men pay for women: "Men are in charge of women, because Allah hath made the one of them to excel the other, and because they [the men] spend of their property [for the support of women]." This verse is invoked by Muslim conservatives to justify men having greater rights in the *shari'a.*[47] It is significant that this very verse is quoted in the text of the Arabic version of Article 20.b, a subsection of an article purportedly concerned with the rights of married women. Its quotation in this context reinforces the idea that male superiority comes from the fact that men support women economically. Women's financial dependence on men is in turn the consequence of other *shari'a* rules that keep women housebound and excluded from remunerative activity. The inclusion of this Qur'anic verse in the Arabic text conveys a very different impression of the implications of the maintenance provisions than does the English version.

Similarly, Article 20.d seems innocuous in the English version, saying that a married woman has a right to inherit from her husband and other relatives in accordance with the law. However, one must recall that the law referred to here is the *shari'a*. *Shari'a* inheritance law discriminates against women generally, allowing them to take only half the share of males, and against widows in particular. In the Arabic version, the impact that this has on a woman's ability to inherit is more obvious. Qur'an 4:12, quoted in the text, assigns the widow [a maximum of] one-quarter of her husband's estate if there are no children and [a maximum of] one-eighth of the estate if there are children. These Qur'anic shares constitute the legal maximum that the widow may take because, according to the prevailing opinion, Islamic law does not allow the spouse relict (widow or widower) to inherit more than the Qur'anic share.[48] One should also bear in mind that the *shari'a* allows the Muslim husband to have up to four wives simultaneously, and if the husband dies and leaves more than one widow, the widows have to divide the one-quarter or one-eighth share that otherwise would go to a sole wife, in which case their shares will be very much reduced. Meanwhile, a widowed husband takes one-half of the estate in the absence of children and one-fourth if there are children, a portion that he does not have to share with any other heir. Thus, in incorporating the Qur'anic standards for inheritance by the spouse relict, Article 20.d reaffirms discriminatory *shari'a* inheritance rules and restricts a wife's right to inherit from her husband in a way that is very much to her disadvantage. This article does not afford protection for any human right as understood in international law, nor does it make an attempt to adjust the inheritance scheme to take into account the erosion of the extended family network that the original Qur'anic scheme assumed would ensure the widow's livelihood.

Regarding divorce, the reader of the English version of Article 20.c, cited above, might interpret the language to mean that a woman who wanted to terminate her marriage could claim a divorce as of right. The article says that the wife "is entitled to seek *and obtain* dissolution of marriage"(emphasis added), which is said to be "in addition to her right to seek divorce through the courts." This suggests that women are being guaranteed a right to divorce, which is not actually the case. When one consults the more authoritative Arabic version of Article 20.c, one sees that no such right is being offered. The Arabic version says that a woman may *ask* her husband to agree to dissolve the marriage via a consensual termination of marriage, known as a *khul'*, or may *ask* a judge for a dissolution within the scope of *shari'a* rules (*fi nitaq ahkam al-shari'a*). The Arabic version offers the authoritative wording of this provision, and when one considers the implications of this wording, one can see that it is not much of a "right" for a wife to be allowed to *ask* her husband to agree to terminate a marriage or to *ask* a court for a *shari'a* dissolution. According to the *shari'a*, the husband is under no obligation whatsoever to grant her request and, except in the doctrines of the Maliki school of law, there are difficult requirements that must be met before a woman can obtain a divorce from a judge over her husband's objections.

After noting the pattern of discrepancies in the English and Arabic versions of the UIDHR that have just been discussed, one cannot help but conclude that the persons responsible for the English version were influenced by public relations concerns in their translation. The material in the Arabic version reassured its audience, which could be expected to be largely Muslim, that the *shari'a* regime of male privilege was being maintained, whereas the English version, the audience for which could be expected to consist largely of non-Muslims, conveys the message that the approach is liberal and better attuned to international norms.

The remaining "rights" that are provided to married women in Article 20 are simply frivolous or meaningless. For example, in Article 20.a, a woman is given the right to live in the house in which her husband lives. This would appear to be a solution to a nonexistent problem under present circumstances in the Middle East, particularly in the urban areas that have grown so quickly in the last decades. Few men today can afford to have homes for themselves while maintaining separate residences for their wives, even if they might wish to live separately from them. In countries like Egypt, where the population pressure is enormous and the stock of urban housing is woefully inadequate, it would be virtually impossible for a husband to find and afford two residences so that he could house his wife separately. Indeed, so serious is the shortage of housing in some urban areas that even couples who are divorced may have to continue to live together in the same dwelling, because neither ex-spouse can find affordable alternative housing. Moreover, since the UIDHR does not abolish polygamy, this "right" might be interpreted to mean that co-wives could not demand that the husband provide separate residences, as they could under the premodern *shari'a* rules, but would have to live together in their common husband's home. The beneficiary of this "right" would be the husband, who would be spared the expense of maintaining them in separate residences.

Article 20.e purports to give a woman a right to have any detrimental information that her husband has about her kept confidential, but it accords the same right to the husband regarding any confidential information that his wife may have about him. Thus, placing this right in the category of rights of married women is misleading. Here, there is no significant difference between the Arabic and the English versions, but in neither case does the principle embodied in the provision rise to the stature of a human right. The provision may relate to a common idea that interspousal communications should be privileged. In the United States, for example, the rules of evidence prevent either spouse from testifying in court over the other's objections about confidential communications made during a marriage. Such an evidentiary privilege is not deemed in international law to embody a right worthy of inclusion in any list of human rights.

Indeed, it is not clear what the intended legal consequences of this provision were, even in relation to *shari'a* tradition. The provision is puzzling, because there is no Islamic legal rule preventing spouses from disclosing detrimental information about each other; on the contrary, the husband may need to do so to annul a marriage and the wife may need to do so to obtain an annulment or a divorce under *shari'a* rules.[49] Depending on circumstances, the ability to disclose evidence about the husband's defects, failings, and misconduct may be the only means a Muslim woman has at her disposal to terminate a marriage.[50] Therefore, such a rule could conceivably be used to inhibit a woman's ability to terminate a marriage over her husband's objections by barring her testimony about relevant evidence. Whatever its purport, this provision adds nothing to the rights of married women. Including it as a right of married women may be an effort to pad the very limited list of rights that are afforded women in the UIDHR scheme.

The Iranian Constitution

The 1979 Iranian Constitution itself does not expressly relegate women to second-class status. As noted in the section on equality, there are even provisions in the constitution that, taken in isolation, might indicate that it was proposing equal status for men and women, such as Article 20, which guarantees men and women equal protection of the law (*qanun*). In various places, the constitution makes reassuring statements about the future of women in Iran's postrevolutionary society. For example, a section of the Preamble called "Women and the Constitution" portrays the revolution as being sympathetic to women's rights, saying that after the overthrow of the shah, people will regain their original identities and human rights (*hoquq-e ensani*) and that, in consequence, women "will be able to enjoy their rights proportionately more." Article 3.14 includes in a listing of the goals of the Islamic

Republic "securing every human right for both men and women, and establishing judicial security for all based on justice and the equality of all before the law [*qanun*]." Article 21.1 calls for the "creation of an environment favorable to the personal growth of women, and to the restoration of their material and spiritual rights."

However, one sees provisions of a very different sort as well, ones that are much more in keeping with the spirit of the Islamic human rights that are under discussion here. It has been noted that the Iranian Constitution provides in Article 20 that citizens' rights are qualified by the Islamic standards and that women's rights are so qualified in Article 21. The negative implications of such qualifications will by now be familiar.

In the section of the Preamble on women and the constitution one also sees that women's function is primarily to be one of bearing children committed to the regime's ideology. The Preamble says, in part:

The family is the basic social unit, and the principal institution for human growth and development. A consensus of beliefs and ideals for the purpose of establishing a family, which provides the basis for the movement of mankind toward perfection, is a cardinal principle of Islam, and the provision of the means to achieve such a goal is the duty of the Islamic government. With the restitution of the noble and respected duty of motherhood, to raise ideological men [*ensanha-ye maktabi*], women will be in the vanguard and in fact the comrade of men in all aspects of active life. Consequently, women will assume greater responsibilities, and from the Islamic point of view they will be held in greater esteem.

In the context of Iranian history and culture, the emphasis on the family and women's role in raising children signaled that the aim was to return Iranian women to a domestic role after decades in which they had made progress in education, employment, entering the professions, and gaining a role in public life. Among Islamic conservatives, emphasizing the family has become a code for programs designed to keep women in the home and out of cultural, economic, and political life. Of course, all these programs are officially justified as being mandated by Islamic law.

This family theme is repeated in Article 10, along with a claim that the framework for family structure should be taken from Islamic rights and morality: "The family being the fundamental unit of the Islamic society, all laws, regulations, and programs which pertain to it shall facilitate the establishment of the family. They shall safeguard the sanctity of the family and the stability of family relationships, based

on Islamic laws and moral concepts [*hoquq va akhlaq-e eslami*]." One
might wonder how this idea of exalting women's role in the family fits
with Article 28, which provides in part: "Every person has the right
to choose the profession he wishes, provided it is not contrary to the
principles of Islam [*mokhalef-e eslam . . . nist*], to the public interest
or to the rights of others."

In the event, one is not forced to rely on the ambiguous formulations
in the text of the constitution in construing the meanings of Articles
10 and 28 because by now there are many years of praxis on the part
of the government of Iran that provide a gloss on these provisions. The
accumulated evidence of the Iranian government's approach to issues
of women's rights indicates that it involves not only the revival of
premodern *shari'a* rules determining women's status in the family but
also the imposition of new rules designed to perpetuate women's subordination, in part by curbing their job opportunities.

One of the first measures that Khomeini took after coming to power
was to nullify in February 1979 the Iranian Family Protection Act of
1967 as amended in 1975. The Family Protection Act was one of the
two most progressive reforms in personal status law (the other is the
Tunisian Code of Personal Status of 1956) enacted in the Middle East
outside of Turkey, where personal status law is entirely secularized.
The Iranian act included rules requiring that all divorce actions be
brought before a court (thereby eliminating the husband's right of
extrajudicial divorce by uttering a divorce formula), significantly broad-
ening the grounds on which women could seek divorce, assigning
custody based on the best interests of the child (instead of saying that
custody automatically reverted to the father after age two for boys and
age seven for girls), and requiring a married man to get a court's
permission before marrying another wife, which would only be given
if he convinced the court of his ability to provide justly for both
wives.[51]

Muslim conservatives claimed that these improvements in women's
rights and curbs on male prerogatives violated the *shari'a* law. With
the abrogation of the Family Protection Act by the Khomeini regime,
shari'a rules were again in force. Since the revolution the regime has
supported the idea of early marriages for girls, lowering the minimum
age for marriage from eighteen to thirteen.[52] Marriages of such young
girls naturally create obstacles to their pursuing higher educations. The
regime has also given strong encouragement to the traditional Twelver
Shi'i institution of temporary marriage, in which a man can contract
for a woman's sexual services for a limited period of time.[53] This is
an institution that has been widely condemned by Iranian feminists as

degrading for women and that is regarded by most Sunni Muslims as a form of prostitution.

In addition to stripping women of legal protections in the area of family law, the regime has interpreted the application of Islamic standards to require drastic curtailment of women's activities outside the home. Women's educational opportunities have been restricted through a variety of devices, they have been fired and excluded from a wide variety of prestigious jobs, and they have been practically eliminated from politics and government. It is particularly revealing that women have been removed from jobs in the field of law, prevented from studying law, and barred from serving as judges. They have been quite deliberately excluded from having a say in the legal order that assigns them an inferior status or from assuming positions where they might challenge the Islamic pedigree of the regime's discriminatory laws. They have been virtually eliminated from employment in the media and the entertainment industry. Their ability to participate in sports activities has been curbed or eliminated by the imposition of requirements that recreational areas be sexually segregated and that women wear cumbersome, baggy, concealing clothing—even while swimming or skiing. Generally, they have been forced to wear all-enveloping chadors in dull colors and have been subjected to harsh criminal penalties for offenses such as not covering every strand of hair or wearing makeup. Revolutionary Guards associated with the regime have engaged in systematic intimidation and harassment designed to discourage women from appearing in public unaccompanied by male relatives. The attempts that women have made to protest the dismantling of the many rights and freedoms that Iranian women had won by the 1970s have been met with the same kind of ruthless repression that the government has meted out to its other opponents.[54]

An incident occurred on January 21, 1986, that perfectly epitomized the official Iranian attitude toward women.[55] In the course of a trip to Zimbabwe, President Ali Khamene'i refused to attend a state banquet in his honor, in part because wine was to be served, but also because women were to be seated at the head table. The Iranian delegation demanded that all women, including a woman cabinet member, be relegated to the table that was farthest away from the head table. The Zimbabwe leadership refused, saying that women were entitled to equal standing with men. The Zimbabweans understood that the Iranian demand that women be confined to the remotest table did not just mean sexual segregation at the dinner but was also symbolic of the inferior status to which the Iranians assigned women. In rejecting the Iranian demand, the Zimbabwean foreign minister noted that the roles played by women in Zimbabwe's struggle for majority rule and for development "entitle them to an equal status and standing in every respect with their male counterparts." President Khamene'i provided additional indications of his animus toward women participating in public affairs and governmental functions by refusing to shake hands with a woman minister and deputy minister who were in the receiving line to greet him on his arrival and by insisting that the female journalists who attended his news conference in Zimbabwe wear veils. By these acts, he was also suggesting that their very persons were offensive and sources of impurity in his eyes.

The parallels between Khamene'i's attitude and conduct and the attitudes and conduct of white supremacists in the United States in the era before civil rights legislation dismantled the traditions of U.S. racism and racial segregation will be striking to persons familiar with the latter. Measures like the physical segregation of an "inferior" group by a more powerful group signals their political subordination. They are suggestive of the enormous ideological gap that separates the rights philosophy of the current Iranian regime and the egalitarian principles of international human rights law. The record, therefore, overwhelmingly establishes that Islamic principles, Islamic law, and Islamic morality have been interpreted in Iran to justify depriving women of any semblance of equality with men, subjecting them to a wide range of discriminatory laws and treatment, and effectively confining them to serving their husbands, performing domestic tasks, and bearing and raising children.

The Sudan Under Islamization

Women's rights were not the focus of the Islamization program undertaken by Nimeiri in the period 1983–1985. However, in the course of the second Islamization campaign, the one undertaken by the military regime of Omar al-Bashir, which came to power in 1989, the imposition of Islamic law became associated with much the same regime of oppression directed at women that one saw in Iran after the Islamic Revolution and in Pakistan under Zia. As of the time of an Africa Watch report of April 9, 1990, the situation of Sudanese women was being transformed along lines proposed by Muslim conservatives. There were systematic dismissals of women from public employment, and women in the legal profession were particularly targeted for dismissal. Women, regardless of age, were prohibited from traveling unless chaperoned by a male relative. Proposals were afoot to restrict women's access to many areas of higher education and to make women students wear veils. The position of the regime, according to statements made by Omar al-Bashir, was that the ideal Sudanese woman was one who took care of her husband and children, did her household duties, attended to her reputation, and was a devout Muslim. There was also a pattern of harassment directed against women who were not supporters of the program of the National Islamic Front, the Islamic fundamentalist faction that was dominant under the military regime.[56] The changes imposed in the Sudan under Islamization resemble those envisaged by the drafters of the Azhar constitution, who likewise represent the Muslim conservative viewpoint.

The Azhar Draft Constitution

The Azhar draft constitution has some features that are very similar to ones in the Iranian Constitution, although the former is a much briefer and sketchier document. It treats the status of women in the section on rules governing "Islamic Society." In the Azhar draft constitution Article 7 provides that the family is the basis of society and that the family's foundations are religion and morality (*ad-din wa'l-akhlaq*), and Article 8 says that safeguarding the family is a state duty. As has been noted, "protecting the family" is a code term used by conservative Muslims for a scheme in which women are kept subordinated and confined to the domestic sphere, so one would expect that this provision would be accompanied by others that fit in with the goals of the scheme.

In the Azhar draft, Article 8 provides that the state should encourage early marriage and provide "the means according to which the wife would obey her husband and look after her children and consider keeping the family the first of her tasks." This provision is highly significant because it shows how in these schemes the state winds up as the enforcer of supposedly traditional values at a time when the tradition itself has crumbled and ceased to have its former normative force. It reflects the Azhar sheikhs' abhorrence of the situation that has developed in contemporary Egypt, where many women are now educated and in full-time jobs, continuing to work after their marriages. There, as elsewhere where similar social changes have occurred, women have been less inclined than they formerly were to see their domestic roles as the center of their lives and have questioned the fairness of a system where men and women both work outside the home but the domestic chores and child care are generally treated as the sole responsibility of the wife, so that she winds up effectively doing two full-time jobs. The earning power of women has also weakened the control that the husband formerly enjoyed by virtue of his providing the wife with maintenance and has made it natural for wives to challenge their husbands' authority and their traditional right to demand obedience from their wives.

The Azhar draft constitution is therefore contemplating a situation where socioeconomic transformations have weakened the power of the husband over the wife and have changed the nature of the spouses' relationship in fundamental ways. The authors realize that they can no longer rely on tradition and that to reestablish the old order of things they must appeal to the state to employ its power to make the wife obey her husband and accord primacy to her duties as mother and housewife. The extensive measures taken by the Iranian government to reinforce male authority and to drive women back to their traditional roles in the domestic sphere demonstrate how a contemporary state may intervene in an attempt to reverse trends affecting women's role in society.

In addition to the general guarantee of the right to work in Article 37 of the Azhar constitution, there is a separate provision in Article 38 that says that women have the right to work within the limits of the precepts of the *shari'a* (*hudud ahkam al-shari'a al-islamiya*). The fact that there is a separate provision for women working suggests that the "Islamic" standards used for judging what work women can undertake will be distinctive. It is significant in this regard that there are no Islamic qualifications imposed on men's right to work—and no idea, therefore, that a man's working might infringe *shari'a* principles. There is no further explanation of what the Islamic limits on a woman's ability to work will be, but extrapolating from the general attitudes of Muslim conservatives, one can presume that women will need their husbands' permissions to work, that they will be allowed to work in only a limited range of jobs deemed suitable for women, and that they will be barred from work that would bring them into inappropriate proximity with men.

The most distinctive provision in the Azhar draft constitution is Article 14, which in the English version provides: "Bedizement [bedizenment, gaudy dress] is forbidden and observing others' feelings is a duty. The government is to pass the laws and decisions to preserve the feelings of the public against profligacy according to the rules of the Islamic Sharia."

Like portions of the English translation of the UIDHR, this English translation of Article 14 seems more than a little disingenuous. The reader of the article may not realize that this prohibition of bedizement is a call for governments to take measures like those that have been taken in Iran to force women to go about veiled and to discourage them from leaving their homes or associating with men from outside the family circle. The use of the term "profligacy" is misleading in this context, since it gives the impression that the concern is for the curbing of wastefulness and dissipation generally, when in reality it is only "shameless" conduct by women that is being prohibited. Thus the bias is obscured by the language chosen in the English translation. When one compares the English with the Arabic version, one sees a disparity like that in the Arabic and English versions of various UIDHR provisions.

In the Arabic version of Article 14 the word corresponding to what should be "bedizenment" in the English version is *tabarruj* and relates to the command in the Qur'an (33:33), which in an English translation that favors archaisms reads, "bedizen not yourselves with the bedizenment of the Time of Ignorance."[57] The verse is widely interpreted to mean that women must avoid immodest or provocative clothing and ornaments, and by Islamic conservatives to mean that heavy veiling and no makeup are de rigueur for women whenever they are exposed to the sight of men who are not members of their own family circles.[58] Wearing the kind of attire normal for women in urban settings throughout the world is considered blameworthy by Muslim conservatives. The ban on "bedizenment" is rarely interpreted as having any bearing on how men dress, however, and Muslim men who abandon traditional Middle Eastern dress and adopt conventional Western styles of clothing are not considered to be committing any offense against public decency. Thus, this provision sets the stage for government-imposed, uniform standards of dress for women, but leaves men free to dress as they please. Their enshrinement of the ban on female "bedizenment" in the early, fundamental provisions of the Azhar draft constitution indicates the mentality of the men involved, their social priorities, and their attitudes toward women's rights.

In the Arabic version of Article 14 the ban on bedizenment is followed by the statements that preserving female honor is a duty (*at-tasawun wajib*). This could be interpreted as justifying the retention of Arab concepts of honor, which have been used traditionally to justify keeping women segregated and secluded and for imposing harsh penalties on women (not men) for violating sexual taboos.[59] This, in turn, correlates with the ideas of Mawdudi about the seclusion of women, which he justified as needed to ensure protection for chastity. The Azhar draft also provides that the state must issue laws to prevent offenses to the public sense of decency according to the principles of the *shari'a* (*ahkam al-shari'a al-islamiya*). This could mean steps beyond just requiring that women be veiled in public; it could be interpreted to entail legislation that allows the kinds of prosecution and harassment of women for "immodest" dress and draconian censorship measures of the media that have been taken in countries like Saudi Arabia, Iran, and Pakistan.[60] These measures include bans on anything that might be objected to as immodest or sexually suggestive by the most reactionary clerics, even if acceptable to the public at large. The definition of indecency is not made precise, and based on the Saudi and Iranian examples, one would expect that this leeway would be exploited by the authorities to justify a wide range of repressive acts and censorship.

Summary of the Islamic Approaches

In these various approaches to women's rights there is an absence of any willingness to recognize women as full, equal human beings who deserve the same rights and freedoms as men. Instead, discrimination against women is treated as something entirely natural—in much the same way that people in the West think it is natural that mentally defective persons and young children must be denied certain rights and freedoms. However, there is a general reluctance to spell out in ways likely to come to the attention of a Western audience the authors' beliefs in inherent female inferiority. In this regard, the invocations of *shari'a* law are very useful, since the *shari'a* qualifications that are placed on rights tend to look harmless to a casual observer but signal the authors' general intentions to an informed audience. The vagueness in the Islamic criteria limiting women's rights also allows great leeway to the authorities in choosing what kind of discriminatory measures they will impose.

On the basis of the standards in international human rights documents, one expects that documents on human rights will aim at protecting human rights, not provide rationales for restricting or denying rights. In contrast, as the examination of these Islamic human rights schemes shows, in the area of women's rights, they actually serve the function of justifying the taking away of rights.

Women's Rights in Islamic and
International Human Rights Schemes

A summary of some areas where the Islamic human rights schemes fail to respect the rights and freedoms that women have been guaranteed in selected international human rights documents will now be presented. Compared to the international standards in the UDHR, aspects of the Islamic human rights schemes that affect women's rights would seem to permit violations of the Article 1 guarantee of equality, the Article 2 guarantee against discriminatory treatment, the Article 7 guarantee of equal protection of the law, and the Article 16 guarantee of the freedom to marry the partner of one's choice. Compared to the international standards in the ICCPR, they appear to permit violations of the Article 2 guarantee against discriminatory treatment, the Article 3 equal rights guarantee, the Article 12 guarantee of liberty of movement, and the Article 26 guarantees of equality, equal protection, and non-discriminatory treatment. Of course, to the extent to which the application of Islamic criteria means that Muslim women are confined in the home and excluded from situations where they will have contact with men, they will be indirectly denied many other freedoms in the areas of education, work, and participation in political and cultural life.

The human rights just discussed are by now well-established principles of international human rights law. To these may be added some newer principles that seem to be in the process of winning international acceptance. These principles set forth expanded protections for women's rights that reflect a determination to eradicate all forms of sex-based discrimination. The principles are based on a full awareness of the complexity of the problems of dismantling regimes of sex-based discrimination. The principles also call for affirmative measures by states to eradicate cultural obstacles in the way of women's achieving full equality. As such, they correlate with attitudes that are the opposites of those of Islamic conservatives.

The Convention on the Elimination of all Forms of Discrimination against Women entered into force in 1981. Measured by the standards in this convention, the treatment of women in Islamic human rights schemes seems particularly deficient and retrograde. The Preamble to the convention states that both parents have a role in the family and in the upbringing of children and specifically provides that the role of women in procreation should not be a basis for discrimination against them. One should recall that Islamic human rights schemes assume that women have the responsibility for looking after the family and for child rearing and that their procreative function sets them apart from men and justifies assigning them a subordinate status. In Article 1 of the convention, discrimination is defined as including "any distinction, exclusion or restriction made on the basis of sex which has the effect or purpose of impairing or nullifying the recognition, enjoyment, or exercise by women, irrespective of their marital status, on a basis of equality of men and women, of human rights and fundamental freedoms in the political, economic, social, cultural, civil, or any other field."

In contrast, the Islamic human rights schemes, while prohibiting certain kinds of discrimination and in some instances seeming to endorse male-female equality, in reality do not rule out discrimination based on sex, which they treat as being justified by *shari'a* requirements. Furthermore, the Islamic schemes have provisions that effectively require drawing legal distinctions along gender lines and imposing discriminatory measures, such as mandatory veiling for women and sexual seclusion and segregation that are purportedly based on concerns for protecting female chastity and honor. They therefore violate the convention's principle of abolishing discriminatory distinctions based on sex.

Other rights provided for in the 1981 convention with which Islamic human rights schemes are in conflict are the Article 11 requirement that all discrimination against women in employment be eliminated and the Article 16 requirement of elimination of all discrimination between men and women in the family and of ensuring that men and women have the same rights and responsibilities during marriage and at its dissolution. In contrast, the references to Islamic criteria in the Islamic human rights schemes open the way for the application of *shari'a* personal status rules that require discrimination against women.

As was already noted, the fact that Islamic human rights schemes justify keeping women at home and segregated from men can mean that women will be prevented from participating in many activities. The Islamic personal status law component in Islamic human rights schemes would violate a number of emerging international standards when it was applied by governments in ways that would oblige women to remain within the confines of the circumscribed role to which conservative interpretations of *shari'a* requirements assign them. Enforcing the regime of personal status law favored by Muslim conservatives would mean violating the obligation imposed on governments in Article 7 of the convention to eliminate discrimination against women in political and public life, in Article 8 to give women opportunities to represent their governments at the international level, in Article 10 to eliminate discrimination in education—including sports and physical education, and in Article 12 to eliminate discrimination in health care. With regard to the issue of health care, one should note that in traditional Islamic milieus disparities in health care often occur. Modesty taboos may keep women from getting medical care from male doctors on the grounds that medical examinations or procedures would constitute a breach of propriety or an infringement of family honor.

Article 2 of the convention calls on states to take all measures necessary to eliminate all discriminatory laws, customs, and practices. There is no indication that the authors of the Islamic human rights schemes endorse such a goal. Their aim seems instead to be one of enlisting the state as the primary enforcer of discriminatory principles taken from the premodern *shari'a,* which confine women within a subordinate role.

The Influence of Sex Stereotyping

The convention recognizes that sex stereotyping constitutes an obstacle to realizing full equality for women and calls on governments to attack the attitudes and practices that stereotype women as inferior beings whose nature disqualifies them from enjoying freedoms on a par with men. Article 5 binds the parties "to modify the social and cultural patterns of conduct of men and women, with a view to achieving the elimination of prejudices and customary and all other practices which are based on the idea of the inferiority or the superiority of either of the sexes or on stereotyped roles for men and women."

One sees no concern for sex stereotyping in Islamic human rights schemes; on the contrary, such stereotyping is a central feature of the schemes, if sometimes only an implied one. All of them show evidence of being shaped by the idea that men and women have fundamentally different natures and roles and should, accordingly, have distinct rights and obligations. Muslim conservatives are dedicated to the proposition that the distinct roles assigned men and women in the premodern *shari'a* and in traditional societies are precisely the ones that nature ordained for them.

I will now survey some details of the sex stereotyping that underlies programs calling for the imposition of premodern *shari'a* rules in the area of personal status law. Not all men who write on Islamic human rights provide expositions of their own stereotypical visions of sex-role differences. However, by examining the substantive provisions in the schemes, one can see whether assumptions about inherent, sex-linked differences are implicit in the schemes and thereby draw some inferences about the authors' attitudes. Whether express or implicit, the stereotypes that correlate with the treatment of women in the Islamic human rights schemes under discussion here are all similar.

Given Tabandeh's general level of candor, it is not surprising that he expressed his sexual stereotypes quite freely and unself-consciously in the course of explaining why Islam cannot accept the human rights accorded women in the UDHR. Women, according to Tabandeh, are touchy and hasty, volatile and imprudent. They are generally more gullible and credulous than men. Their sexual desire makes them easy prey for the blandishments of salacious individuals.[61] He invoked these female characteristics to justify the restrictions that he argued that Islam imposes on women's ability to obtain a divorce, but, obviously, these same female failings would justify male superiority in other areas as well. In Tabandeh's opinion, nature made men and women capable of different functions. Women were designed for "cooking, laundering, shopping, and washing up," as well as for taking care of children. Men, in contrast, were created for field work, warfare, and earning a living.[62] Women are deficient in the intelligence needed for "tackling big and important matters," and they fall into mistakes and lack long-term perspectives. For this reason, he said, they must be excluded from politics.[63] They cannot fight in war because they are "timorous-hearted," affected by physical weakness, and might get frightened and run away.[64]

Mawdudi took a similar line, although not in his publication on human rights, where, as noted, he attempted to steer clear of any discussion of the awkward issue of his unwillingness to accord women equal rights. In his book on purdah he argued that nature has designed men and women for different roles, treating menstruation, pregnancy, and nursing as incapacitating disabilities.[65] Women, he asserted, are created to bear and rear children. They are tender, unusually sensitive, soft, submissive, impressionable, and timid. They lack firmness, authority, "cold-temperedness," strong willpower, and the ability to render unbiased, objective judgment.[66] Men have coarseness, vehemence, and aggressiveness, which suit them for roles like generals, statesmen, and administrators. The education of men should, therefore, aim at training them so that they can support and protect the family, whereas a woman should be educated to bring up children, look after domestic affairs, and make home life "sweet, pleasant, and peaceful."[67]

Similar observations are made by Ayatollah Javad Bahonar, a cleric who was briefly Iran's prime minister before being assassinated. Bahonar was one of Khomeini's closest aides, and his thinking may be taken as representative of many of the leading clerics in Khomeini's regime who fashioned or supported the regime's policies vis-à-vis women. In an article on Islam and women's rights in an English-language journal distributed in the West by the Iranian regime, Bahonar said that men are bigger and stronger and have larger brains, with more of the brain section "dealing with thought and deliberation."[68] A relatively larger portion of the smaller female brain is "related to emotions," and women have more in the way of the affection and deep tender sentiments that suit them for child care and nursing. Women's sentiments and emotions make them ill equipped to cope with earning a livelihood, which calls for farsightedness, perseverance, strength, tolerance, coolness, planning, hardheartedness, connivance, and the like—characteristics that women lack. Therefore, it is men who are equipped by nature to deal with "the tumult of life," and who can fight on the battlefield or manage the affairs of government and society.[69] A note at the end of the article offers some statistics on female physical inferiority, including the comment that "a man's brain weighs 100 grams more than a woman's." Bahonar summed up his evidence by saying that the "differences in physical structure are reflected in the mental capacities of the two sexes."[70]

Bahonar included in his recital of women's natural deficiencies and infirmities the assertion that "Islam considers men and women equal as far as the basic human rights are concerned."[71] However, even if one did not know of his role in the Iranian government and his close association with Khomeini, by the evidence he offered of his views of the innate deficiencies of the female sex, one could predict that any human rights scheme that he might devise would be bound to relegate women to the subordinate status mandated by his sex stereotypes of female weakness and physical and mental inferiority. Indeed, although Bahonar proposed many ways that men and women share similar religious and moral obligations—for example, both have to pray, be faithful and obedient believers, command the good and prohibit the evil, keep their looks cast down, and be punished for crimes—the only rights that he actually lists that the two sexes share on an equal basis are the rights to own and use property and to inherit.[72]

We do not have direct expressions of the sex stereotypes that were on the minds of the authors of the Azhar draft constitution or the UIDHR, but in those documents we can see implicit many similar prejudices regarding women. Like the other Islamic human rights schemes, rather than serving the goals of the 1981 convention of dismantling discrimination or eliminating stereotypical ideas of the different roles of men and women, they provide Islamic rationales for maintaining the de jure inferiority of women.

Because the Islamic legal tradition developed in traditional, patriarchal milieus and because to this day the authoritative works on the legal status of women in Islam are exclusively by men, it is not surprising that male stereotypes of women were incorporated into that tradition and that they have been retained as part of Islamic schemes for relegating women to subordinate status. However, there is very little in the original Islamic sources that supports these stereotypes, and there is, moreover, nothing distinctively Islamic about the self-interested and biased appraisals of women's characteristics that they offer.

In fact, the sex stereotyping that one sees in the Islamic tradition resembles very closely that developed in other contexts, such as in a variety of Christian faiths. For example, it can be seen in the Catholic church, only one of the many denominations where sex stereotyping was used to support the position of the exponents of Church doctrine— all males—to the effect that women had to be kept subjugated due to their "natural" inferiority to males. It is not a coincidence that Catholic theologians, having stereotyped women in much the same way that Muslim jurists had, developed a similar set of rules discriminating against women and restricting their freedom and opportunities. To be reminded that sex stereotyping has common features that can be projected into very dissimilar religious traditions, one should briefly consider what has occurred in the West under the influence of the Christian tradition. Among the characteristics that the Church Fathers attributed to women were fickleness, shallowness, garrulousness, weakness, slowness of understanding, and instability of mind.[73] Saint Augustine asserted that in comparison with men, women were small of intellect.[74] Two priests in a book designed to persuade Catholic women that, due to their sex, their "entire psychology is founded upon the primordial tendency to love," asserted that a woman's brain "is generally lighter and simpler than man's."[75]

Pope Pius XII in 1945 in a public speech to women described "the sensibility and delicacy of feeling peculiar to woman, which might tempt her to be swayed by emotions and thus blur the clearness and breadth of her view and be detrimental to the calm consideration of future consequences."[76] He asserted that as a result of their characteristics, women were suited for tasks in life that called for "tact, delicate feelings, and maternal instinct, rather than administrative rigidity."[77] A Jesuit theologian who offered an outline of a divine plan for women asserted in the course of his discussion of the nature of a woman: "She has not lost the dispositions of impressionability and mobility which Eve had manifested in the initial drama of humanity. She remains fragile, more subject to an unreflected impulse, and more accessible to seduction."[78]

As a major feminist critic of Catholic doctrine has pointed out, the sex-role stereotypes upheld and disseminated by men in the Church hierarchy became closely intertwined with the Catholic teachings calling for the subordination of women, because "the very emancipation which would prove that women were not 'naturally' defective was denied them in the name of that defectiveness which was claimed to be natural and divinely ordained."[79]

The same nexus between culture-bound presuppositions about inherent female characteristics and religious doctrine exists in the Islamic tradition. Therefore, when it is apparent that an Islamic human rights scheme embraces rather than repudiates the sex stereotyping that has provided the justification for so many discriminatory rules on the status of women, one can be sure that the scheme will not interpret Islamic requirements in a way that will allow full equality for women or afford full protection for the other rights guaranteed women in international human rights principles. As in the case of sex stereotypes that have been ascribed to religious authority in the West, the question remains whether the sex stereotypes associated with Islamic doctrine really are supported by the Islamic sources or are being read into them by male interpreters according to their own interests in preserving a patriarchal order.

CHAPTER 7

Islamic Human Rights Schemes and Non-Muslims

The Treatment of Religious Minorities in Muslim Countries

The peculiar historical background of the question of the rights of non-Muslim minorities makes any discussion by a Western observer of this issue perilous. Critical assessments of the use of Islam as a rationale for discriminatory treatment of non-Muslims are likely to be interpreted as being prompted by Western and Orientalist biases. The historical background is summarized here in an attempt to show that important distinctions should be made between the past, in which there were imperialist campaigns aimed at undermining the sovereignty of Muslim countries by exploiting the issue of the treatment of non-Muslim minorities, and the present, in which the equality of all citizens of Muslim countries is an issue of international human rights law. A review of the background is also needed to show how Muslims have been conditioned to look at this problem as part of a broader historical relationship with the West and how their perceptions, influenced by that history, have tended to impede their recognition of the human rights implications of traditional patterns of according unequal status to non-Muslims.

For centuries, the status of non-Muslims in the Middle East was determined by *shari'a* law in a situation where Muslim rulers enjoyed unchallenged hegemony over their non-Muslim subjects. At the time of the growth of European commercial connections with the Ottoman Empire, European states claimed that the treatment afforded non-Muslims under the *shari'a* was unacceptable. European powers were able to wrest concessions from the Ottomans for their own citizens, who were given extraterritorial status. This was done via capitulations, agreements that exempted their citizens from the jurisdiction of local courts. Subsequently, Europeans who settled in the Middle East were able to gain legal exemptions from *shari'a* law and *shari'a* courts.[1] In the face of mounting European military, political, and economic power, exemptions of non-Muslims from *shari'a* standards became historically associated with the growth of European imperialism, which eventually eroded the sovereignty of almost all Muslim countries.

In the nineteenth century, European powers with political ambitions in the Middle East appointed themselves the protectors of the various local Christian minorities, and Europeans began to monitor aggressively the treatment of non-Muslim minorities, using allegations of mistreatment of non-Muslims as pretexts for interfering in Middle Eastern politics. European pressures were a factor in the promulgation by the Ottoman sultans of special edicts in 1839 and 1856 that formally granted equality to non-Muslim Ottoman citizens.[2]

The treatment of non-Muslims thus became a bone of contention between Middle Eastern governments and European countries with imperialist ambitions. The Europeans, where they succeeded in dominating Middle Eastern societies, inevitably favored non-Muslim minorities, the most important instance being Britain's use of its mandate over Palestine to foster the development of a Jewish homeland.[3] In addition to according privileged treatment to the non-Muslim segment of the population, Europeans invoked the need to protect the non-Muslims from oppression by the Muslim majority as a rationale for their rule.[4] Since European powers were notably lacking in sympathy for the aspirations for freedom on the part of the Muslim population of the Middle East and concern for Muslim rights and well-being, European expressions of solicitude for non-Muslims naturally became associated with hypocrisy and selfish political ambitions. Christian missionary activities in the Middle East, which flourished when these countries were under European domination, suggested that there was a Christian plot against Islam, which was seen as a barrier to the complete subjugation of the local populace to Europeans. In this context European expressions of concern for rights of local non-Muslims could not be severed from political agendas of European powers.

Eventually, Europe was forced to abandon its colonial ambitions, and the countries of the Middle East became independent of European domination. In most cases this happened in the wake of World War II—though it was decades earlier in the case of Turkey. When full independence was achieved, many members of non-Muslim minority communities emigrated. For example, most Jews left for Israel or the West, the French left Algeria, Greeks left Turkey, the Italians left Libya, and people from various European countries and Middle Eastern minority communities left formerly cosmopolitan cities like Alexandria and Cairo. While the old Christian communities of Egypt, Syria, and the Levant largely remained in place, the proportion of non-Muslims in the Middle East dwindled, leaving relatively few people who today are affected by the treatment of non-Muslims under the *shari'a*.

Events since World War II, particularly Western support for establishing Israel as a homeland for Jews, have tended to exacerbate Muslim resentment of Western politics regarding religious minorities. Muslims were aggrieved that the former colonialist powers par excellence, Britain and France, should ignore the right of self-determination of the native Palestinian population in order to house the remnants of a Jewish community long persecuted by European Christians. This disregard for the right of Palestinian self-determination and the strong U.S. support for Israel has reinforced the impression that there is a link between neocolonialist designs of Western powers and their commitment to protect religious minorities in the Middle East and to further the cause of Zionism. In particular, U.S. policies in the Middle East are seen as part of neocolonialist designs to oppress the largely Muslim population of the region, one of the strategies being dismantling Islamic law.[5] Against this background, Muslims, when reviewing past Western disregard for the rights of Muslims, may respond with anger to contemporary Western criticisms that judge the human rights policies of independent Muslim countries in a hypocritical and self-righteous manner.[6]

As a consequence of all these factors, many Muslims inevitably tend to view any discussion of the status of non-Muslims in the Middle East in relation to this particular historical background. The West's record of exploiting this issue to obtain political advantages at the expense of local sovereignty is cited, and resentment over the double standard that the West has continued to employ in this area is stirred up. Naturally, any critical comparisons of *shari'a* standards for the treatment of religious minorities with those in international law—Western in origin—are bound to provoke negative reactions on the part of Muslims who suspect that they are motivated by neocolonialism.

An examination of the present context of the issue of the status of non-Muslims shows that the implications of criticizing the rights accorded non-Muslims in Islamic human rights schemes are different from the implications of criticisms of the treatment of non-Muslims in the colonialist era. With the exception of Saudi Arabia, independent Muslim countries have themselves imported constitutional models from the West and have adopted modern concepts of citizenship designed for use in the nation-state. Conservative proponents of Islamization, who demand the adoption of Islamic forms of government and the imposition of laws discriminating against non-Muslims, are engaged today in a struggle not with alien forces bent on dominating their countries but with other political factions inside their own societies that favor the perpetuation of modern norms of constitutional government and equality of citizens. Thus, Muslim conservatives are reacting to institutions that are now part of the political systems of independent states. In this context, critical assessments of the countermodels proposed by Muslim conservatives who oppose existing constitutional norms do not serve to undermine the sovereignty of the existing states. On the contrary, it is the forces calling for Islamization that are challenging the authority of existing regimes of independent Muslim countries.[7]

Furthermore, the significance of *shari'a* rules for religious minorities is changing. Islamization has serious implications for the rights of religious minorities: Their status has been increasingly tied to the rights of religious minorities or dissidents who consider themselves Muslims but who are not deemed such by those who set the standards of Islamic orthodoxy in the states where they live. That is, the standards for treatment of religious minorities are relevant for the rights not just of persons who are avowedly non-Muslim but also of religious minorities and dissenters generally—including dissenters and sects within the Muslim community that are opposed to the version of Islam endorsed by the government. The question of the rights and status of non-Muslims has also become relevant for the scope of religious freedom accorded to Muslims. Thus, the traditional nexus between the status of non-Muslims and that of the local Jewish and Christian communities is crumbling and with it one basis for asserting that Western concern for religious minorities relates to favoritism for Jewish and Christian communities. In the light of these altered conditions, it is time to discontinue automatically associating critiques of the status of religious minorities accorded under *shari'a* rules with neocolonialist attitudes and objectives.

Standards Prohibiting Religious Discrimination

Just as it is not permissible under international human rights norms to deny people equal protection of the law or to discriminate against them on the basis of sex, so it is not permissible to do so on the basis of religion. This principle is enshrined in the UDHR in Article 2, and in the ICCPR in Articles 2 and 26. More recently, the Declaration on the Elimination of All Forms of Intolerance and of Discrimination Based on Religion or Belief, proclaimed by the UN General Assembly on November 25, 1981, reaffirmed this principle in Article 2, elaborating on it in Article 2.2 to define impermissible discrimination as "any distinction, exclusion, restriction or preference based on religion or belief and having as its purpose or as its effect nullification or impairment of the recognition, enjoyment or exercise of human rights or fundamental freedoms on an equal basis."

Article 4.1 requires all states to take effective measures to prevent and eliminate discrimination on the grounds of religion. Article 4.2 calls on governments to take affirmative steps to dismantle patterns of discrimination and eliminate religious prejudice: "All States shall make all efforts to enact or rescind legislation where necessary to prohibit any such discrimination, and to take all appropriate measures to combat intolerance on the grounds of religion or belief in this matter."

Shari'a Law and the Rights of Non-Muslims

Retaining the premodern *shari'a* rules affecting the status of non-Muslims is incompatible with the relevant standards of international human rights law. Those *shari'a* rules were formulated by Islamic jurists at an early stage of the history of the Islamic community and are tied to its circumstances. The nascent community was weak and beleaguered, faced with the difficult task of absorbing non-Muslim communities in territories to which it expanded while having to meet the military threat of powerful non-Muslim foes.[8]

In Islam, Christians and Jews are regarded as the recipients of previous divine revelations, revelations which were deemed to have culminated in God's final Revelation to the Prophet Muhammad. They are known as *ahl al-kitab*, or people of the book, an indication of Islamic respect for their scriptures.

In the early Islamic conquests, numerous Christian and Jewish communities became subjugated to Muslim rule, but many of those conquered refused to embrace Islam as the culmination and perfection of their own faiths. A major concern of the leaders of the new Islamic community became how to treat the Christians and Jews who continued in their old beliefs.[9] The *jihad,* or Islamic holy war, was undertaken both to expand the territory subject to Muslim control and to spread the Islamic religion.[10] However, contrary to Western images of Muslim conquerors presenting the conquered peoples with a choice of conversion to Islam or the sword, conquered Christians and Jews were allowed to persist in their beliefs because Islamic law opposes compelled conversions.

Although the premodern doctrines of *jihad* remain part of the Islamic cultural legacy and *jihad* may be proclaimed in a variety of military or political contexts by contemporary leaders, conducting holy war is obviously incompatible with the modern scheme of relations between nation-states. Muslim governments know that under international law they cannot invoke religious doctrines to justify military campaigns to conquer the non-Muslim world. In practice, many of the premodern doctrines regarding *jihad* and treatment of non-Muslims have been discarded, having been recognized as anachronisms in present circumstances, when the Muslim community has burgeoned to about 1 billion adherents and is certainly not threatened with extinction.[11] Those *jihad* doctrines as well as many ancillary principles for relations with non-Muslims that are no longer of practical relevance will not be discussed here. The aspects of the *shari'a* doctrines that do remain relevant for the status of non-Muslims do need to be summarized.

Jews and Christians ruled by Muslims had the political status of *dhimmi*s, being accorded toleration in return for submitting to Muslim rule and accepting a number of conditions governing their conduct.[12] *Dhimmi*s had to pay a special capitation tax known as the *jizya* and were excluded from serving in the military, since, as non-Muslims, they could not be expected to fight in holy wars on behalf of Islam. Depending on the jurists' opinions, *dhimmi*s could be either excluded from serving in government altogether or excluded from high government positions. Although they were generally subject to *shari'a* law, *dhimmi*s were allowed to follow their own rules of personal status, but they were subject to Islamic law in mixed cases—those in which persons of different faiths were involved and especially when the other party was a Muslim.[13]

In theory, other faiths were not tolerated. In premodern *shari'a* doctrine, non-Muslims who were not Christian or Jewish were categorized as polytheists or unbelievers. When conquered by Muslims, they theoretically had either to embrace Islam or to die; there was no place for them on the territory subject to Muslim rule.[14] In practice, as Islam expanded eastward, the premodern doctrines had to be adjusted and Muslims had to learn to coexist with Hindus and other polytheists.[15]

Despite incidents of discrimination and mistreatment of non-Muslims, it is fair to say that the Muslim world, when judged by the standards of the day, generally showed far greater tolerance and humanity in its treatment of religious minorities than did the Christian West.[16] In particular, the treatment of the Jewish minority in Muslim societies stands out as fair and enlightened when compared to the dismal record of Christian European persecution of Jews over the centuries.[17]

With the rise of secular nationalism in the Muslim world in the nineteenth century, it seemed that the distinctions between Muslim and non-Muslim were destined to dwindle in significance.[18] Although the *shari'a* prohibitions affecting intermarriage persisted and seemed well entrenched and most Muslim countries retained the legal requirement that the chief of state be Muslim, de jure discrimination against non-Muslims continued to diminish in the twentieth century. In most respects they gained the legal status of citizenship on a par with Muslims.

Today, as the influence of secular nationalism has waned and the influence of Islam as a political ideology is mounting, Muslims are divided on the merits of reinstating the premodern *shari'a* rules on *dhimmi*s. Because of demands for reinstating *shari'a* law and establishing Islamic states, issues of the status of non-Muslims that seemed until recently closed have been reopened.[19]

In addition to secularists who assume that Islamization entails discrimination against non-Muslims and who thus oppose the reinstatement of premodern *shari'a* rules affecting non-Muslims, one finds Muslims who believe that Islamic law, when properly understood, does not stand in the way of observing international human rights standards prohibiting discrimination based on religion. One must note, however, that the kind of robust, vigorous advocacy of the feminist position within the Islamic tradition that one commonly encounters today is not matched when one moves to the area of equal rights for non-Muslims. Still, one finds Muslims representing a variety of currents of Islamic thought who have taken the position that Islam can accommodate equal treatment for non-Muslims. For example, the Lebanese scholar Subhi Mahmassani argued in his work on Islam and human rights that there can be no discrimination based on religion in an Islamic system.[20] His approach seems basically to be one of assuming that there must be harmony between Islam and international law, which entails tacitly suppressing or discarding any features of the *shari'a* that would be incongruous in the scheme of international human rights. Mahmassani places great emphasis on aspects of the original sources and examples from early Islamic history that demonstrate the tolerant and egalitarian strains that have from the beginning constituted important components in the Islamic tradition.[21]

The conviction that there must be a natural affinity between Islam and the principles of international human rights law has led other Muslims, as well, to embrace the principle that full equality for all citizens is compatible with Islam.[22] So deep is the conviction on the part of some that full equality must comport with Islamic norms that the provision of arguments justifying this conclusion may be relegated to an afterthought. For example, the Egyptian political theorist Tariq al-Bishri, concerned with the status of Egypt's Copts and insisting that they should be equal to Muslims, has called on specialists to reconcile this equality with Islamic law but has expressed confidence that in a tradition as flexible and egalitarian as the Islamic one this should present no great problem.[23] However, he has also considered the implications of the political changes in the Muslim world that are relevant for evaluating whether the premodern *shari'a* rules remain applicable. Al-Bishri noted that the nature of the modern state is so different from the kind of government envisaged by medieval Islamic theorists that the *shari'a* restrictions on non-Muslims holding high political office no longer logically apply.[24] The interpretations of the requirements of Islamic law that have been offered by Abdullahi An-Na'im show much more concern than al-Bishri's for establishing the methodological basis for deriving the rule that Islam allows absolute equality of Muslim and non-Muslim.[25] An-Na'im's system is based on the teaching of the late Mahmud Muhammad Taha, who said that the applicability of legal rules in various Qur'anic verses must be rethought. By distinguishing verses that were meant to apply in the circumstances of the early stages of the Islamic community from those that were meant to have enduring validity, he was able to derive Islamic human rights principles that abolish the status of *dhimmi*s and mandate an end to all discrimination on a religious basis.[26]

Against such persons are arrayed Muslim conservatives like Tabandeh and Mawdudi, who want either to preserve or to revive discriminatory *shari'a* rules affecting non-Muslims. Even where the documents in the Islamic human rights literature do not expressly advocate assigning non-Muslims to an inferior position, they have been deliberately drafted so as to accommodate the continued application of discriminatory *shari'a* rules. However, with the exception of Tabandeh, the authors of these human rights schemes formulate their provisions regarding non-Muslims in such a manner that their intention to retain premodern *shari'a* rules regarding non-Muslims will not be too obvious. That is, just as in the case of their evasive treatments of the status of women, they are reluctant to state forthrightly that they refuse to endorse the principle of equality as understood in international law.

Tabandeh and the Rights of Religious Minorities

Tabandeh demonstrated a rare candor in his willingness to concede that, according to his conception, the *shari'a* precludes equality between Muslims and non-Muslims. In commenting on the UDHR Article 1 guarantee of equality, Tabandeh insisted that the principle of equality does not apply when it comes to differences of religion, faith, or conviction. This is because "nobility, excellence and virtue consist in true worship of the One God and obedience to the commandments of Heaven."[27] According to Tabandeh, the *ahl al-kitab* deserve respect because of their belief, but "since their faith has not reached the highest level of spirituality, but obeys commands which we believe to have been abrogated, and puts other laws in place of these revealed through Islam by the means of the Prophet and most righteous Judge, therefore [the *shari'a*] makes certain difference between them and Muslims, treating them as not on the same level."[28] Therefore, because Christians and Jews, instead of accepting God's final Revelation, adhere to earlier and less perfect versions of God's message, they must be discriminated against. For those non-Muslims who are not *ahl al-kitab,* he has only contempt. Humanists, he said, are "the gangrenous members of the body politic,"[29] and those who have not accepted the one God are "outside the pale of humanity."[30] Given his attitudes, Tabandeh naturally cannot concede that persons in the latter categories are deserving of any human rights protections.

The view that non-Muslims who are not among the *ahl al-kitab* are not entitled to the status of legal persons is common among Muslim conservatives. This idea corresponds to features of the premodern *shari'a,* but it means a sharp conflict with international human rights norms, which do not recognize that a person may be denied legal personality because of religion or belief. The ICCPR says in Article 16 that everyone has a right to recognition everywhere as a person before the law.

Tabandeh's conviction that the polytheist must be treated as a nonperson also comes up in comments regarding the issue of intermarriage. He insisted that it is necessary to preserve the premodern *shari'a* rules that absolutely prohibited marriage with polytheists and said, "your idolater has so far rejected sound sense and the inheritance of humanity that he worships objects other than God, and thereby puts himself outside the pale of mankind."[31]

He is equally adamant about keeping the premodern *shari'a* rule that prevents a Muslim woman from marrying a Christian or Jew, while allowing a Muslim man to marry a woman from those faiths.[32] According to him, the marriage of a Muslim wife and a non-Muslim husband is invalid, a child born of it is illegitimate, and if she knew before the marriage that her husband was a non-Muslim, the woman must be punished.[33]

It is at this point in Tabandeh's argument that one sees how the inferior status of women and the inferior status of non-Muslims are linked—a linkage that is made by many Muslim conservatives. Tabandeh argued:

The scripture says: "Men are guardians of women and guarantors of their rights" [Qur'an IV:34]. The wife must obey her husband. But, if she weds a non-Muslim husband it means that she as a Muslim is subordinating herself: and Islam never allows a Muslim to come under the authority of a non-Muslim in any circumstance at all, as is made perfectly plain in "God will never make a way for infidels (to exercise lordship) over believers" [Qur'an 4:41]: and therefore He never granted permission that Muslims should by marriage voluntarily subordinate themselves to non-Muslims. . . . In Islam every distinction is abolished except the distinction of religion and faith; whence it follows that Islam and its peoples must be above infidels, and never permit non-Muslims to acquire lordship over them.[34]

Here one consequence of the anti-individualistic approach taken by Muslim conservatives is apparent: The rights of the individual man and woman who wish to marry despite religious differences are totally absent from Tabandeh's concerns. Instead of the concern that one finds in international human rights law for the freedom of the individuals involved, the concern is for the prestige of the Muslim community, the honor of which is sullied if one of their number is subordinated to a member of the inferior group, the non-Muslims. What is more, the assumption is that, just as Muslims are placed above non-Muslims, so men are placed above women, meaning that wives are necessarily subordinated to their husbands. Therefore, the Muslim man who marries a female *dhimmi* does not infringe the hierarchy of status, since by virtue of her sex the non-Muslim wife will be subordinate to her husband, who as a Muslim and a male ranks above her on two counts. In contrast, the Muslim woman who marries a *dhimmi* violates the rules of status, since as a wife she has lower status than the man to whom she is married even though by virtue of her adherence to the Islamic religion she should rank above him. One can see that these *shari'a* rules regarding marriage have the effect of allowing Muslim men to exercise the powers that they enjoy as husbands both over their own women and *dhimmi* women, while allowing *dhimmi* men to exercise their marital prerogatives solely over women who are likewise relegated to *dhimmi* status.

On the questions of political rights and freedom of expression, Tabandeh proves himself to be opposed to according to non-Muslims rights that are guaranteed in international human rights standards. Non-Muslims, he said, must be entirely excluded from the judiciary, the legislature, and the cabinet.[35] Furthermore, no "propaganda" for any non-Muslim religion may be allowed.[36]

Religious Minorities and the UIDHR

The disposition of the authors of the UIDHR to evade hard questions regarding the compatibility of *shari'a* rules with international human rights law has already been established in connection with discussions of the treatment of equality and equal protection. Where the status of non-Muslims is concerned, the authors of the UIDHR are much less forthright than Tabandeh in spelling out the specific discriminatory rules that will apply to non-Muslims in their version of Islamic human rights, preferring to circumvent the important rights issues involved.

The UIDHR addresses the situation of non-Muslims in Article 10. This article does not guarantee equal treatment for religious minorities or state that discrimination based on religion is impermissible. It provides in Article 10.a that the religious rights of non-Muslim minorities are governed by the principle that there is no compulsion in religion, which is based on the Qur'an 2:256. The traditional interpretation of this verse is that *dhimmi*s should not be forced to convert to Islam. In contrast, it has not traditionally been interpreted to mean that the prohibition against compulsion in religion precludes *dhimmi*s or other non-Muslims being subjected to discrimination based on their religion. Its quotation in this context thus offers very little protection for the rights of non-Muslims.

What the UIDHR seems to contemplate is the use of the *millet* system that flourished under the Ottoman Empire, in which the various non-Muslim communities were governed under their own religious laws in internal matters and for lawsuits involving members of the same faith while being subject to the *shari'a* in mixed cases and in all other matters. In most Muslim countries today, remnants of this system persist, since personal-status matters remain for the most part governed by the religious law of the parties involved.

In the English version of Article 10.b, "religious minorities" are given the right to be governed either by Islamic law or their own laws on personal-status or civil matters. Not limited in terms to Christians and Jews, Article 10.b appears to go beyond the premodern *shari'a* rules, which gave only *dhimmi*s the right to be judged under their own law. The article seems to allow all non-Muslims to follow their own laws in personal or civil matters. However, the Arabic version of the same provision resurrects the old distinction between Christians and Jews, on the one hand, and other non-Muslims, on the other, suggesting that only members of the *ahl al-kitab* enjoy this right. In a peculiar formulation, the Arabic version of Article 10.b provides that non-Muslims may appeal to Muslims for judgment, but that if they do not do so, they must follow their own laws, provided that they (seemingly, the non-Muslims) believe that the latter are of divine origin. This would seem to mean that where non-Muslims did not elect to be governed by the *shari'a,* their subjective convictions that the laws of their own communities were divinely inspired would mean that their laws would be controlling. However, the references in the same provision to the Qur'an verses 5:47, dealing with people of the Gospel, and 5:42, dealing with the followers of the Torah, give reason to believe that this right of religious minorities to be bound by their own religious rules actually pertains only to Christian and Jewish minorities. That is, as in the premodern *shari'a,* no provision is made allowing non-Muslims who are not Christians or Jews to follow their own religious law in civil and personal-status matters among members of their own communities. This leaves open the question as to what status is contemplated for such non-Muslims, who under the *shari'a* were nonpersons.

International human rights law assumes that a neutral, nondiscriminatory law will be applied to all citizens of a country. In contrast, the UIDHR contemplates the general application of the *shari'a.* It is important to note that there is no indication that the UIDHR intends to repudiate any of the discriminatory features of the premodern *shari'a.* Furthermore, the UIDHR allows only Christians and Jews to opt out of the *shari'a* to follow their own laws in personal status and civil matters. Although the UIDHR does not discuss choice of law problems, one can presume that the normal *shari'a* choice of law rules would apply to limit this already narrow exemption from the applicability of the *shari'a* to those cases arising among members of the same non-Muslim community. Therefore, in most matters non-Muslims would appear to be subject to discriminatory *shari'a* rules, including rules affecting non-Muslims that are in violation of international human rights norms.

In another article the UIDHR echoes an idea put forth by Mawdudi in his human rights pamphlet saying that Muslims must show respect for the feelings of non-Muslims. Mawdudi stated that Islam does not allow Muslims to use abusive language that may injure the religious feelings of non-Muslims.[37] The UIDHR says in Article 12.e that no one shall hold in contempt or ridicule the religious beliefs of others. Both of these principles seem to be ethico-moral injunctions rather than enforceable legal rights. Again, as so frequently happens in Islamic human rights schemes, they are not directed against laws or governmental action, which are the most common sources of infringements of liberty, but against private individuals, whose actions are less likely to have as great an impact on non-Muslims as discriminatory laws and governmental policies.

Article 12.e of the UIDHR elaborates on this idea, saying that "people" should not incite hostility toward non-Muslims. This is a laudable ethico-moral precept, and the Islamic Council is performing a valuable public service by taking a stance condemning such incitement, which, in the volatile Middle Eastern setting, can be a prelude to violence. However, for this principle to have teeth—and legal force— further definition of what constitutes such impermissible incitement to violence would be required. As the UIDHR now stands, it lays down no guidelines for enforcing this principle. All speech is allowed within the limits of the *shari'a,* according to Article 12.a, a standard that is far too vague to determine what kinds of speech would constitute unacceptable incitement to public hostility toward non-Muslims.[38]

Religious Minorities and the Iranian Constitution

The article of the Iranian Constitution dealing with religious minorities seems to contemplate a model similar to the *millet* system. It contemplates a system where there are two categories of persons, Muslims and the *ahl al-kitab.* Article 13 provides: "The Iranian Zoroastrians, Jews, and Christians are the *only* recognized minorities, who, within the limits of the law [*dar hodud-e qanun*], are free to perform their own religious rites, and who, in matters relating to their personal affairs and teachings, may act in accordance with their religious regulations"(emphasis added).

That is, aside from acts of religious observance and personal status matters, the *ahl al-kitab* in Iran (here treated as including Zoroastrians) are subject to the principles of Iranian law. As has already been discussed, Iranian laws are subordinate to Islamic law, which, under Article 4 of the constitution, is treated as the norm to which all laws must conform. This means that, as a matter of law, the *ahl al-kitab* will be discriminated against. The nonrecognition of religious minorities other than the *ahl al-kitab* in this *shari'a*-based system means that they can claim no constitutional protections. The problems of non-Muslims who are not accorded the status of recognized minorities will be discussed after a review of the implications of constitutional provisions for the rights of recognized minorities.

The human rights record of the postrevolutionary regime vis-à-vis religious minorities shows that the disabilities imposed on non-Muslims have been serious. In many instances the deprivations of rights and freedoms actually have gone beyond those that would be required under the rules of premodern *shari'a.* Since in the postrevolutionary Iranian environment, Islam is interpreted to be an ideology—much as communism used to be in the East Bloc countries—the fact that non-

Muslims are persons who by definition do not subscribe to the official Islamic ideology of Iran has provided additional grounds for discriminating against them. Iran has imposed tests of ideological purity on applicants for public employment that effectively excluded non-Muslims.[39] Of course, Muslims who oppose the peculiar ideologized version of Islam that is sponsored by the regime are also excluded from employment because they are unable to pass ideological screening tests.

One might parenthetically note at this point that using adherence to an ideological version of Islam as a device to justify discrimination is not a uniquely Iranian idea. Mawdudi, for example, believed that Islam must be the official ideology of Muslim countries. Although he did not discuss this in his human rights pamphlet, elsewhere he indicated that he considered discrimination against persons who did not share this official Islamic ideology perfectly reasonable.[40] An example of the consequences of ideologization of Islam can be seen in the Iranian Constitution. There is an ideological test for those who wish to serve in the Iranian military. A close reading of Article 144 reveals that non-Muslims will be excluded from the military, just as *dhimmi*s were in premodern Islamic civilization. The article provides: "The Army of the Islamic Republic of Iran shall be an Islamic army. It must be an ideologically-oriented and democratic army and it must accept competent people who will be faithful to the goals of the Islamic revolution and will be self-sacrificing in the attainment of these goals." Obviously, Iran's non-Muslim minorities will have no place in an Islamic army set up under these criteria, as they do not share the Islamic ideological orientation that is called for.[41]

Article 14 of the Iranian Constitution provides: "The Islamic Republic of Iran and Moslems shall treat non-Moslems according to the dictates of virtue and Islamic justice, and to honor their human rights [*hoquq-e ensani*]. This principle will be applicable only to those who do not become involved in conspiracies and activities which are anti-Islamic or are against the Islamic Republic of Iran." Far from granting non-Muslims protections for the rights to which they are entitled under international human rights standards, this article, in subjecting them to Islamic justice, reinforces the principle that all rights are subject to *shari'a* qualifications, which is expressly set forth in Article 20. Here honoring non-Muslims' "human rights" in conjunction with the application of "Islamic justice" would seem to entail the application of discriminatory features of *shari'a* law.

In addition, Article 14 provides that the human rights that non-Muslims enjoy, which one may assume will be very limited to begin with, are to be forfeited if the non-Muslims become involved in "anti-Islamic" activities, a vague standard that would afford a broad range of potential justifications for curbing their rights. It is interesting that this article provides special grounds for denying non-Muslims their human rights for opposition to the Islamic Republic, even though there is already a general provision in Article 26 that enables the government to curb the activities of groups, including "minority religious associations," if they are "contrary to the principles of Islam or the Islamic Republic." The Article 14 provision seems to contemplate an even more extensive pattern of deprivations of human rights than the mere deprivation of the freedom of association, as in Article 26. Together they would indicate that the consequences for non-Muslims of oppositional activities are intended to be harsher than for Muslims who are guilty of such activities. It also seems to betoken a belief on the part of the drafters of the constitution that non-Muslims are likely to be more disposed to oppose Iran's Islamic Republic than members of the Muslim population. Of course, since the ideological version of Islam envisaged in the constitution legitimizes discrimination against non-Muslims and relegates them to second-class status, such opposition could certainly be anticipated.

Although Iran denies Jews, Christians, and Zoroastrians many basic rights, the latter are distinctly better off than non-Muslims who do not qualify for *dhimmi* status as *ahl al-kitab*. Such non-Muslims are excluded from the Article 13 status of "recognized minorities." The exclusion from this status has been particularly sinister in the case of Iran's Baha'i community in the past several years.

The Baha'i religion, sometimes called Babism, originated in Iran in the nineteenth century. It is named after one Baha'ullah, who in 1863 announced that he was a messenger from God and espoused liberal and ecumenical teachings. It teaches veneration for the founders of all the major world religions and insists on the brotherhood and equality of all persons, stressing that men and women are meant to be equal. Baha'ism denies that clerics are needed to understand religion, calling instead for universal education so that individuals can pursue the path of enlightenment. It also supports the idea of a world government and world peace.[42] Baha'i doctrines appealed to many of Iran's Muslims and led them to convert away from Islam to the new faith. Baha'ism has elements that reveal its Iranian origins, but it aims at being a universalist religion. It has spread to many countries.

In Iran, the position of the Baha'i community has always been precarious and its members have suffered from periodic waves of persecution. Iran's Shi'i clerics have often been the leading forces in anti-Baha'i campaigns. From the beginning, Baha'ism has been perceived as a threat by Iran's clerics, and many of them have been violently hostile toward the religion and its adherents. Shi'i clerics have, since the nineteenth century, supported attempts to eliminate Baha'ism from Iran through massacre, torture, intimidation, and discrimination.[43] This clerical animus had several grounds. Baha'ism challenged the doctrine of the finality of God's Revelation to the Prophet Muhammad. It aimed at winning converts from Islam in violation of the *shari'a* prohibition of any conversion away from Islam to another faith. Its egalitarian doctrines challenged the hierarchy of privilege mandated by the *shari'a,* according to which men were superior to women and Muslims superior to non-Muslims. Its members showed no inclination to defer to the views of Iran's clerics, whose authority they denied.

Given this long history of clerical animosity toward the Baha'i community, which by the time of the Iranian Revolution may have numbered 200,000–300,000, it was natural that when Shi'i clerics achieved political dominance in the postrevolutionary regime, they would exploit their power to try to eliminate Baha'ism once and for all from the soil of Iran. The government, sometimes acting directly and at other times indirectly through allied groups, has carried out a campaign of terror against Baha'is. They were fired from jobs, their property was confiscated, their homes were subject to invasion at any time by persons bent on harassment and plunder in the guise of investigating crimes, and they were murdered with impunity. Hundreds of Baha'is were arrested, imprisoned, and subjected to brutal torture, and Baha'i leaders were executed on a variety of trumped-up charges. In addition, their shrines and houses of worship were destroyed and desecrated, and all of their associations were forcibly disbanded. The widespread persecution of the Baha'is has been extensively documented and has been noted by neutral observers and international human rights organizations.[44]

It is thus obvious that it was not coincidental that Baha'is were denied the status of a "recognized minority" in Article 13. This is one of many instances in Islamic human rights schemes where principles deviating from the international model point to an intention to deny human rights that are guaranteed under international law.

Mawdudi and Religious Minorities

Mawdudi's treatment of equality has already been mentioned in an earlier section, but his vague, ambiguous position merits further examination in connection with his views on the rights of non-Muslims. Just as he avoided detailing his views on women's rights in his human rights pamphlet, so he steered clear there of any specifics on how the *shari'a* affects non-Muslims. He merely mentioned *dhimmi*s in passing, saying that their lives and properties are as "sacred" as those of Muslims.[45]

However, his views on this subject are on record in other publications. Mawdudi advocated discrimination against non-Muslims. According to him, Muslims are to be accorded superiority over non-Muslims. He favored the reimposition of the *jizya* tax traditionally imposed on *dhimmi*s,[46] excluding them from military service,[47] and eliminating them from high positions in government.[48] He asserted that Islam "does not permit them to meddle with the affairs of the State."[49] Because he said that Islamic law should control personal status matters as long as one party is a Muslim,[50] the *shari'a* prohibitions regarding intermarriage would obviously be retained in his scheme. Thus, although Mawdudi did not follow Tabandeh in acknowledging in the course of his discussion of human rights in Islam that he supported a regime of discrimination against non-Muslims, he was similar to Tabandeh in believing that they are to be relegated to an inferior status.

Mawdudi's Jama'at party was also among the instigators of the Pakistani campaigns against the Ahmadi minority, who were later to be badly affected by Pakistan's Islamization. In an era in which governments are adopting official versions of Islamic requirements as the law of the land, it is not just persons who formally adhere to religions other than Islam who need to be concerned about the status assigned to non-Muslims: Muslims who adhere to minority sects or schools of thought may be assigned by governmental policy to the category of "non-Muslims." The treatment of the Ahmadi Muslim minority in Pakistan, which may number about 1 million, provides a good illustration of how this can happen.

The Ahmadi sect was founded by Mirza Ghulam Ahmad (d. 1908) in India. Ahmadis, their opponents charge, treat their founder as a prophet, thereby violating the Islamic doctrine of the finality of the Prophethood of Muhammad. Ahmadis have energetically campaigned to spread the ideas of their founder in Pakistan and around the world and are active in projects such as constructing mosques and distributing Qur'ans. Although Ahmadis fervently believe that they are Muslims, they are considered heretics by many Muslim conservatives in Pakistan. For a variety of reasons, Mawdudi's followers in the Jama'at-i-Islami and the Ahmadiya became bitter foes, and the Jama'at was implicated in the serious disturbances that resulted from their anti-Ahmadi agitation in the Punjab in 1953.[51] Mawdudi wrote an anti-Ahmadi tract and was even incarcerated after being convicted of a leading role in anti-Ahmadi agitation.

In a concession to anti-Ahmadi sentiment, Prime Minister Bhutto decided to have the constitution amended in 1974 to declare the Ahmadis non-Muslims. President Zia, who was closely allied with the Jama'at and right-wing clerics, went further and in 1984 issued a decree, the "Anti-Islamic Activities of the Quadiani Group, Lahori Group and Ahmadis (Prohibition and Punishment) Ordinance XX of 1984," forbidding Ahmadis to call themselves Muslims or their religion Islam, to use Islamic terminology, to use the Islamic call to prayer, to call their houses of worship mosques, and to preach or propagate their version of the faith—all prohibitions under sanction of criminal law.[52] In the wake of this decree, it became a criminal offense for Ahmadis to act as if they still considered themselves Muslims, and many were prosecuted for so doing.

The 1984 decree was challenged in the Pakistani Federal Shariat Court as being un-Islamic. In the face of overwhelming evidence to the contrary, the court held that the ordinance did not interfere with the Ahmadis' freedom of faith or the right of Ahmadis to profess or practice their religion. It also ruled that the decree was not contrary to the Qur'an and *sunna*.[53] In ruling that the law was not "un-Islamic," the court effectively decided that Islamic law did not protect Ahmadis from being singled out for discriminatory treatment as non-Muslims by a regime that decided that their particular views on Islam were not in keeping with the standards of Islamic orthodoxy. With the Ahmadis helpless to obtain relief from the courts, their exposure to criminal prosecutions made their situation increasingly difficult and perilous.[54]

It is obvious that Islamization aggravated the discrimination experienced by this religious minority. The rights deprivations that ensued were largely prompted by the past agitation of Mawdudi against the Ahmadis and by the demands of his conservative followers. The situation of the Ahmadis shows how discriminatory features of contemporary Islamic rights schemes are relevant for religious minorities generally, not just for the rights of non-Muslim minorities.

Summary

The Islamic human rights schemes discussed here do not provide any real protections for the rights of religious minorities comparable to those found in international human rights law. In fact, to the extent that they deal with the question of the rights of religious minorities, they seem to endorse premodern *shari'a* rules that call for non-Muslims to be relegated to an inferior status if they qualify as members of the *ahl al-kitab* and for them to be treated as nonpersons if they do not qualify for such inclusion. The Azhar draft constitution avoids dealing with the status of non-Muslims. In the context of a document that seems to support the general applicability of premodern *shari'a* rules, the failure to address the issue suggests that the intent was to retain such rules to govern the status of non-Muslims.

Not only does the record of the treatment of religious minorities in countries undergoing Islamization show that there are policies afoot of relegating religious minorities to second-class status, but it also establishes that Muslim conservatives are in some instances ready to go much further and engage in actual campaigns of religious persecution. The experiences of the Sudan, which will be discussed in Chapter 8, provide another illustration of this tendency.

CHAPTER 8

Freedom of Religion in Islamic Human Rights Schemes

International Human Rights Law and the Shari'a Rule on Apostasy

In the West, people do not tend to think of the freedom to change religion as the central concern of provisions guaranteeing religious freedom. There, the right to freedom of religion is most often conceived of as a guarantee against religious persecution and protection from the kinds of discriminatory treatment meted out to disfavored religious minorities. Although such discrimination was common until recently, government-imposed constraints on conversion from one religion to another and the concept of apostasy as a criminal offense have virtually vanished in the West.

In Muslim milieus the perspective is different, and the question of whether there should be freedom to convert is alive. Muslim attitudes are still influenced by the premodern *shari'a* that forbade Muslims to convert from Islam. Under the interpretations of the medieval jurists, apostates were to be given an opportunity to repent and return to Islam, but if they refused, they were to be executed if they were male and imprisoned until they changed their minds if they were female. Premodern *shari'a* rules also provided that apostasy constituted civil death, meaning, among other things, that the apostate's marriage would be dissolved and the apostate would become incapable of inheriting. Naturally, the *shari'a* imposed no penalties on converts to Islam from other faiths. Given this background, when one evaluates Islamic versions of human rights with respect to religious freedom, it is particularly important to see whether the schemes contemplate the retention of the *shari'a* ban on apostasy.

International human rights law allows no constraints on a person's religious beliefs: Freedom of religion is an unqualified freedom. One of the most influential statements of this freedom is in Article 18 of the UDHR, which does not place any qualifications on this freedom. Article 18 states: "Everyone has the right to freedom of thought, conscience and religion; this right includes freedom to change his religion or belief, and freedom, either alone or in community with others and in public or private, to manifest his religion or belief in teaching, practice, worship and observance."

It is historically significant that the phrase guaranteeing the right to change religion was added to this article at the behest of the delegate from Lebanon (a Christian). Lebanon in the 1940s and 1950s was an oasis of toleration, where large Christian, Muslim, and Druze communities coexisted in a pluralistic society. The Lebanese Christian community did object to *shari'a* rules like the ban on conversions from Islam. Not surprisingly, when the Lebanese representative proposed this language be added, he faced strong objections from some Muslim countries.[1] The Saudi Arabian representative was particularly outspoken in condemning this provision on the grounds that Islam did not permit Muslims to change their religion. A voice on the Lebanese delegate's side was Pakistan's representative, an Ahmadi, who spoke forcefully in defense of the proposition that freedom of religion as presented in this article was fully consonant with Islam. In the end, all Muslim countries other than Saudi Arabia overcame their scruples and voted for the UDHR.[2] Objections similar to those that had been raised by Saudi Arabia were later raised by Iran in discussions of the 1981 Declaration on the Elimination of All Forms of Intolerance and of Discrimination Based on Religion or Belief, expressing the government's positions that Muslims were not allowed to convert from their religion and were to be killed if they did so.[3] These public statements by Muslim governments indicated the degree to which the *shari'a* ban on apostasy continued to be regarded as a legitimate feature of their criminal law.

In this, they were placing themselves at odds with the codifications of international human rights in subsequent conventions and declarations. Freedom of religion is unqualified in the ICCPR Article 18.1. Although the wording is basically similar to the UDHR Article 18, this ICCPR provision does not specifically mention the freedom to change religion. The 1981 Declaration on the Elimination of All Forms of Intolerance replicates the ICCPR Article 18.1 in its Article 1.1. Article 1.2 provides that no one shall be subject to coercion that would impair his freedom to have a religion or belief of his choice. This would seem to bar any use of coercion to prevent a person from freely choosing a religion and therefore appears to include the freedom to change religion.

Since attempts to convert from Islam are uncommon, one might object that the issue of whether Muslims are free to convert to other religions in the Middle East is an academic rather than a practical one.

After all, one can point to the facts that Islam is the world's fastest growing religion and that Muslims rarely seem motivated to convert to other faiths, even where there are no legal constraints to prevent them from doing so. In these circumstances, the number of persons whose freedom of religion might be expected to be affected by the imposition of the *shari'a* ban on conversion would be expected to be minimal. It is necessary to explain why the ban on conversion from Islam has broader ramifications and potentially limits the rights of a much larger segment of the populations of Muslim countries than one might initially expect.

As the ban on apostasy has been interpreted, it can affect people who are born into a non-Muslim religion but whose parents, grandparents, or even remoter ancestors converted from Islam. The notion that Baha'is are renegades from Islam has been one basis for the recent wave of prosecutions and persecutions of the Baha'is in Iran since the revolution. The targeted individuals had not changed their religion, but they followed a religion that in Iran is believed to be largely composed of persons who are descendants of Muslims who converted to Baha'ism. As the example of Iran shows, such persons may be punished and persecuted as "apostates" by virtue of their ancestors' defections from Islam.

The ban can also affect Muslims who adhere to doctrines that are out of keeping with whatever standard of orthodoxy is currently being espoused by a government pursuing Islamization. Although premodern Islamic culture was generally tolerant of diverging views on questions of Islamic theology and law, when contemporary Middle Eastern governments have pressed forward with Islamization campaigns, they have tended to impose a uniform standard of orthodoxy on their Muslim citizens and to reject the legitimacy of the positions of Muslim groups that do not accept what is being presented as the official norms of Islam. As the official orthodoxy becomes identified with the regime's own ideology and legitimacy, modern governments have shown themselves inclined to label Muslims who do not accept the official Islam as "heretics" and "apostates." The example of how the Ahmadi minority in Pakistan became officially designated "non-Muslim" and made a target of discrimination and persecution under official Islamization policies has already been discussed. Likewise, the Sudanese Republicans officially became "apostates" from Islam under Nimeiri even though they never repudiated Islam and believed themselves to be following authentic Islamic teachings. Thus the ban on apostasy has become a curb on the religious freedom of Muslims—not only on their freedom to convert from Islam, but also on their freedom to follow their consciences in selecting what Islamic teachings to follow. In the climate of intolerance that has been fostered by official Islamization campaigns, even if Muslim minorities are not executed for beliefs that are officially deemed heretical, they may have to contend with discrimination, harassment, and jailing where they follow disapproved theological or legal doctrines.

Furthermore, the ban on conversion from Islam has implications for the freedom of Muslim women, since it means that they cannot escape their subjugation to the rules of premodern *shari'a* law. This subjugation follows from the choice of law rules in force in most Muslim countries, where religious affiliation decides the law applicable to personal status issues. Only in rare instances, like the reforms in Turkey and Tunisia, have Muslim countries so modernized their personal status rules that one national standard can apply to all citizens. Elsewhere, *shari'a* law still applies to personal status questions where one or both of the parties is Muslim.[4] Thus, for example, by virtue of being Muslim, a Muslim woman may have to abide by such premodern *shari'a* rules as the severe restrictions on divorces by the wife without the approval of the husband that one finds in the Hanafi School, the requirement of obtaining the consent of a male marriage guardian in order to marry, or submitting to the husband's right to demand obedience and to keep his wife confined inside the house.

In such systems, if there were no ban on conversion, a Muslim woman could change the personal status law applicable to her simply by abandoning Islam or converting to another religion. Conversions would not be inspired by theological considerations but would be undertaken for quite practical reasons, to avoid the application of an unfavorable law. In the Middle East, conversions from one religion to another—and sometimes switches from one Islamic sect or school of law to another—have long been used to change the applicable law in personal status issues. These conversions are the equivalent of forum shopping in the United States, where litigants, by changing domicile, can alter the law applicable to family law and inheritance issues— "shopping" for the law of a forum that is favorable by changing residence from one state to another.

Conversions—including those to Islam—potentially enable parties to accomplish objectives impossible to achieve under their original personal status law. For example, a Roman Catholic woman married to a Catholic would be barred from divorcing, but if she wanted a divorce, she could sever her marital tie by converting to Islam. Then her marriage would become void, for she would get the benefit of the *shari'a* rule that a Muslim woman cannot be validly married to a non-Muslim. In the Middle East it seems largely to be men who have converted to other religions to gain temporary advantages in litigation.

Non-Muslim men have converted to Islam for reasons of expediency, in order to get the benefit of its more favorable personal status rules. Penalizing conversion from Islam can be utilized to deter "conversions" undertaken only out of expediency and prevents these men from converting back to their original faiths after achieving the results they hoped to obtain by changing their personal status law.[5]

One of the options, admittedly a drastic one, open to Muslim women who seek to sever their ties with their husbands but are unable to get divorced is that of apostasy. By virtue of becoming apostates, Muslims incur civil death, regardless of whether a criminal penalty is imposed, and civil death of one party terminates a marriage. Thus, the Muslim woman who is willing to incur civil death can escape both from her marriage and from the applicability of *shari'a* law.

In the past, there were many informal social and cultural factors inhibiting Muslim women from taking such a radical course, but these inhibitions must be crumbling under the impact of modernization. In intact traditional communities, the ostracism that apostasy from Islam entails would make women reluctant to resort to it, but such communities are being undermined by phenomena like rapid urbanization and economic changes that make it possible for women to become independent and self-supporting. Improved educational opportunities, exposure to different social models via the media, growing skepticism among women regarding the authoritativeness of Islamic models of female subordination, and other factors may lead women to chafe under onerous marital obligations that they formerly would have accepted. They contemplate with more interest than before the prospects of freedom that apostasy can bring them.

That Muslim women may be tempted to abandon Islam concerned Tabandeh, who has identified a number of discreditable reasons for which Muslim men might convert, while positing a Muslim woman's desire "to exploit easier conditions for divorce obtaining under other religions" as the only reason for apostasy in a woman's case.[6] His sense that the temptation to escape a marriage by apostasy is a real threat and that a strong deterrent is necessary to prevent women from using apostasy this way led him to propose a penalty that has no counterpart in the *shari'a:* life imprisonment at hard labor for the female apostate.[7]

In Kuwait, where a Muslim woman's ability to opt out of the *shari'a* system has likewise been perceived as a threat, a different legal solution was found. There, a law was enacted discarding the premodern *shari'a* rule that a Muslim woman's marriage would be automatically dissolved by her apostasy. The reason for this change is offered in an explanatory memorandum accompanying the text of the law reform: "Complaints have shown that the Devil makes the route of apostasy attractive to the Muslim woman so that she can break a conjugal tie that does not please her. For this reason, it was decided that apostasy would not lead to the dissolution of the marriage in order to close this dangerous door."[8] In the Kuwaiti treatment of apostasy, one clearly sees that fidelity to the *shari'a* takes second place to concerns for preserving the patriarchal order intact; the *shari'a* principle of civil death for the apostate is abandoned where it would permit the wife to sever a marital tie over her husband's objections. With the change in the law, Muslim women in Kuwait can no longer open "this dangerous door" to independence from their husbands.

When one considers the significance of apostasy for women's status, one sees the connection between the desire to retain the regime of premodern *shari'a* personal status rules, which all the Islamic human rights schemes seem to share, and the failure of these schemes to endorse freedom of religion and the freedom to change religion. The authors of the Islamic human rights schemes, because they relegate Muslim women to an inferior status at a time when the latter are emerging from their traditional roles and when modern ideologies favoring equal rights for women are percolating through the culture, expect that Muslim women will resist the imposition of premodern *shari'a* rules. In such circumstances, where *shari'a* rules are converted into a scheme for controlling and subjugating one-half of the population, it is essential that there be no means by which the subjugated half may evade the applicability of the *shari'a* via the manipulation of choice of law rules. All this leads to rules that deny the legitimacy of a woman's decision to change religion and fail to protect religious freedom according to the international standards.

Given this background, one can see that in the Middle East the freedom to change religion constitutes a more significant dimension of religious freedom than it does in the West. However, until recently, the progressive Westernization of Middle Eastern legal systems seemed to promise that the practical importance of *shari'a* concepts in this area would diminish. Because of the secularization that took place in the nineteenth and twentieth centuries in the area of criminal law, the application of the *shari'a* death penalty for apostasy from Islam became a rarity.

In this regard, the impact of Islamization on Middle Eastern legal systems has made a great difference. What until recently had seemed to be an anachronism has been revived in ways that have led to serious breaches of international human rights in the name of applying *shari'a* law. With mounting pressures in Muslim countries for the reinstatement of Islamic law, including Islamic criminal law, it seems that the former inhibitions on imposing the death penalty for apostasy are being weakened.

Even in countries where Islamic law plays a marginal role there have been pressures for the formal legislative adoption of the rule that converts from Islam should be killed. For example, in Egypt since the 1970s there have been insistent demands by Muslim conservatives for a revival of the death penalty for apostasy from Islam. These have met energetic resistance and condemnation on the part of Egypt's large Coptic population and have also been opposed by liberal Muslims and secular elements. Although the Egyptian government has managed to thwart attempts to have the death penalty for apostasy from Islam enacted into law, these defeats do not seem to have discouraged Muslim conservatives from pursuing the issue.[9]

In some legal systems where the impact of Islamization campaigns has been far-reaching, even in the absence of formal incorporation of a rule allowing the imposition of the *shari'a* death penalty for apostasy as part of the criminal codes, governments may nonetheless execute people for apostasy from Islam. As will be evident in the case of Mahmud Muhammad Taha and his followers in the Sudan, people may be executed as apostates simply by reference to the *shari'a* rules that are set forth in medieval juristic treatises—as if the *shari'a* rules are binding even in the absence of corresponding provisions in the criminal code. It is important to be aware of this possibility, since it seems that even those governments that intend to execute people as apostates from Islam are reluctant to adopt laws that publicly confirm that the death penalty applies to persons who convert from Islam. Thus, for example, Iran does not officially kill Baha'is as apostates; instead, they are executed for supposedly committing secular offenses, such as spying for Israel or treason, even though the fact that their "crimes" are pardoned if they recant and return to Islam reveals that they are in practice being prosecuted for apostasy.

Rethinking the Shari'a Rule on Apostasy

It is ironic that the apostasy penalty of the premodern *shari'a* has been revived after developments had suggested that many thoughtful Muslims were prepared to reform or discard the principles of premodern Islamic jurisprudence on this topic and accept the concept of religious freedom. There are contemporary Muslims who have repudiated the penalty, saying that the premodern juristic interpretations were unwarranted by the texts of the Islamic sources and out of keeping with the principle "no compulsion in religion" (based on the Qur'an 2:256).[10] The principle of tolerance of religious difference, which figures prominently in the

Islamic value system and tradition, supports the notion that religious adherence should be left a matter of conscience. This position is strengthened by the fact that there is no verse in the Qur'an that stipulates any earthly penalty for apostasy, and the premodern jurists' rules on apostasy were extrapolated from incidents in the Prophet's life and from historical events after his death that actually lend themselves to a variety of interpretations. Relying on the distinctions between the Qur'anic concern for freedom of conscience and the public order concerns that led jurists to conclude that the apostate should be punished by death, one Muslim scholar has concluded that the Qur'anic principle of religious liberty shares common foundations with the Western concept of religious liberty.[11]

Contemporary scholars have found many indications that the premodern *shari'a* rule that the apostate must be killed should not be taken to be the definitive interpretation of the Islamic sources in this area. For example, the Lebanese scholar Subhi Mahmassani asserted that the circumstances in which the penalty was meant to apply were intended to be narrow ones. He pointed out that the Prophet never killed anyone merely for apostasy. Instead, the death penalty was applied when the act of apostasy from Islam was linked to an act of political betrayal of the community. This being the case, Mahmassani argued that the death penalty was not meant to apply to a simple change of faith but to punish acts such as treason, joining forces with the enemy, and sedition.[12] The position has also been taken that the death penalty that was imposed on the tribes that abjured Islam after the Prophet's death was tied to a peculiar historical situation, and that there is no Islamic precedent for imposing the death penalty in the case of individual decisions to change religion.[13] Another interpretation that has been offered is that the apostate from Islam must be won back to Islam by reason and persuasion and should be given an indefinite—and indefinitely extendable—grace period in which to overcome the doubts that led to the apostasy.[14]

Muslims who currently call for the execution of apostates are not compelled to do so by unambiguous Islamic authority supporting the death penalty. There is diversity of opinion and ample ground for deciding that the premodern *shari'a* rules on apostasy no longer apply. Muslims can select alternative interpretations of the Islamic rules on apostasy that are more in keeping with the tenor of the Qur'an and with modern human rights norms on religious freedom. Where they elect not to do so and insist that apostates should be executed, one must wonder whether they are in reality motivated by opposition to the principle of religious freedom and are constructing Islamic rationales to legitimize that opposition.

Tabandeh

Not surprisingly, Tabandeh is the most direct of the authors treated here in calling for the retention of premodern Islamic rules restricting religious freedom. As we have seen, in his view, *dhimmi*s do enjoy the right to follow their own religions, but this is not so in the case of adherents of other religions. Because they are largely descended from Muslims who converted, members of the Baha'i faith are considered by Tabandeh and Iranians who share his conservative views to be defectors from Islam who must be forced to recant and return to the fold. In what appears to be a thinly veiled attack on the Baha'i faith, Tabandeh asserted that

followers of a religion of which the basis is contrary to Islam, like those who demand Islam's extirpation have no official rights to freedom of religion in Islamic countries or under an Islamic government, nor can they claim respect through their religion, any more than in certain countries definite political parties which are contrary to the ideology of the regime can claim freedom since they are declared to be inimical to the welfare of the land and people.[15]

Tabandeh also stated that in Islam religion and politics are not separated and the government cannot be divorced from the official religion.[16] Here Islam is effectively ideologized and treated like a political philosophy. With this analogy in place, Tabandeh can compare freedom of religion to the curbing of a political party with goals "inimical to the welfare of the land and people." This implies that in executing followers of a religion like Baha'ism, Iran would be acting like a state that executed people for political acts of treason rather than doing something extraordinary.

Tabandeh said that "propaganda" for any religion other than Islam must be prohibited.[17] His position on this is a consequence of his unyielding insistence that conversion from Islam should not be tolerated. In his view there is no conceivable justification for abandoning the Islamic faith:

No man of sense, from the mere fact that he possesses intelligence, will ever turn down the better in favor of the inferior. Anyone who penetrates beneath the surface to the inner essence of Islam is bound to recognise its superiority over the other religions. A man, therefore, who deserts Islam, by that act betrays the fact that he must have played truant to its moral and spiritual truths earlier.[18]

The reasons why a person might desert Islam include, according to a speech by the Egyptian UN representative and cited by Tabandeh, duress, bribes, and a woman's desire "to exploit easier conditions for divorce obtaining under some other religions."[19] As other possible inducements to abandon Islam, Tabandeh listed false promises by another religion, spite on the part of a Muslim who has been injured by another Muslim, or being led astray by carnal lusts that Islam forbids.[20] The nature of these reasons means, according to him, that conversions from Islam should not be given encouragement, "let alone by an international law." A person born in Islam who deserts after coming of age must be killed since he is "diseased . . . gangrenous, incurable, fit only for amputation."[21] A person who was not born Muslim but converted to Islam and then leaves it is given three days to reconsider his apostasy, after which, if he fails to return to the faith, he must be executed.[22] To illustrate the solicitude of Islam for women's welfare, Tabandeh pointed out that the female apostate is not killed but is condemned, instead, "only to life imprisonment with hard labor."[23] In contrast, Tabandeh noted that "a person who gives up some religion other than Islam to accept Islam's sound faith is received and respected."[24]

It is obvious that this kind of attitude is incompatible with the protection of religious freedom; for Tabandeh, there are only the categories of truth and error. Seemingly unaware that such an approach is incompatible with international norms, he assumes that it is feasible to project these categories into international law. He apparently imagines that once those who make international law are made to understand the reasons why Islam forbids conversion, international law will also decree that conversions from Islam should be banned.[25] Tabandeh's attitudes on conversion from Islam are shared by many conservative Muslims, which explains why concepts of human rights involving religious freedom have been only very superficially assimilated in some Muslim milieus.

It is worth considering how Tabandeh's arguments for banning conversion from Islam relate both to central premises underlying the Islamic human rights schemes and to those underlying international human rights law. Tabandeh and Muslims who share his values start with the premise that one must accord primacy to the interests of Islam and the Muslim community when deciding whether individual freedoms are permissible. If it turns out that the interests of the religion or the community dictate that the individual should be deprived of freedom, this is entirely acceptable to them. Tabandeh's arguments on this point provide an excellent illustration of the anti-individualistic attitudes shared by the authors of the Islamic human rights schemes.

In contrast, in international human rights law a central premise is that the individual is the best judge of his or her interests, because the individual ultimately has more insight into what he or she needs to be happy than does any other person or institution. International human rights is based on the assumption that exercising the freedom to choose, a fundamental right, is part of what is involved in being human and achieving dignity and self-respect.[26] It is therefore disposed to afford very strong protection for the individual's freedom of choice in a matter like religious belief and has little concern for whether the interests of a religious institution or the community in which the individual lives are served by that choice.

The UIDHR

The UIDHR purports to treat the "Right to Freedom of Belief, Thought and Speech" in Article 12.a, but, again, it uses formulations in the English and Arabic versions that convey very different impressions. In the English, Article 12.a states: "Every person has the right to express his thoughts and beliefs so long as he remains within the limits prescribed by the Law. No one, however, is entitled to disseminate falsehood or to circulate reports that may outrage public decency, or to indulge in slander, innuendo, or to cast defamatory aspersions on other persons."

At first glance this provision appears to impose neutral, secular restraints on freedom of expression, while sidestepping the issue of freedom of belief. It also appears to indicate that slanderous, defamatory speech can be curbed by law, an idea that most human rights advocates would find unobjectionable. The standards for curbing freedom of expression in this article are broad enough to allow for government interpretations that make serious inroads in the area of freedom of expression, but if one assumed that the qualifications would be interpreted narrowly, one might find this formulation in substantial conformity with international norms.

The Arabic version of Article 12.a conveys a very different message because it reveals that Islamic criteria limit freedom of expression. It states: "Everyone may think, believe and express his ideas and beliefs without interference or opposition from anyone as long as he obeys the limits [*hudud*] set by the *shari'a*. It is not permitted to spread falsehood [*al-batil*] or disseminate that which involves encouraging abomination [*al-fahisha*] or forsaking the Islamic community [*takhdhil li'l-umma*]."[27] The first sentence of this provision thus expressly provides that *shari'a* rules set limits not just on freedom of expression but also on the freedoms of thought and belief. Limitations on such freedoms using the criteria of one religion are unacceptable under international human rights norms.

One can surmise what specific rules in the *shari'a* would be likely to be employed to curtail these freedoms. For example, one would expect that in a system based on the *shari'a,* people would be prohibited from converting from Islam and forbidden to speak disparagingly of the Prophet. However, since the original *shari'a* rules were not elaborated as part of a philosophy of rights, there exist no established standards for how extensive the *shari'a* limits on the kinds of freedoms involved here may be. Therefore, the scope of the *shari'a* restraints that could be imposed under this provision is left vague and uncertain.

The significance of the second sentence is difficult to ascertain. The English version seems to be establishing that defamation and slander are categories of expression that are not protected, but the Arabic version appears to deny protection to quite different categories of expression. Expression that constitutes falsehood or encouragement of abomination or forsaking the Islamic community could be banned, but since these vague, value-laden terms have no settled meanings as they apply to limit human rights, one cannot really predict how the authorities would interpret the scope of restrictions on the freedom of expression. It is conceivable that any speech that might threaten to diminish adherence to the local version of Islamic orthodoxy or that might tend to lead Muslims to question the doctrines of their faith could be banned. The provision would also seem to allow broad censorship in order to protect standards of morality. Here, as in other instances, the open-ended terms of the qualifications offer so many opportunities for restricting and denying rights that they have the potential of emasculating the very freedoms that are ostensibly being granted.

"Right to Freedom of Religion" is the rubric for Article 13 of the UIDHR. Article 13 states in the English version that everyone has the right to freedom of conscience and worship in accordance with his religious beliefs. The wording is different from the wording of comparable international human rights principles, but the difference is a relatively subtle one.[28]

The significance of the difference between Article 13 and the relevant international standards is more readily ascertained if one consults the Arabic version, which says that everyone has freedom of belief and freedom of worship according to the principle, "you have your religion, I have mine." This line is taken from the Qur'anic Sura "al-Kafirun," 109:6. *Al-kafirun* can mean "unbelievers," "infidels," or "atheists" but in any case has strong negative connotations. The complete Sura runs as follows, in Pickthall's flowery translation: "Say: O disbelievers [*al-*

kafirun]! I worship not that which ye worship; Nor worship ye that which I worship. And I shall not worship that which ye worship. Nor will ye worship that which I worship. Unto you your religion, and unto me my religion." The Sura contemplates a situation where people are divided between Islam and "unbelief." It lays the groundwork for coexistence but does not attempt to establish any principle of freedom of religion comparable to the one in international human rights documents. If there is a right implied in this provision, it is the right to follow one's own religion, which in a *shari'a*-based system would be a freedom accorded only to Muslims and, within limits, to the *ahl al-kitab*. As a consequence of being obliged to follow their own religion, Muslims would be bound by *shari'a* rules. If the rules followed were like those used in Iran and the Sudan, this would mean that they would not be allowed to convert from Islam and could be executed if they did so.

One of the *shari'a* rules that one could expect would apply pursuant to Article 13 would be the double standard regarding conversion, according to which conversions to Islam are encouraged but none from Islam are allowed. This result would be consistent with the Arabic version of Section 7 of the Preamble of the UIDHR. The English version of this section looks quite neutral and innocuous, calling for a society in which "all worldly power shall be considered as a sacred trust, to be exercised within the limits prescribed by the Law and in a manner approved by it, and with due regard for the priorities fixed by it." In sharp contrast, the same section in the Arabic version is an expression of a commitment to a society where all people will believe that Allah alone is the master of all creation. This is tantamount to a commitment to seeing the world convert to Islam, a commitment that is not compatible with the attitudes that shaped the international human rights norms regarding freedom of religion.

To establish an effective guarantee for religious freedom that would meet international standards, Article 13 would have to indicate that the premodern *shari'a* rules in this area were being discarded. Instead, the UIDHR has carefully refrained from including any provisions that would stand in the way of the applicability of the premodern *shari'a* rules.

The Azhar Draft Constitution

The Azhar draft of an Islamic constitution is less evasive than the UIDHR on the issue of protection for freedom of religion. It says in the English version of Article 29 that "within the limits of the Islamic Sharia, the Government provides for the natural basic rights of religious and intellectual beliefs." In this obscure formulation, there is no mention of any freedom of religion. Given this omission, the article could mean the same kind of "right" to follow one's own religion—without any right for Muslims to change religion—that was set forth in Article 13 of the UIDHR, which has already been discussed. In contrast, the same article of the Azhar draft constitution expressly mentions "freedoms" of labor and expression and personal "freedom." The omission of the mention of "freedom" (*hurriya*) of religion is unlikely to be accidental, particularly given the fact that the rights set forth in the article are being offered only "within the limits of the Islamic Sharia." Any doubts about whether the application of these limits is intended to restrict the freedom of religion in accordance with premodern *shari'a* rules are removed by Article 71 of the draft constitution, which provides for the application of the death penalty for apostasy. Since the *shari'a* sets the governing standards, this can only refer to apostasy from Islam. The relative candor of the Azhar draft with respect to the death penalty for apostasy from Islam is in striking contrast to the evasiveness one normally encounters on this issue.

The willingness of al-Azhar to call openly for the execution of persons who abandon Islam is probably the result of several factors. The al-Azhar University is the oldest institution of higher learning in Islam and the most prestigious center for training in the Islamic sciences in Sunni Islam. Despite the great differences between the Muslim and Catholic traditions, one can say that in a general way al-Azhar has had an institutional mission of guarding the tenets of orthodoxy that is reminiscent of the mission of the Vatican in protecting Catholic doctrine. In modern times the Azhar has generally taken conservative positions on contentious issues.

Conservative Sunni clerics, who could be expected to have great input into any document emanating from al-Azhar, have tended to feel very strongly that conversions from Islam must be barred. Given the emphasis on the study of traditional Islamic sciences and premodern jurisprudence in the Azhar curriculum, Azhar clerics are unlikely to be heavily exposed to modern liberal, democratic values or well versed in international human rights norms. Clerics might also be expected to be less uneasy than the average Muslim about proposing rules that could seem retrograde by modern standards of constitutional jurisprudence.

The Azharites may have felt political circumstances in Cairo obliged them to take a tough position on the apostasy penalty. The question of whether to execute apostates was at the time of the drafting of the Azhar constitutional model very hotly contested in Egypt, a relatively cosmopolitan country with a large Christian minority. Moreover, in

Egypt conversions had been occurring with enough frequency to anger Muslim clerics and to mobilize conservative Muslim opinion behind proposals to enact a law imposing the death penalty for apostasy. Given the centrality of the controversy about the death penalty for apostasy, it would have been difficult for a Cairene institution like al-Azhar to sidestep the issue of the legality of apostasy even if the Azharites had been motivated to do so.

Furthermore, the Azhar draft was not an actual constitution but only a proposal for what standards Muslim conservatives would ideally like to see incorporated in a constitution. Because their exercise was an academic one, the authors of the Azhar draft were not forced to accede to political compromises with disaffected Egyptian Copts. Nor did the drafters have to deal with politicians and jurists who were abreast of modern trends in constitutionalism, which might have diluted or eliminated the more extreme features of the draft, such as the apostasy penalty. It is instructive to contrast the candor of the Azharite draft constitution on this point with the ambiguities and ambivalence in the UIDHR and the Iranian Constitution. The ambivalence in the latter is particularly striking since the evidence shows that the Iranian government ultimately shares the same view as the Azharites, that apostates from Islam should be killed.

Mawdudi

Mawdudi was not prepared to confess in the text of his human rights pamphlet that he supported killing those who convert from Islam. As was his habit when he realized that his views were so far out of keeping with international human rights standards that, by expressing them, he would undermine the credibility of his human rights scheme, he simply avoided the issue. There is, therefore, no discussion of the problem of freedom of religion in his human rights pamphlet. However, Mawdudi is on the record elsewhere as supporting the death penalty for conversion from Islam.[29]

The Iranian Constitution

The rights provisions of the 1979 Iranian Constitution also do not deal with the issue of religious freedom as such. However, Article 23 does forbid interrogating or attacking people because of their beliefs. This provision might be interpreted as meaning that religious persecution should be outlawed. Whatever the original intent or hopes of the drafters of this article may have been, the Iranian government has certainly not interpreted it as a guarantee of freedom of religion or as protecting religious minorities from persecution.

One is entitled to consider the conduct of the Iranian government as a gloss on the meaning of the protections afforded by Article 23. The extensive persecutions of Iran's Baha'is unequivocally establish that the Iranian government does not believe that Article 23 prevents interrogating or attacking members of disfavored religious minorities because of their religious beliefs. Baha'is have been put under enormous pressure to recant their beliefs and return to Islam. It is well established that the Baha'is are persecuted on the basis of their religious beliefs, because the trumped-up criminal charges of spying and accusations of other offenses against Iran's secular laws have been dropped when and if accused Baha'is were willing to repent of their theological errors and proclaim their adherence to Islam.[30] The religious nature of the persecution can also be seen in the fact that Baha'is are treated as persons who have incurred civil death, the consequence of apostasy from Islam under *shari'a* law. Thus, for example, all Baha'i marriages have been declared invalid, sexual intercourse between the former spouses has been treated as fornication (punishable by death), and the children of the dissolved marriages have been declared illegitimate, thereby depriving their parents of any claim to them.[31]

It is significant that despite the extensive evidence that the persecution of the Baha'is is religiously motivated, in communications designed for international audiences, the Iranian government has gone to great lengths to portray Baha'ism as a political movement and to justify executions of Baha'is on the grounds that the deceased had been guilty of political crimes. Executed Baha'is are routinely alleged to have been in league with Iran's enemies, and accusations that Baha'is were guilty of spying for Israel or the CIA have commonly been made. In international forums, the Khomeini regime insisted that Baha'is who are not guilty of antiregime activities are not molested and repeatedly asserted that Iran does not persecute Baha'is for religious reasons.[32]

A comment published by the Iranian attorney general intended to debunk charges that Baha'is were being persecuted for religious reasons is revealing of the regime's attitude:

> Now, if a Baha'i himself performs his religious acts in accordance with his own beliefs, such a man will not be bothered by us, provided he does not invite others to Baha'ism, does not teach, does not form assemblies, does not give news to others, and has nothing to do with the administration [of the Baha'i community]. Not only do we not execute such people, we do not even imprison them, and they can work within society. If, however, they decide to work within their administration, this

is a criminal act and is forbidden, the reason being that such administration is considered to be hostile and conspiratorial and such people are
conspirators.[33]

According to this official statement, Iran was not persecuting Baha'is
for their beliefs but for conduct manifesting their beliefs or for associations with Baha'i religious institutions ("their administration"). Even
if one accepted this disavowal at face value, one would see that the
regime had acknowledged its anti-Baha'i policies and its refusal to grant
Baha'is religious freedom on a par with adherents of other faiths. At
the same time that the attorney general was denying that Iran was
killing Baha'is because of their religious beliefs, he effectively admitted
in this statement that the religion and its institutions were officially
associated with treasonous, conspiratorial activities, making it impossible for Baha'is to worship or associate with each other without risking
criminal prosecutions.

In trying to argue to an international audience that the prosecution
of the Baha'i population was political rather than religious in character,
the Iranian government pretended that a distinction was being made
in Iran between political and religious crimes. However, this is a
distinction that by the terms of Article 168 of the Iranian Constitution
cannot, in fact, exist. The second sentence in Article 168 reads: "The
definition of a political crime, the manner in which the jury will be
selected, their qualifications and the limits of their authority shall be
determined by law, based upon Islamic principles [*mavazin-e eslami*]."
One sees in this article that it is not the secular law that defines political
crimes, but law based on Islamic principles. That is, religious categories
and rules determine the definitions of political crimes; thus political
crimes are, ultimately, also religious crimes.

The lack of candor on the part of the Iranian government in its
official representations to the international community about the reasons
for its persecutions of Baha'is correlates with the patterns of obfuscation
and evasiveness that one sees in Islamic human rights schemes generally.
However, it seems surprising in the Iranian context for several reasons.

Based on past clerical demands for the execution of Baha'is, one
could anticipate that killing Baha'is as apostates would win general
approval in clerical milieus as a correct implementation of *shari'a* rules.
Given the fact that in the Iranian Constitution Islamic principles are
treated as the supreme law of the land, one might expect that the
legality of the executions of the Baha'is in Islamic terms would be
Iran's only concern, that it would publicly admit its policy of killing
apostates, and that the government would cite *shari'a* rules in response
to any foreign critics of its actions. The Iranian government might,

therefore, be expected to take a position like that taken in the Azhar draft constitution, where there was forthright endorsement of the rule that apostates were to be killed. However, in reality, the Iranian government is painfully aware that appealing to *shari'a* standards that entitle it to kill people for their religious beliefs will only create embarrassment for it. It is cognizant of the fact that the persecutions and executions of Baha'is violate international human rights standards and that it is by reference to these international standards that the quality of Iran's Islamic justice will largely be judged—by Muslims as well as by non-Muslims.

The government of Iran is actually very anxious to avoid being found in breach of international human rights norms, a kind of condemnation that it understands has the potential to tarnish its image among Muslims as well as to harm its standing in the international community. This has led it to resist allowing UN and other observer teams to monitor the human rights conditions in the country and to pretend that the executions of Baha'is result from their being convicted of secular political offenses. Reclassifying Baha'is as "traitors," "spies," and "conspirators" enables Iran to pretend that its criminal justice system follows a more conventional model than it actually does. In trying so hard to hide the fact that it is applying the premodern *shari'a* rules penalizing apostasy, the government of Iran reveals that it does not really have confidence in the normative force of the *shari'a* rules on apostasy and, at the same time, that it implicitly recognizes the authoritative, universal character of the international human rights standards.

Like Tabandeh, Khomeini was relatively uninfluenced by the standards of international law. In the Salman Rushdie case, Khomeini himself assumed the role of spokesperson for Islam, which meant that the veil that more diplomatic and cosmopolitan members of the regime had sought to draw around the regime's policies of rejecting the principle of religious freedom was lifted in this case. Khomeini personally and quite deliberately courted international notoriety in the Rushdie affair, seeking thereby to buttress his faltering image as the leader of militant Islam, an image that had been undermined by his having had to accept a UN plan to end the Iran-Iraq War, which he had earlier promised to pursue till victory was achieved and Saddam Hussain overthrown.

Khomeini issued his death sentence for Salman Rushdie on February 14, 1989, claiming that Rushdie's book *The Satanic Verses* was an attack on Islam, the Qur'an, and the Prophet. On February 19 he added to the death sentence the order that even were Rushdie to repent of his offense, he would still have to be executed.[34]

Muslims' responses to Khomeini's death sentence proved that they were divided about whether the command that Rushdie be executed was legitimate under *shari'a* law. There was also no consensus as to whether it could be reconciled with secular rights concepts of freedom of religion and freedom of speech.[35] Demonstrations by irate Muslims in many parts of the world revealed that Khomeini was far from alone in his belief that blasphemous statements by a Muslim in a work of literature might justify his execution as an apostate. There were strong disincentives for Muslims who would have wanted to speak out against the death sentence, and fears were augmented by the assassination of a moderate Islamic leader in Belgium on March 29 who had taken a public stance against the death threats.[36] Despite this, courageous Muslims did occasionally raise their voices in protest over the death sentence, at considerable risk to their own lives. Furthermore, it is noteworthy that not a single Muslim country opted to support Khomeini's death threat, even though on March 16, 1989, the Organization of the Islamic Conference did label the book blasphemous and Rushdie an apostate.[37]

Iran itself seemed in its subsequent propaganda to lack confidence in the legitimacy of killing Rushdie solely on grounds of his expression of ideas that indicated he had abandoned the Islamic faith. As the regime attempted to justify Khomeini's call for Rushdie's execution, more and more efforts were made to portray Rushdie, in actuality a leftist supporter of Third World causes, as an antirevolutionary agent of the forces of capitalism and Zionism, an agent of both the CIA and the Mossad, and a participant in a British imperialist plot to destroy Islam. That is, just as in the case of the Baha'is, there was an attempt to portray the criminal charges as being based on secular offenses, not on religious beliefs.

The Rushdie death sentence seems to have been Khomeini's own initiative, and the paucity of endorsements by distinguished Iranian theologians suggested that he was relatively isolated on the question. However, when Khomeini died and the more moderate Rafsanjani regime came to power, there was no retraction of the order for Rushdie's execution, perhaps because the new rulers feared that they would be attacked by powerful factions supporting Khomeini if they backed away from a policy so closely identified with the late leader.

The Rushdie case and the Taha case, which will be covered in "The Sudan Under Nimeiri," aptly illustrate a point made earlier in this chapter and in Chapter 7, that in today's circumstances it is often Muslims who suffer under governmental policies supposedly designed to implement *shari'a* law where these conflict with international human rights norms in the area of freedom of religion.

The Sudan Under Nimeiri

The sinister implications of the treatment of freedom of religion in Islamic human rights schemes are borne out by what happened in the Sudan when versions of *shari'a* law endorsed by Muslim conservatives superseded other legal and constitutional norms. The execution of Mahmud Muhammad Taha, the leader of the Sudanese Republican movement, as a heretic and apostate from Islam, indicates that regimes committed to Islamization may use the *shari'a* death penalty for apostasy to silence their Muslim critics. Taha's execution proves that the endorsement by Muslim conservatives of the death penalty for apostasy is not an academic issue. Moreover, it exemplifies the conflict that exists between governmental attempts to use Islam as a justification for violating international human rights and the beliefs of private Muslims that their religion supports the very international human rights norms that the government, by appeals to Islam, is denying. One can see Taha's execution as resulting at least in part from the Nimeiri regime's outrage over the delegitimizing impact of a challenge to the regime's Islamization policies, a challenge that was itself based on Islamic principles.

Taha had led a liberal school of thought in the Sudan known variously as the Republicans or the Republican Brothers. Republicans viewed Islam as establishing an egalitarian order that was fully compatible with the norms of international human rights law. Taha offered a controversial interpretation of the history and aims of the revelation of the Qur'anic verses with legal content. According to his interpretation, much of what had come to be regarded as timeless *shari'a* rules was actually legislation that had been intended to deal only with the peculiar circumstances of the early Muslim community. In accordance with this interpretation, Taha was able to justify discarding *shari'a* rules that violated modern human rights norms, saying that they were never meant to be permanently binding on Muslims.[38] In particular, Taha and his followers believed that Islam, correctly interpreted, supported complete equality between men and women and Muslims and non-Muslims.

Taha's liberal, reformist views were anathema to many Muslim conservatives. For example, in 1976 al-Azhar officially declared him to be an apostate from Islam.[39] His views were also attacked by the Ikhwan, or Muslim Brothers, a conservative Islamic movement that has been very influential in both the Sudan and Egypt. One segment of the Ikhwan was closely involved in Nimeiri's Islamization scheme.

The Republicans criticized the human rights violations that came about as a result of Nimeiri's Islamization campaign of 1983–1985.[40] They condemned the violations of rights of the non-Muslim southern Sudanese, who were both strongly opposed to Islamization and also often the victims of the criminal prosecutions undertaken as part of the Islamization campaign. The Republicans brought several suits claiming that the imposition of the premodern *shari'a* rules violated the constitution by discriminating against non-Muslims and women; these suits were not successful.[41]

Nimeiri was aggrieved by the charges that his application of Islamic law in the Sudan was violating the rights provisions in the Sudanese Constitution, and he reacted by violently condemning those who made such charges. He tried to counter charges that his Islamization campaign violated human rights, insisting in a speech that "Islam was the first to declare human rights." An official commentary on the same speech claimed that persons who charged that the application of Islamic law in the Sudan contradicted human rights principles were actually opposed to Islam as a religion and a way of life that could unite Muslims.[42] In this way, the government sought to associate critics of human rights violations resulting from Nimeiri's Islamization program with enmity toward Islam.

As a result of their criticisms of Nimeiri's policy and their campaign demanding respect for human rights, many Republicans were thrown in jail. Taha, who had been briefly released after nineteen months of detention without any charges being brought against him, was rearrested along with a group of his followers and tried in January 1985. He boycotted as illegal and unconstitutional his original trial for offenses against the Sudan Penal Code of 1983 and the State Security Act of 1973. On review, the trial court's judgment, which did not deal with apostasy, was replaced by the higher court ruling convicting Taha of the additional offense of apostasy from Islam. He was condemned to die. Both the legal and the constitutional dimensions of this case warrant discussion, as they illustrate the impact that Islamization had on the system of justice.

As we saw in Chapter 2, Nimeiri's plan to rewrite the Sudanese Constitution to make it suit his ideas about Islamic government came to naught. Given his attitudes, it is likely that any Islamic constitution adopted under Nimeiri's leadership would have taken the position that official interpretations of Islamic requirements could override conflicting constitutional rights provisions. However, instead of an Islamic constitution, the Sudan still had its 1973 constitution at the time of the Taha trial. Nimeiri suspended the constitution and all rights protections during a state of emergency that lasted from April 29 to September 29, 1984. After the end of the state of emergency, the constitutional rights protections had come back in force. In these circumstances, Taha's execution violated the operative constitutional norms. The constitution provided in Article 70 that no person could be executed for a crime that was not set forth in the law at the time when the act was committed and in Articles 47 and 48 that freedom of thought, belief, and expression were guaranteed. The court simply ignored the provisions in the constitution that would be violated by the conviction.[43]

One must stress that there was no Sudanese law in effect in 1985 establishing that apostasy from Islam constituted a crime. Even though a number of rules designed to revive the more archaic features of *shari'a* criminal law such as the *shari'a* crucifixion penalty were enacted into law in 1983 and even though the government did not hesitate to impose *shari'a* penalties like amputations of limbs, the *shari'a* death penalty for apostasy from Islam had not been restored. One presumes that the failure to reinstate that rule at a time when so many other rules of *shari'a* law were being revived was a result of the kind of ambivalence about this issue that was illustrated by Iran's unwillingness to admit publicly that it executed Baha'is as apostates from Islam. In addition, the Nimeiri regime may have been inhibited from formally reinstating the death penalty for apostasy out of fear of the southern Sudanese reaction. Even without placing that penalty on the books, the Islamization program had led in 1983 to a renewed outbreak of the Sudan's protracted civil war. Disaffected southern Sudanese, who were largely animist and Christian, interpreted Islamization as a policy of relegating them to second-class status. Non-Muslim Sudanese have seen in the *shari'a* apostasy standards a rule that if enacted into law, would constitute an official endorsement of the proposition that Islam and its adherents rank above other religions and non-Muslims. Thus, reviving the apostasy penalty would have made it even more difficult to win back disaffected southerners and to keep the Sudan united.

It is interesting to see how the appellate court reached its conclusion that Taha was an apostate. Because there was no actual trial of the apostasy issue, there was little evidence on the trial record on which the appellate court could rely in holding Taha guilty of this offense. To establish his apostasy, the court referred to an ex parte civil proceeding that had been brought in Khartoum in 1968 by private plaintiffs offended by Taha's opinions on Islam. That case had resulted in a ruling that he was an apostate. Because of the trial court's lack of proper jurisdiction over this civil case and its constitutional invalidity, this judgment had been unenforceable. In ruling Taha an apostate, the appellate court also relied on declarations by al-Azhar and the Muslim World League to that effect.[44]

It accompanied these rulings by asserting that "the Republican Brothers was an infidel group and renegade faction that must be dealt with in the same manner as other infidel groups. All books and publications of Mahmud Muhammad Taha and the Republican Brothers shall be seized from all libraries and destroyed to prevent circulation and printing. The activities and meetings of the group will be banned throughout the country."[45] In ordering that Taha be hanged, the court imposed a number of conditions, including that "no prayers should be said for him, nor should he be buried in a Muslim grave. His estate will be distributed among Muslims after payment of any outstanding debts."[46] When the judgment calling for the execution of Taha as a heretic was referred to President Nimeiri, he said that he was upholding it "on the basis of Shari'ah law to protect the nation from the danger of Mahmud Muhammad Taha and his slander of God and his insolence towards Him [God] and to protect this homeland from heresy."[47]

Taha's followers were also declared apostates from Islam. This meant that, like the Baha'is in Iran, they incurred civil death in accordance with the premodern *shari'a* rules regarding apostasy. Among the consequences were that Republicans' marriages were dissolved, sexual intercourse between the erstwhile spouses became punishable as a capital offense under the then-prevailing Islamic penal standards, and their children became illegitimate.

Taha was publicly hanged on January 18, 1985, in a prison courtyard in Khartoum. According to reports, he conducted himself in his last moments with the utmost dignity and calmness while surrounded by a taunting mob of members of the Ikhwan and other supporters of Nimeiri, who hailed his execution as a great victory for Islam.

Although decreeing that Taha be executed without being given a chance to repent of his heresy, the court ruled that the four other Republicans who had been convicted would be given a month "to repent and return to Islam." In an effort to get those of Taha's followers who had been convicted with him to recant their beliefs, proceedings were held in which Taha's followers were interrogated, threatened, and browbeaten by a tribunal of clerics who insisted that they renounce Taha's teachings and endorse the supposedly more orthodox doctrines espoused by the clerics. The Nimeiri regime, proud of leading this campaign against the allegedly apostate Republicans, instead of trying to disguise the religious nature of the prosecutions—as the Iranian regime had prudently done in the case of its proceedings against Baha'is—had the heresy trials of Taha's followers broadcast on Sudanese television.

Undoubtedly, the regime's calculation that Taha's execution and the heresy trials would bring it credit for its zealous defense of Islam and win it support was correct in the case of Muslims who condemned Taha's philosophy or who adhered to groups like the Muslim Brothers. However, the calculation was very wrong in terms of anticipating the reaction of the average Sudanese. Outrage and disgust over the execution and televised heresy trial prevailed, even among Sudanese Muslims who had no personal sympathy for Taha's theological positions.[48] The revulsion over the execution of the peaceable, elderly religious leader provided a strong impetus for mobilizing the popular coalition against Nimeiri that succeeded in toppling him from power on April 6, 1985. Owing to the policies of Nimeiri, Islam became associated with an act of medieval barbarism, but many Muslims considered the execution a violation of fundamental Islamic values.

The costs of Nimeiri's decision to proceed openly against the Republicans on religious grounds were high, and the execution of Taha as a heretic made Nimeiri the target of international opprobrium. More astute Muslim politicians can calculate more accurately than Nimeiri did the political costs of openly executing people on the grounds of their religious beliefs. Those politicians may have this in mind when they disguise their intentions to apply the *shari'a* rules on apostasy and try to deceive the international community about their willingness to respect the principle of freedom of religion.

Summary

The Islamic human rights schemes that are being described here are evasive on the question of protections for freedom of religion. Since they deal with freedom of religion against a background of the tradition of prohibiting conversion from Islam, their failure to repudiate the *shari'a* rules is strongly suggestive of an intent to retain them. The lack of an unequivocal endorsement of freedom of religion in this context indicates a lack of support for the idea that people should be free to follow the religion of their choice. It also means that there is no commitment to the proposition that self-professed Muslims should be protected from being declared apostates by governments that classify their beliefs as unorthodox or heretical. Not only do the Islamic human rights schemes under discussion here fail to mitigate the harshness of the premodern rule on apostasy, but they also evince a general lack of sympathy for the idea of freedom of religion that is such an important component of modern human rights law. The failure of a single one of these Islamic human rights schemes to take a position against the application of the *shari'a* death penalty for apostasy means that the authors of these schemes have neglected to confront and resolve the main issues involved in harmonizing international human rights and *shari'a* standards.

The lack of support for the principle of freedom of religion in the Islamic human rights schemes is one of the factors that most sharply distinguishes them from the International Bill of Human Rights, which treats freedom of religion as an unqualified right. The authors' unwillingness to repudiate the rule that a person should be executed over a question of religious belief reveals the enormous gap that exists between their mentalities and the modern philosophy of human rights.

The sponsorship of campaigns of persecutions against religious minorities by regimes conducting Islamization campaigns in Iran, Pakistan, and the Sudan has proved that the failure of Muslim conservatives to recognize the principle of religious freedom is not a mere theoretical problem. In real life it can mean adverse consequences for rights protections of people, including Muslims, who espouse religious positions unacceptable to Muslim conservatives and ideologues of Islamization.

The insensitivity of Muslim conservatives to human rights concerns in this area has created a gap dividing them from other Muslims who share the international ideals of human rights. Conservative factions like the Muslim Brothers probably did not realize that killing Taha as a heretic would make him into a martyr for the cause of freedom, a cause that many Muslims strongly support. Arab human rights activists selected the anniversary of Mahmud Muhammad Taha's date of death as the day on which Arab Human Rights Day was to be annually commemorated—a sign that in his opposition to human rights violations perpetrated in the name of Islamization, Taha did not stand alone.

CHAPTER 9

An Assessment of Islamic Human Rights Schemes

Deviations from International Human Rights Principles

The Islamic human rights schemes devised by conservatives are being promoted in an environment in which international human rights are established as the authoritative, universal standard. Thus, it is natural to examine provisions of Islamic human rights schemes in relation to their international counterparts.

Although the Islamic human rights schemes impose many restraints and qualifications that conflict with the rights protections afforded by international law, they have been presented in formats and terminology designed to lead people to assume that they constitute valid counterparts of the rights norms set forth in international documents and the bills of rights in the constitutions of modern democracies. The similarity in formats and terminology naturally invites comparisons, but these inevitably reveal the inadequacies of the Islamic schemes according to the criteria of the international documents that they superficially emulate. In every case where the Islamic human rights provisions prove to have distinctive features, it turns out that they are ones designed to dilute, if not altogether eliminate, the corresponding civil and political rights found in international law.

The authors evince little real sympathy for the ideals of individual rights and freedoms. Instead they accord priority to rationalizing governmental repression, protecting and promoting social cohesion, and perpetuating traditional hierarchies in society, which means discriminatory treatment of women and non-Muslims. They call for obedience to authority and give political leaders complete leeway in determining the scope of permissible freedoms. Political authorities are allowed to curb rights and freedoms by reference to vague Islamic criteria, which the authors do not bother to define. They assert the supremacy of

Islamic principles in all areas relevant for the protection of human rights, thereby providing a justification for overriding international human rights standards by appeals to "Islam."

The authors do not seem to have approached their task with methodological rigor, as the many inconsistencies and deficiencies in their work indicate. At times the contents of their rights provisions lead one to conclude that they have managed to attain only a tentative grasp of what the concept of a human right entails. Certainly, they have neglected to think through the historical connection between the values and philosophical premises of international human rights and the nature of the protections afforded civil and political rights in international law. Little effort appears to have been expended in pondering the jurisprudential adjustments that would be needed to accommodate human rights within a framework dictated by the concerns of premodern Islamic law.

The disparities between the rights protections afforded by international law and those provided by Islamic human rights schemes devised by Muslim conservatives prompt questions regarding the nature of the latter. The very inadequacies of the Islamic schemes are interesting from the standpoint of the general problem of the reception of international human rights in dissimilar cultures and, particularly, in cultures in the developing world. There cultural traditions and religious loyalties may be invoked by political leaders and entrenched elites as pretexts for refusing to adopt the guarantees for rights provided in the international norms.

Because these Islamic rights schemes contain references to Islamic sources and values associated with traditional societies, they appear to represent one form of culture-based resistance to international human rights. However, a careful examination of the Islamic tradition and the diversity of Muslims' current views on human rights indicates that Islamic culture does not by itself account for the distinctive features of these schemes. Instead, such study proves that the Islamic legal heritage is rich in elements that support principles of equality, freedom, democracy, and respect for human dignity and that at the grass-roots level there is also widespread culture-based receptivity to human rights in Muslim milieus.

One could argue that with all their defects, Islamic human rights do constitute a step forward in that they suggest that even Muslim conservatives have become persuaded that human rights can be integrated in Islamic culture—albeit only tentatively and partially. For example, some drafters of the UIDHR may have believed that even if the UIDHR did not measure up to international standards, its promulgation would nonetheless enhance the legitimacy of human rights in the eyes of some Muslims by associating Islam with human rights. Furthermore, given the reality that the traditional cultures are waning or besieged because of the disruptive impact of modernization, it is possible to see the phenomenon of Islamization of human rights as representing a temporary and transitional stage in the process of assimilating international human rights principles. Perhaps the indigenization of international human rights requires—at least for many Muslims who are still attached to aspects of traditional culture—that human rights concepts initially pass through a transitional stage, one in which international human rights schemes are disassembled and reconstructed to coincide with familiar categories and readjusted to fit conservative values and mores. The merit of such transitional rights formulations would be to introduce rights gradually and conditionally so as to avoid excessive clashes with the traditional social order, which was in any case in the course of erosion.

In this connection, one might speculate that some of the obfuscation and confusion that one sees in these schemes could facilitate the reception of human rights by avoiding specifics that might reveal inherent conflicts. Although the evidence reviewed suggests that Tabandeh, Mawdudi, and the authors of the Azhar draft constitution have little sympathy for human rights in their international formulations, one cannot be sure that all the persons who participated in designing the rights provisions of the Iranian Constitution and the UIDHR were equally unsympathetic. It may have struck some engaged in drafting the Iranian Constitution and the UIDHR that it would be politically expedient at this stage of introducing human rights norms in the matrix of Islamic legal culture to defer confronting the more sensitive and controversial problems that would arise in reconciling the two. By expedient evasive tactics and intentionally ambiguous formulations, the authors may have intended in some cases to avoid a premature break with the heritage of premodern *shari'a* rules and associated cultural traditions, a break that could be exploited by adamant opponents of human rights eager to show that human rights principles are violative of Islamic law.

If one took an optimistic stance, seeing in Islamic human rights a basically benign, transitional phenomenon, one might hope that the Islamic features that have been grafted onto the imported human rights norms would be eventually discarded when further social and economic development made the international standards more palatable to conservative opinion. Against that, one could adopt a more pessimistic view, predicting that deficiencies of Islamic human rights schemes would harm the prospects for realizing human rights, not serve as a means to facilitate their eventual reception. The presence of this vague and inadequate Islamic human rights literature could actually hinder the development of an awareness of the kinds of human rights that are guaranteed in the International Bill of Human Rights and the rights formulations that would be needed to enable people in the Middle East to mount effective challenges to denials of human rights and, particularly, rights violations perpetrated in the name of "Islam." Given the political power of conservative Islamic factions in many countries, it is very likely that the pattern of exploiting Islam to justify government policies violating rights will continue to be a serious problem. Thus, any literature that gives governments grounds for saying that there is Islamic authority for denying the rights afforded under international law could be exploited in ways that would have a nefarious impact on rights.

Once embodied in law, Islamic criteria undermining rights protections could stand in the way of the adoption of genuine human rights principles based on the international models. For example, the incorporation of Islamic limitations on human rights in the text of the 1979 Iranian Constitution means that what were previously informal obstacles in local custom and tradition to realizing international human rights protections have been elevated to the stature of formal constitutional norms, which affirm Islamic restrictions on rights. These formal limitations on rights may prove difficult for subsequent generations of Iranians to dismantle. That is, the distinctive Islamic features of Islamic human rights schemes could be seen less as a natural transitional stage in the absorption of alien institutions than as weapons in a strategy designed to forestall the influence of international rights concepts.

In evaluating the significance of Islamic human rights schemes it is helpful to examine the ways that other Western ideologies or institutions have been transformed when transplanted to developing societies. One might consider in this regard a phenomenon like the reformulation of imported Catholicism in a host environment like Brazil's. There, for many persons who retain links to African culture and institutions, the alien precepts of Catholicism are acceptable only insofar as they are presented in a syncretic version combining Catholicism with features of African tradition. Thus, in the Africanized Brazilian version of Catholicism, African priests and priestesses retain their traditional authority, African folklore has been joined with Catholic worship, and analogies are drawn between Catholic saints and African gods and goddesses.[1] The resulting syncretic religion is neither strictly Catholic nor strictly African, but a blend of two very dissimilar traditions concocted by people who had been exposed to both and needed to find an accommodation between the two. For African Brazilians, the syncretizing of the two makes congenial what would otherwise seem to be an alien system, one threatening to their culture and social organization.

Although their hybrid religion hardly conforms to the standards of orthodoxy of the Roman Catholic church, a powerful institution in Brazil, it is tolerated by the Church hierarchy. Some members of the Brazilian Catholic church may feel that it is better to accept an Africanized version of Catholicism than to resist Africanization and be left with a situation where there would be no Catholic influence on local religion. That might result were the Brazilian Catholic hierarchy to insist rigidly that no deviations from Roman norms would be tolerated. Although to an outsider this toleration might seem surprising, since elements of Catholicism and African religion appear conflicting and incompatible, to those interested in promulgating Catholicism in Brazil, the resulting hybrid may seem an acceptable compromise stage en route to converting Brazilians to a more orthodox understanding of the Catholic religion that might be expected to come with more education and economic development.

A comparison with this Africanized Catholicism clarifies the significance of Islamic human rights. Certainly, the Islamic human rights schemes discussed here are syncretic in nature, combining categories and terms taken from international human rights with elements of *shari'a* rules and some cultural values historically associated with premodern Islam. The combinations can, however, be distinguished from the blending of elements of Catholicism and African culture and religion in Brazil, a grass-roots phenomenon, not one imposed from above. Brazilian Africans are free to choose between African religion and Catholicism but have instead opted for a hybrid blend of the two. Brazilian Africans' religious ideas grew organically out of a situation in which the people confronted a confluence of an imposed Western religion and an indigenous African tradition.

In contrast, the Islamic and international elements in Islamic human rights schemes have been artificially cojoined by members of clerical and political elites and other legal "experts." Africanized Catholicism in Brazil is a manifestation of popular culture, but popular culture did not provide the impetus for creating the diluted human rights that one finds in Islamic human rights schemes. Islamic human rights have emerged under the auspices of repressive regimes or the sponsorship of conservative clerics and their intellectual allies and serve their interests. In the cases of regimes pursuing Islamization programs, the leeway afforded by Islamic schemes of rights has been exploited to legitimize repression and dismantling of the rule of law. The curious combinations of Islamic and international legal elements that make Islamic human rights interesting from the standpoint of comparative legal history are what causes their deficiencies as rights.

One could speculate that these Islamic schemes of human rights might have broad popular appeal by virtue of their simultaneous association with both Islam and human rights. To the extent that their Islamic labels gave them legitimacy, they could serve to distract Muslims from campaigns being waged for the observance of human rights according to international law, which may have been one of the objectives that their authors had in mind.

In fact, there is little evidence that the Islamic labels on the enfeebled rights protections in these Islamic rights schemes make them more attractive to the average Muslim than the stronger rights guarantees found in the International Bill of Human Rights. Muslim human rights advocates and human rights associations that emerged in Muslim countries in the 1980s have campaigned to realize the norms of human rights set forth in international law, not watered-down "Islamic" alternatives like the ones examined here. Awareness of what the international guarantees of rights and freedoms mean is spreading. As the world is brought closer together by modern communications, it becomes more difficult even for the most repressive regimes in the world to block the penetration of ideas of democracy and human rights, which in the late 1980s resoundingly demonstrated their popular appeal and capacity to undermine the legitimacy of despotic governments around the globe. Precisely because Muslim countries have human rights records that range from the mediocre to the atrocious, they provide fertile soil for conversions to the ideals of international human rights, which address the problems actually faced by contemporary Muslims victimized by repression and denials of rights.

Moreover, the idea that premodern Islamic norms should override and cancel out international human rights principles has not been endorsed by Muslims in any kind of democratic process. In the course of Islamization campaigns, the policy that respect for human rights is incompatible with the imposition of Islamic law has been consistently pressed by the governments involved—but only in the face of popular resistance. When Muslim voters had the opportunity to vote in relatively free elections in the Sudan in 1986 and in Pakistan in 1988 after experiences of the suspension of constitutional rights protections and the implementation of official Islamization programs, the candidates who identified with Islamization did poorly. In contrast, candidates promising a return to democracy, freedom, and human rights did relatively well.[2]

It seems significant that since the Islamic Revolution Iran has not allowed elections in which voters were allowed to vote for candidates opposed to clerical rule and the country's official Islamic ideology. From the fact that Iranian voters have never been permitted to express any potentially negative reactions to being governed by a regime that uses Islam as a pretext for denying rights, one can infer that the regime fears that the official policy of denying rights on Islamic pretexts lacks a popular mandate.[3] In 1990, after having had a decade to consolidate their hold on the country, Iran's clerical rulers still felt so threatened by demands that were being made by members of Bazargan's Freedom Movement and other Iranians for more democracy and respect for human rights that the government imprisoned the signatories of an open letter calling for, among other things, respect for the rights and freedoms in Iran's own constitution.[4] Since the June 1989 military takeover in the Sudan, which brought militant members of the National Islamic Front to power, the regime has felt compelled to resort to extensive and brutal repression to stifle popular dissent and quell opposition to its rigid Islamization policy.[5]

To identify what is at stake, one needs to ask who would benefit and who would lose if international human rights provisions were enacted into law and effective mechanisms to ensure their observance were set in place. The benefits of international human rights would be felt by the population as a whole, which would enjoy the freedoms and the rights protections that come from a government's being held accountable to the citizenry. Implementation of the international norms would mean enhanced rights for women and religious minorities, who would be freed of the discrimination that relegates them to a vulnerable and inferior status. The losers would include the unpopular, dictatorial governments in the region and groups whose dominance could not survive under democratic conditions and whose interests are closely linked to the preservation of the regime of inequality based on ingrained social hierarchies. Muslim men would forfeit their privileged status both within the family and, to a lesser extent, in the society at large.

Comparisons with Shari'a Law

The provisions in Islamic human rights schemes often do show the influence of rules developed by medieval Islamic jurists and the values of traditional societies. These rules and values are incorporated without examination of the historical context in which they arose and without critical assessment of the degree to which they may be appropriately employed in the radically different political and social circumstances of modern nations. There is no evidence of any serious inquiry into the reasons why human rights principles as such were not developed in premodern Islamic legal culture. The implications of this lack of rights concepts in the premodern *shari'a* are neglected, even though they are relevant for working out how medieval rules need to be adjusted before rights can be accommodated.

It must be stressed that the consequences of using Islamic sources for designing schemes of rights or protorights are not self-evident, as the great diversity of Muslim opinion in this area establishes. Thus, all conclusions about the implications of the Islamic sources necessarily rest on interpretations of the sources, interpretations that, depending on the philosophy of the interpreters, have led to the production of rules that were in some instances favorable to, and in others, opposed to rights norms.

The conservative versions of Islamic human rights do not simply replicate principles stated in the Islamic sources, even though they often include references to the sources. They also cannot accurately be said to be representative of the premodern juristic tradition or Islamic philosophy as a whole but represent only one side, reflecting the authors' own preferences for antirationalist, antihumanistic currents in Islamic thought. Thus, from an array of options in Islamic civilization, Islamic human rights schemes include those elements that present obstacles to the accommodation of modern human rights principles—obstacles that are then attributed to Islam. If the authors' aim had been to foster protections for human rights in Muslim milieus, they could have constructed rights principles reflecting currents in premodern Islamic thought that emphasized the roles of reason and humanistic concerns. These could provide the basis for constructing a viable synthesis of Islamic principles and international human rights norms. The authors could have chosen, as other Muslims have done, to review the Islamic sources in the light of concerns for what best serves the welfare of Muslim societies in present circumstances.

The creation of conservative versions of Islamic human rights thus represents only one of the possible responses that contemporary Muslims have had to the question of how premodern Islamic doctrine should affect the reception of human rights in contemporary Muslim societies. The attitudes and values of conservatives are not more Islamic in the sense of corresponding to a definitive Islamic cultural model of rights than the attitudes and values of Muslims who endorse international human rights norms.

The Islamic human rights schemes are not solely the products of efforts to mine the Islamic tradition for guidance. Instead of relying exclusively on the Islamic sources, which, in the Muslim view, are divinely inspired, the authors have also engaged in extensive—though unacknowledged—borrowings from ideas and formulations in Western constitutions and international rights schemes. In presenting human rights principles that purportedly correspond to authentic Islamic criteria, the authors in fact employ a variety of terms and concepts that are patently taken from international and Western models. These frequent borrowings and the use of principles like "equal protection of the law" that are without precedent in the premodern *shari'a* are puzzling in terms of the criteria of Islamic jurisprudence, according to which rules not established using Islamic sources and criteria are irrelevant. One would expect professedly "Islamic" human rights schemes to rest on methods that ensure that the schemes set forth pure, undiluted Islamic principles on the subject—not awkward hybrids of premodern Islamic and modern non-Islamic principles. The hybrid results suggest that even conservative Muslims who are ostensibly dedicated to reviving authentic Islamic teachings are disposed to borrow from the international models when they deal with questions of human rights. This calls for an explanation of the theoretical underpinnings of these schemes, but a clear methodology is never given. The resulting schemes are admixtures of undigested principles from international law and incompatible rules and values derived from the premodern Islamic heritage. It is not surprising that the principles show little coherence.

While mining the Islamic heritage for rules and values that could be used to thwart rights, the authors attempt to make the Islamic schemes look as much as possible like the corresponding international and Western formulations of rights, which in turn involves appropriating material from non-Islamic sources. The attempts to disguise disparities between Islamic rights schemes and the international human rights documents are incongruous in terms of the authors' stated legal philosophies, which consistently maintain that Islamic law is superior to and overrides all conflicting secular legal principles. If any comparisons were made between human rights principles that were derived from the Islamic sources and the international standards, a Muslim committed to upholding the *shari'a* would be expected to accord primacy to the Islamic rules and to dismiss other rights principles as incorrect where they diverged. Tabandeh, as noted, actually did this at certain points. However, he is exceptional in his readiness to acknowledge that there are occasional conflicts between the premodern *shari'a* rules and international human rights norms. He said candidly that where the two differ, the international standards are defective. Tabandeh argued that Muslims should assert the superior merits of Islamic human rights. He asked:

> Why do we not simply put into practice our own Islamic laws? Indeed, why do we not put them forward at the United Nations Assembly and at its various Commissions and Conferences? Why do we not orientate the compasses of the nations of the world by the pole-star of Islam, and

publicly glory in our possession of laws that so exactly fit the human condition? Why do we not demonstrate the value of these laws, and illustrate their excellence in our words and in our practice? Why do we not invite the United Nations to express their Conventions in the terms already laid down in the Islamic Canon?[6]

With the exception of Tabandeh, the authors are reluctant to state openly that following Islamic criteria entails departures from the norms of international law.

In part because the authors of these Islamic human rights schemes have complicated and ambivalent relationships to the system of international law and in part because of impact of the authors' own political preferences, their relationship to the Islamic legal and cultural heritage is not straightforward. Although the Islamic schemes have some features in common with the premodern Islamic tradition, they are something other than simple restatements of *shari'a* rules.

Cultural Nationalism

Some of the features of the Islamic human rights schemes discussed here are influenced by their being produced in an environment where feelings of cultural nationalism and resentment of Western cultural dominance are very potent. The perspectives of the authors of the human rights schemes are influenced by cultural nationalism, and the schemes are also designed to appeal to sentiments of cultural nationalism as a means of winning acceptance by a non-Western audience. The approach taken in the literature on Islamic human rights is a manifestation of the unease that is felt in the Muslim Middle East over the extent of the region's cultural dependency on the contemporary West. Resentment of this dependency leads Middle Easterners to strive for cultural autonomy, to defend institutions associated with their own cultural heritage against charges of backwardness, and to construct Middle Eastern countermodels of Western ideas and institutions.[7]

Campaigns for Islamization of law are in part reactions to imported Western law and are based on the notion that the imposition of Western law was part of an imperialist plot both to undermine the independence of Muslim states and to demean the Islamic heritage. The impetus behind campaigns for reinstatement of Islamic law and casting aside laws associated with the era of Western domination is as much nationalist as it is religious.

In the course of reacting against Western law, proponents of Islamization do not necessarily achieve the goal of banishing the influence of the Western legal culture. The thrust of these campaigns is to show that Islam and indigenous culture have institutions comparable to those in the West and that they are equally "advanced." But what is "advanced" is constantly being defined in modern, Western terms. This leads to cultural confusion in drawing up Islamic counterparts to Western legal models because the Islamic counterparts are constructed with constant reference to the Western models that they are designed to replace. The *shari'a* is reformulated to fit borrowed Western categories, such as constitutional rights provisions, categories that have no precedent in the *shari'a* legacy The result is an admixture of Islamic and Western elements, replicating alien formulations of human rights and constitutional principles—albeit often only in a superficial manner and without incorporating their philosophical premises.

For examples of this cultural confusion, one could refer to two of the authors who most energetically condemn the West: Both Mawdudi and Tabandeh sensed that the authority of the *shari'a* rules used to restrict human rights depends on their finding Western examples and precedents that confirm their soundness. In his book explaining why the Western model of emancipation for women is bad and should be repudiated by Muslims, Mawdudi relied extensively on findings of Western "scientists," "experts," and "authorities" to establish that Western freedoms have led to social and moral disaster—with the corollary that *shari'a* rules mandating female subjugation and seclusion are sound.[8] Tabandeh, despite his claiming to believe in the superiority of *shari'a* law, found a clinching argument to support his assertion that under *shari'a* rules women should be excluded from politics in the fact that women were denied the vote in Switzerland, "one of the most civilized and most perfect societies of the world."[9] These arguments are revealing: The criticisms they fear are those that emanate from Muslims who are familiar with Western approaches to rights. Therefore Mawdudi and Tabandeh have felt compelled to devise rationales for *shari'a* rules that derive from Western science—or pseudoscience—and Western examples and experience. This approach manifests the reactive character of cultural nationalism. Such Western-inspired rationales are, however, utterly irrelevant from the standpoint of Islamic jurisprudence and would play no role in any rights scheme that was actually based on Islamic sources and a more rigorous methodology.

The factor of cultural nationalism also helps explain why authors of Islamic human rights schemes insist, despite the overwhelming historical evidence to the contrary, that human rights originated in Islam, pretending that the Western and international principles from which they are heavily borrowing are the derivative ones. Because the sources of Islamic law date from the seventh century, and all Islamic law is in theory derived from these sources, the authors seem to have concluded that human rights must be shown to have been established in Islamic principles that date from the beginning of Islamic legal history. Thus, Islamic human rights principles have to be projected back into the seventh century. There is an utter failure to deal with the historical reality that although the Islamic sources may have foreshadowed ideas that were later developed into human rights principles, the study of Islamic civilization shows that the potential of the sources as statements of rights principles was not developed until the twentieth century.

What one sees in these Islamic human rights schemes is a manifestation of a broader phenomenon that has been commented on by French scholars observing contemporary developments in Islamic thought. Called *concordisme* or *concordisme pieux* (harmonization or pious harmonization), the practice involves strained attempts by Muslims to project modern intellectual developments that have emerged outside the Muslim world back into the Islamic past. The impetus behind this *concordisme* is a desire to show that Islam anticipated all valued achievements of modern civilization. It entails retroactively Islamizing these by inventing supposed Islamic antecedents. However, in this process readings of Islam are being forced to conform to external models, at the same time that comparative intellectual history is being distorted. To one who bears in mind the need to avoid acknowledging an intellectual debt to Western civilization, the claims for the Islamic origins of human rights become intelligible. They result from cultural nationalism and a desire to establish that the West is indebted to Islam for advances that the West has wrongfully claimed as its own.

The foreword to the UIDHR states that "Islam gave to mankind an ideal code of human rights fourteen centuries ago [as calculated using the Islamic lunar calendar]." In the 1980 Kuwait seminar on human rights in Islam the conclusion was drawn that "Islam was the first to recognize basic human rights and almost 14 centuries ago it set up guarantees and safeguards that have only recently been incorporated in universal declarations of human rights."[10] In the keynote address at the same seminar, it was claimed: "To the student of the Qur'an not one word, in the preamble or in the objectives of the [UN] Charter and not a single article in the text of the 'Universal Declaration of Human Rights' will seem unfamiliar . . . the 'Universal Declaration of Human Rights' must follow as a basic corollary, or an extension of the Qur'anic programme."[11]

Tabandeh, for all of his professed disappointment with certain features of the UDHR, argued that Islam anticipated all the declaration's provisions and projected it back into the Islamic past, asserting that the UDHR "has not promulgated anything that was new nor inaugurated innovations. Every clause of it, indeed, every valuable regulation needed for the welfare of human society . . . already existed in a better and more perfect form in Islam."[12] Despite the fact that the details of Tabandeh's commentary on the UDHR reveal a deep philosophical antipathy toward the individual rights and freedoms provided for in the UDHR, Tabandeh obviously feels that Islam will be considered deficient if it cannot be shown to have anticipated the ideas embodied in contemporary human rights norms.

It is instructive to contrast the attitudes of authors of Islamic human rights schemes with those of the authors of the International Bill of Human Rights, which betray none of the defensiveness of the former. When one considers the improbability of a drafter of an international human rights document being moved to boast that the *shari'a* had not promulgated anything that constituted an innovation in relation to international human rights or to claim that the provisions in the international document were more perfect than those in the *shari'a,* one is able to appreciate the great difference in perspectives and the significance of the defensive stance that Tabandeh is taking. From the standpoint of specialists in international law, there is no need to assert its superiority vis-à-vis the *shari'a* because the authority of international law is taken as a given. The idea of the potential relevance of the *shari'a* as a rival authority or more prestigious standard never even occurs to them. In contrast, to establish the authority of their own models, Tabandeh and others like him must try to discredit the international models.

Mawdudi, who, as has been shown here, espoused ideas that are in fundamental conflict with international human rights norms, likewise attempted to defend the thesis that human rights originated in Islam, while castigating Westerners for their presumptions to have produced human rights. In keeping with his general concern for showing that Islam and the Middle East are wrongly accused of being culturally backward and underdeveloped, he complained that "people in the West have the habit of attributing every beneficial development in the world to themselves."[13] After presenting his ideas on human rights, which clearly embody philosophical positions that would preclude the development of human rights along the lines of the international norms, Mawdudi asserted:

> This is a brief sketch of those rights which 1400 years ago Islam gave to man. . . . It refreshes and strengthens our faith in Islam when we realize that even in this modern age, which makes such loud claims of progress and enlightenment, the world has not been able to produce more just and equitable laws than those given 1400 years ago. On the other

hand, it is saddening to realize that Muslims nonetheless often look for guidance to the West.[14]

Mawdudi clearly meant to argue that Muslims should for religious reasons abandon reference to the allegedly derivative Western rights concepts and refer instead to the original models, which are Islamic rights.[15] His disappointment with Muslims who seek intellectual guidance in the West did not reflect the teachings of Islam, the doctrines of which are free of nationalist bias and which do not set any geographical limits on where Muslims may look in the search for wisdom and enlightenment. His injunctions to Muslims not to look for guidance in Western rights principles reflected his espousal of the cause of cultural nationalism.

One sees that cultural nationalism lies behind some of the confusion in these Islamic human rights schemes. If Islam is treated as having anticipated the most influential post–World War II human rights documents, Islamic human rights and constitutional rights provisions must somehow be made to look like those in the international documents and Western constitutions. This means that instruments like the UDHR effectively set the agendas for presentations of the Islamic human rights that are designed to replace them. There is therefore extensive borrowing from Western models and terminology. In such an endeavor, there is no room for critical examination of whether the rules and priorities of the *shari'a* tradition that the authors seek to preserve are compatible with human rights. Internal contradictions and inconsistencies are the inevitable result of the authors' casual appropriation of the formulas and terminology of the international human rights schemes without first assessing the intellectual foundations on which they rest.

Another feature of the literature on Islamic human rights that indicates the influence of cultural nationalism on these schemes is the frequent reference to practice in the West (from any period in the history of Western civilization) that deviated from modern human rights norms. There is also an unwillingness to deal with actual problems of oppression and discrimination in the Muslim world that occurred at any time since the advent of Islam. The golden age under the Prophet Muhammad and his immediate successors in the seventh century is treated as the model of how Islamic rights work in practice—as if the perfections ascribed to *shari'a* law meant that all Muslim societies over the centuries have conformed to the ideals of the golden age of Islam. The failure to examine critically the rights situation in Muslim societies throughout history reflects this literature's apologetic, defensive function—to denigrate Western accomplishments and to exalt the heritage of Islamic civilization rather than to come to grips with human rights problems that contemporary Muslims actually face and the historical origins of these problems.

Of course, governments in both the West and the Muslim world have engaged in conduct that would constitute egregious violations of rights by the standards of modern human rights norms. Judged by contemporary standards, both Western and Muslim governments have over the centuries accumulated records of violations of civil and political rights and of engaging in oppressive and discriminatory practices. However, despite many serious lapses, Western countries since the nineteenth century have generally been moving in the direction of affording greater protections for the human rights of their citizens and imposing limits on the abilities of governments to infringe on these rights. Today, the rights protections afforded in the law of industrialized democracies of the West, although far from perfect, are nonetheless better developed than elsewhere. In contrast, in the Muslim world the current human rights situation is generally a dismal one, even worse than it was under traditional, despotic regimes. The oppressive rule of the centralized, authoritarian or totalitarian regimes that predominate in the Middle East is stifling in its impact on freedom because the state has greatly increased its power and a variety of social and economic changes have made individuals more vulnerable to governmental coercion.[16] Thus, in lieu of progress in the direction of enhancing rights, the actual trend has been in the direction of reducing individual autonomy and freedom.

The realities of oppression and rights violations by governments in the Muslim world are neglected by the authors of Islamic human rights schemes. Instead, where Muslim conservatives do treat real human rights problems, they tend to focus on Western human rights violations in an attempt to show that Western human rights protections are inadequate and ineffectual and that Westerners who criticize human rights abuses in the Middle East are hypocritical.[17] By alluding to the violations of human rights that have been perpetrated by the West, the authors seem to think they are discrediting both the Western rights models and potential Western critics of their Islamic human rights schemes. Thus, the record of rights violations in the West, which was touched on in the Kuwait seminar, was somehow deemed relevant to understanding the comparative merits of Islamic human rights.[18]

However, the question remains open why, if their Islamic human rights theories have the perfection that they attribute to them and if their principles date back to the seventh century, as they argue they do, they are so disinclined to discuss the actual historical record of how these rights were either respected or violated over the many centuries of Islamic civilization. The proponents of Islamic human rights at the 1980 Kuwait seminar on Islam and human rights expressly denied that Islamic human rights could be evaluated by reference to the historical record, saying, "It is unfair to judge Islamic law (Shari'a) by the political systems which prevailed in various periods of Islamic history."[19]

The statement would be correct if it meant that one should distinguish between the conduct of governments and the teachings of the Islamic religion, but it would be misguided if it suggested that the efficacy of human rights guarantees could not be evaluated by the degree to which they are realized in practice. The historical record of the centuries in which Islamic law was officially the governing standard indicates that efficacious human rights guarantees were practically nonexistent.

The West preoccupies Muslims as they seek to denigrate its achievements and, at the same time, to maintain that their own culture surpasses these achievements. In contrast, from a Western or international perspective on rights, neither the rights practice of Muslim countries nor Islamic rights principles are treated as having any normative force whatsoever. No Western writer would try to deflect criticism of his or her government's violations of human rights by pointing out that serious violations of human rights had occurred in Muslim countries. This in turn relates to the historical record of human rights violations and denials of democratic freedoms in Muslim societies, which discredits them as models.

Actual Human Rights Concerns in the Middle East

As has been noted, the Islamic human rights literature avoids dealing with actual human rights problems in the Middle East, but the people of the Middle East are engaged in struggles to deal with these problems and end rights violations. Even in the face of considerable dangers, there have been many attempts by Middle Eastern political and legal groups to campaign for greater freedom and stronger guarantees for human rights.[20] It is noteworthy that Muslim human rights activists have been prepared to face imprisonment and even death in their efforts to promote human rights protections according to the international standards.

In striking contrast to the silence of Islamic human rights schemes regarding the actual human rights problems facing the people in Muslim countries today, a very thoughtful and exceptionally outspoken critique of the human rights situation in the Arab world was publicly issued by a group of Arab intellectuals after a meeting in Tunis in 1983. Portions of their critique, which also applies, mutatis mutandis, to many aspects of the rights predicaments in non-Arab countries in the region, will be summarized and paraphrased here to show how Middle Easterners who are not swept up in the politics of cultural nationalism and who are not engaged in apologetic enterprises vis-à-vis the West appraise the dimensions of human rights problems in the region.

The critique asserts that under various pretexts—such as the needs of socialism, development, realization of pan-Arab unity, protecting national sovereignty, and fighting Israel—demands for democracy have been denied. It claims that freedom, aside from its social usefulness, is a value in and of itself, one that all Arabs long for and all regimes deny. Not only are Arabs prevented from free expression and from participating in the determination of their fate, but also they are always exposed to repression. Fear of imprisonment, murder, mass murder, and torture dominates their lives. The Arab individual is so humiliated, his or her personal sphere of personal freedom so restricted, and the individual so crushed into silence and subjugation that he or she becomes prone to despair and incapacity to act. These repressive measures are condemned in the critique, along with institutions like emergency courts and police-state practices; the statement demands that trials be conducted according to law. It calls on Arab governments to respect civil rights and not to infringe personal freedoms guaranteed by the UDHR. The first priority is affirmed to be equal treatment for all citizens regardless of belief, descent, or sex.

The critique maintains that its emphasis on political repression should not obscure the fact that a parallel, deformed understanding of authority shapes social and cultural patterns in the family, school, work, and religion and also in party and union organizations. In the latter groups, authority is not held accountable and therefore is exercised arbitrarily. In most Arab countries, authority, the critique asserts, is based on the oppression and subjugation of citizens. The consequences are confusion in values and norms and a lack of critical thought. A monolithically structured, hermetically closed system of authority dominates the scene, leaving no room for political or intellectual pluralism or for genuine culture. The participants called for guarantees for freedoms, especially freedom of belief, freedom of opinion and expression, freedom to participate, freedom of assembly, and freedom to form political organizations and unions. Women's and minorities' rights were also said to need guarantees. An independent judiciary was demanded as well.[21]

It is useful to bear in mind this critique because it proves that intellectuals who are genuinely concerned about protecting human rights in the Middle East are prepared to speak out to denounce the actual patterns of human rights violations by present governments and that they do not hesitate to invoke international human rights norms in their criticisms of the human rights abuses that Middle Eastern governments have perpetrated in the areas of civil and political rights. It also confirms that the common forms of oppression by Middle Eastern regimes are not just objectionable by Western standards but are perceived by people within these societies, especially the members of the educated elite, to be impermissibly harsh in their impact on individuals and stultifying in terms of their impact on society and culture. The comments show that the kinds of justifications that are offered by government officials for patterns of repression are not necessarily accepted by people in these societies and that the latter do not consider participatory democracy an exotic, Western luxury; instead, they attribute many of the problems afflicting their own societies to its absence.

An important study of the connections between the lack of democracy and the violations of human rights in the Arab world, recently published in Egypt, developed many of the themes discussed in the Tunis declaration.[22] It is noteworthy that a work produced by Arabs, one that undertakes a critical evaluation of rights problems, did not bother to discuss Islamic human rights schemes; the implication is that they are irrelevant. There are many indications that the kinds of Islamic human rights schemes that have been concocted by Muslim conservatives do not impress Muslims sincerely committed to finding realistic formulas for resolving human rights problems.

It is highly significant that the Islamic human rights schemes discussed here, in contrast to the kinds of critiques just mentioned, insist on the absolute perfection of abstract Islamic ideals while ignoring altogether the myriad problems of institutionalizing and implementing human rights protections and democratizing closed systems in the Middle East. They talk of Islamic human rights as if they enjoyed unquestioned authority and automatic efficaciousness by reason of their divine provenance, owing to which no government would dare to tamper with them. For example, in its Preamble, the UIDHR says of Islamic human rights that "by virtue of their Divine source and sanction these rights can neither be curtailed, abrogated or disregarded by authorities, assemblies or other institutions, nor can they be surrendered or alienated."[23]

The authors must ignore the grim reality of the human rights situation in the Middle East, because to admit its dimensions and the lack of respect that governments have routinely shown for the law, including norms of Islamic law, would entail confronting the fact that the religious pedigrees of Islamic rules are not by themselves sufficient to guarantee that they will be respected in practice. Before Western incursions and influences that led to the displacement of Islamic law in the Muslim world, there was a long record of cruel and tyrannical rulers, who were not inhibited by Islamic norms from exploiting and mistreating their subjects. Since civil society had not developed and there were no political institutions to hold rulers accountable to those whom they ruled and judges and courts did not enjoy independence from the political authorities, there were no effective means for restraining despots and protecting individual freedom. To a large extent these systemic problems have persisted in contemporary Muslim countries. Muslims who are sincerely committed to realizing human rights and who understand the prerequisites for establishing a free and democratic order realize that it is systemic change and not the appeal to abstract Islamic ideals that can lay the groundwork for the rule of law and effective protections for human rights.

Summary

As this assessment has indicated, these Islamic human rights schemes are products of the political context in which they emerged. Their Islamic pedigrees are dubious, and the principles they contain do not represent the outcome of rigorous, scholarly analyses of the Islamic sources or a coherent approach to Islamic jurisprudence. Instead, they seem largely shaped by their conservative authors' negative reactions to the model of freedom in Western societies and the scope of rights protections afforded by the International Bill of Human Rights.

In producing their Islamic human rights schemes, the authors used material from the Islamic heritage, often confused with the values found in traditional societies, in highly selective manner, resulting in a one-sided representation of Islamic teachings relating to rights that suited those authors' conservative political dispositions. Anti-Western attitudes and cultural nationalism have also influenced the way the authors perceive the Islamic tradition. They have been disinclined to seek a synthesis of Islamic and international human rights norms, a synthesis that could serve the cause of curbing the actual patterns of human rights violations that afflict the inhabitants of contemporary Muslim countries.

CHAPTER 10

Islam and Culture-based Resistance to Rights

The significance of Islamic culture for the reception of human rights in contemporary Muslim countries is not only a topic of interest to scholars of comparative law but also an issue that is of practical consequence both for proponents and opponents of human rights. A major preoccupation of contemporary Islamic thought is sorting out the relationship between Islamic law and the international legal system, which has been identified by some Muslims with a hostile Western civilization. The principle of the supremacy of international law is a given in the modern international order. The reality of this supremacy confronts Muslims at a time when there are calls for the revival of Islamic law and efforts to develop elements of the Islamic legal tradition to encompass contemporary problems. This is occurring as part of a general effort to marshall tradition in order to withstand the inroads of Western cultural influences, which threaten to overwhelm local culture and obliterate Islamic institutions. The emergence of Islamic schemes of human rights may be seen as one manifestation of ongoing processes of Islamic cultural reassertion, processes that are reactive in character.

Lacking the legitimacy of democratic governments, oppressive regimes in Muslim countries consider Muslims' growing tendency to demand the observance of international human rights to be a threat to those regimes' dominance. Regimes whose entire legitimacy is tied up with the imposition of premodern *shari'a* rules are particularly threatened by the ascendancy of international human rights models. They face a dual crisis of legitimacy in which both the oppressive, undemocratic political orders and the interpretations of Islam offered by conservative defenders of the premodern *shari'a* are vulnerable to challenges based on the model of international human rights. The perfect example of a regime struggling with this dual crisis of legitimacy is Saudi Arabia, where both the autocratic ruling family and a powerful faction of conservative Sunni clerics allied with the ruling house of Saud are committed to the perpetuation of a monarchical regime. To refuse demands for democratization, the regime relies on clerics' interpretations of premodern *shari'a* rules. One of the few weapons that they have at their disposal to combat the appeal of human rights and democratization is manipulation of religious sentiment.

The heritage of premodern *shari'a* law, which still retains prestige in Muslim milieus, can, if selectively employed, buttress authoritarian ideologies and provide rationales for inequality, discrimination, and denials of freedom. Muslims committed to preserving *shari'a* formulations that serve the cause of forestalling change and modernization have been prepared to argue that demands for respect for international human rights can be equated with hostility toward Islam. In this connection, one sees why in the conservative versions of Islamic human rights, where the standards of rights protections fall below the international norms, efforts are made to identify the positions taken on rights with the tenets of the Islamic religion.

To the critical observer, the Islamic rationalizations that are offered for resistance to human rights in countries like Saudi Arabia smack of cynical self-interest on the part of the ruling family and the dominant clerical faction. However, one must bear in mind that, from the point of view of conservative Muslims in a society like Saudi Arabia's, preserving Islam may have become so closely identified with the preservation of the traditional order that the two are indistinguishable. Therefore some conservatives equate challenges to the political status quo that are based on the principles of democracy and international human rights with challenges to the legitimacy of Islam itself. Consequently, one must be open to the possibility that the invocations of Islam by conservatives to discredit human rights may be motivated by sincere beliefs on the part of at least some of the participants in the debates. However, it seems that on the whole Muslims themselves are disposed to question the good faith of governments and clerics who rely on premodern *shari'a* norms to discredit advocates of democratization and to rationalize subjecting people in Muslim countries to a lower standard of rights protections than those afforded people outside the Muslim world.

Until Muslims' thinking on the relationship between Islam and international human rights becomes definitively settled and one doctrine supported by a general consensus of Muslim opinion emerges, at the level of theory there will be conflicts between factions of Muslims who rely on premodern Islamic rules to curb rights and other Muslims committed to human rights as embodied in international law. These conflicts will inevitably center around whether there is real Islamic authority for distinctive Islamic human rights schemes and whether fidelity to Islam stands in the way of the adoption of the international norms.

The premodern Islamic juristic culture did not address "human rights" as such, providing no explicit Islamic model of rights principles. Appeals to "Islam" to justify deviations from the international norms of human rights would seem to presuppose the existence of such a model. The Islamic tradition does include many elements that bear on rights, but no monolithic body of Islamic doctrine that is generally accepted by Muslims as the definitive statement on rights exists. The Islamic heritage is rich in sources and materials that offer a vast array of principles and values relevant for rights. These sources can be utilized both by Muslims advocating and by those opposing human rights in support of their respective positions. But only one component of the Islamic heritage—Muslim conservatives' readings of the sources and the values of the premodern tradition—has been selected for incorporation in the Islamic human rights schemes examined here. Furthermore, conservatives' treatments of rights are by no means simple replications of Islamic doctrines. Their treatments are in reality legal hybrids that comprise many concepts borrowed from international human rights models and Western constitutions. The authoritativeness of these schemes as epitomes of Islamic rights doctrines is in consequence open to question.

However often the terminology and references invoke religious sources and authority, the stakes in the battle over human rights standards are ultimately political. The religious tenor of the discourse should not obscure the fact that the questions being addressed deal with the rationales for preserving the features of premodern political and social orders and for refusing to democratize political systems. These underlying issues and concerns are hardly unique to Muslim milieus, and elements of the strategies being employed by Muslim conservatives to discredit advocates of human rights have counterparts elsewhere.

The varied responses to human rights in Muslim countries should be viewed, not in isolation, but in relation to general trends in other regions. As developments in the late 1980s have shown, international human rights standards today enjoy popular support in environments where the values and institutions of Western liberal democracies either have previously never existed or have long been suppressed and condemned by those in power as being incompatible with the official ideology or indigenous culture. Events in countries as diverse as China, Tibet, Burma, Argentina, Chile, the USSR, Albania, Czechoslovakia, Kenya, South Africa, Algeria, and Tunisia have demonstrated that international human rights norms are enthusiastically supported by people in societies with a wide variety of religious and cultural traditions. The growing evidence of the universality of the appeal of international human rights brings into question the motives behind the insistence by governments and leaders of traditionalist movements resisting human rights that the local culture and values stand in the way of their adoption.

It is important to bear in mind that appeals to a supposed cultural specificity as the rationale for rejecting the validity of international human rights are not limited to Muslim milieus. Louis Henkin, a distinguished scholar of international human rights law, has observed common features in attempts to justify denying human rights. Maintaining that human rights are legally and politically universal (which is not the same thing as saying that they are universally respected in practice), Henkin has concluded that the strongest challenge to their universality has been culturally based resistance.[1]

An instructive counterpart to Islam-based cultural resistance to human rights can be seen in the attempts by the Communist Chinese government to argue not only that rights issues fall within Chinese domestic jurisdiction but also that China has its own standard of human rights, opposing the idea that human rights are universal. It is noteworthy that this is a position endorsed by the ruling elite, but one that events in spring 1989 suggested is not necessarily accepted by the Chinese people, the same people whose culture the regime ostensibly is trying to protect.

The idea that adherence to a separate Chinese model excuses the deficiencies in rights protections in China has been criticized by the distinguished Chinese scientist and human rights activist Fang Lizhi, who insists that Chinese people aspire to the same human rights as do peoples in other cultures. He has proposed that there are analogies between the resistance to human rights by the Communist elite today and Chinese rulers' rejection of modern astronomy in the eighteenth century on the grounds that Chinese culture had its own astronomy. Not surprisingly, investigation revealed that there were vested political interests behind the Chinese rulers' upholding of the authority of the traditional Chinese astronomical model. The old Chinese feudal aristocrats opposed the idea of the universal validity of science and even killed five astronomers, Fang Lizhi explained, because modern astronomy undermined the basis for their claims to divine right of rule—and, hence, their legitimacy. In the same vein Fang Lizhi observed that acknowledging the universality of human rights norms would destroy the legitimacy of the present Chinese rulers. Thus, they must promulgate the notion of a distinctive Chinese cultural version of human rights to legitimize their opposition to democratization.[2] That is, Fang Lizhi found that the political interests of the present Chinese leadership, which seeks to preserve the status quo, actually prompt the claims that distinctive features of Chinese culture justify deviating from international human rights norms.

One sees obvious parallels between the use of a Chinese model of astronomy to resist the destabilizing impact of modern science in the old Chinese system and the contemporary political use of Islamic human rights models that are designed to obviate recourse to international rights. Just as it was necessary to refer to the science of astronomy to evaluate the political functions of the Chinese model of astronomy, so it is necessary to compare Islamic rights models with their international counterparts to ascertain their significance.

Even though there may be individuals in Chinese as well as Muslim society who are convinced that there is a local cultural specificity that is out of keeping with international human rights, when such rationales for denying human rights are offered by governments, they smack of politically inspired attempts to manipulate and exploit cultural loyalties. Particularly in cases where the governments professing their commitment to the respect for traditional culture are ones that aspire to all the attributes of modernity in areas where these could enhance their ability to control those they rule, their devotion to preserving traditional culture must be suspect. It is possible in such circumstances that the loyalties to the local culture or tradition that they invoke may involve artificial constructs, designed for use in consolidating governmental authority and having no real popular roots. This is one of many reasons why the tenets of cultural relativism must be applied warily and sparingly when analyzing culturally based resistance to human rights.

According to Henkin, the current popularity of human rights has led to the muting of the philosophical and religious opposition that human rights formerly encountered.[3] Now, the enemies of freedom, rather than condemning human rights, may find it expedient to sponsor alternative and weaker versions of them. In these circumstances, one must be alert to the possibility that opponents of human rights may be obliged to disguise their real attitudes and adopt much of the language of human rights proponents.

Opposition to rights in the Muslim world now tends to be expressed more obliquely than was formerly the case. At present, governments and ideologues who are hostile to democracy, freedom, and equality are much more on the defensive than Muslim conservatives opposed to rights were at the earlier stages of reception of Western ideas of freedom and equality and in the years immediately following 1948, when the Universal Declaration of Human Rights was promulgated.

Although Muslim conservatives from countries like Saudi Arabia once felt comfortable denouncing human rights principles outright, today such an absolute rejectionist stance is infrequently encountered and more subtle and indirect tactics for discrediting the international norms are preferred. With the growth in the prestige and influence of the international human rights models, Muslim conservatives do seem to perceive the need to design measures that permit them to co-opt the popularity of these models. To combat the appeal of international human rights, conservative Muslims from a variety of countries and from both Sunni and Shi'i communities have found it expedient to arm themselves with alternative "Islamic" versions of human rights. All the alternatives employ religious criteria to dilute and even negate rights protections while giving lip service to the ideals of human rights.

The areas where Islamic rationales are employed to combat the influence of international human rights also fit the general patterns of culture-based resistance to rights that Henkin has noted. Henkin concluded that the human rights particularly susceptible to cultural challenge are those involving freedom of expression, freedom of conscience and religion, equality, and bans on discrimination based on race, ethnicity, or gender.[4] As the comparative assessment of Islamic human rights schemes undertaken here has shown, these are precisely the areas where the Islamic countermodels of rights have tended to deviate sharply from international norms—with important and commendable exceptions in the area of discrimination based on race or ethnicity.

That is, based on Henkin's assessment of patterns of culture-based resistance to human rights, one might have predicted that the recourse to Islamic criteria to justify resistance to international human rights norms would lead, as in fact it did, to deviations from the international standards in areas like freedom of expression, freedom of conscience and religion, and the norms of equality and equal protection of the law. Culture-based resistance to human rights will tend to invoke the values typical of traditional societies, and traditional societies tended to resemble each other in the features that set them apart from modern societies. Values and priorities that one typically finds in traditional societies, such as anti-individualism, preserving established hierarchies and patriarchal orders, and enforcing social cohesion and conformity, are ones that can be exploited by opponents of democratization and conservative forces hostile to the expansion of freedom to legitimize their resistance to "alien" concepts of human rights. This culture-based resistance to human rights may represent authentic responses of persons immersed in traditional culture who are unaffected by the impact of modernization. However, such resistance is likely to rest on artificial constructs of traditional culture when it is pursued by educated, urbanized elites long after traditional societies have crumbled under the onslaught of modernization processes and after governments of nation-states have come to exercise centralized control over all aspects of society in ways that were never contemplated in traditional societies. All this draws one to conclude that the patterns of diluted rights in Islamic human rights schemes should not be ascribed to peculiar features of Islam or Islamic culture but should be seen as part of a broader phenomenon of attempts by beneficiaries of undemocratic and hierarchical systems to legitimize their opposition to human rights by appeals to supposedly distinctive cultural traditions.

Notes

Chapter 1

1. Excellent analyses of this problem can be found in the work of Bassam Tibi, *The Crisis of Modern Islam. A Preindustrial Culture in the Scientific Technological Age,* Judith von Sivers, trans. (Salt Lake City: University of Utah Press, 1988), and *Islam and the Cultural Accommodation of Social Change,* Clare Krojzl, trans. (Boulder, Colo.: Westview Press, 1990).

2. A useful survey of human rights groups that have recently emerged can be found in the articles assembled in *MERIP Middle East Report,* November-December 1987.

3. This attempts to summarize the comments in Alan Watson, *Legal Transplants: An Approach to Comparative Law* (Edinburgh: Scottish Academic Press, 1974), 6–9.

4. The writings of Abdullahi An-Na'im, cited throughout this study, are important exceptions. His most recent work is *Toward an Islamic Reformation: Civil Liberties, Human Rights and International Law* (Syracuse: Syracuse University Press, 1990). Sami Aldeeb Abu Sahlieh's work is also significant. See his "Les Droits de l'homme et l'Islam," *Revue general de droit international public* 89 (1985), 625–716; "Liberté religieuse et apostasie dans l'Islam," *Praxis juridique et religion* 3 (1986), 43–76. Critical appraisals are also presented in Jack Donnelly, "Human Rights and Human Dignity: An Analytic Critique of Non-Western Conception of Human Rights," *American Political Science Review* 76 (1982), 306–16; Jack Donnelly, *Universal Human Rights in Theory and Practice* (Ithaca: Cornell University Press, 1989), 50–52; Lucie Pruvost, "Declaration Universelle des Droits de l'Homme dans l'Islam et Charte Internationale des Droits de l'Homme: Convergences-Divergences, *IslamoChristiana* 9 (1983), 141–57.

5. It is not coincidental that the people who tend to oppose open discussion of sensitive issues are largely not specialists in international law, for one sees that combined expertise in Islamic law and international law can provide the basis for undertaking critical comparative study of the two. A scholar of international law, Professor Abdullahi an-Na'im, formerly of Khartoum University Law School, is a rare scholar who dares to attempt to examine seriously the relationship between Islamic law and international law.

6. Edward Said, *Orientalism* (London: Routledge & Kegan Paul, 1978).

7. These comments echo remarks made in an elegant summation of how misdirected responses to Said's *Orientalism* can recreate rather than correct Orientalist biases. The summation is in Sadiq Jalal al-'Azm, "Orientalism and Orientalism in Reverse," in *Forbidden Agendas: Intolerance and Defiance in the Middle East,* selected and introduced by Jon Rothschild (London: Al-Saqi Books, 1984), 349–81. Although not dealing with human rights issues, al-'Azm's arguments are especially relevant for these. See especially his comments on 366–73.

8. A good illustration of this position can be found in Admantia Pollis and Peter Schwab, "Human Rights: A Western Construct with Limited Applicability," in *Human Rights: Cultural and Ideological Perspectives,* Admantia Pollis and Peter Schwab, eds. (New York: Praeger, 1979), 1–18.

9. Ibid., 14.

10. United Nations General Assembly. Thirty-Ninth Session. Third Committee. 65th meeting, held on Friday, 7 December 1984, at 3 p.m. New York. A/C.3/39/SR.65.

11. Fernando Teson, "International Human Rights and Cultural Relativism," *Virginia Journal of International Law* 25 (1985), 875.

12. Donnelly, *Universal Human Rights,* 114.

13. Of course, Saudi Arabia is the exception in this regard, having no constitution and preserving a traditional monarchical system of government.

14. John Kelsay, "Saudi Arabia, Pakistan, and the Universal Declaration of Human Rights," in *Human Rights and the Conflict of Cultures: Western and Islamic Perspectives on Religious Liberty,* David Little, John Kelsay, and Abdulaziz Sachedina, eds. (Columbia: University of South Carolina Press, 1988), 35–36.

15. Ibid., 36–37.

16. I have not run across a single instance where a Muslim conversant with the international human rights norms who felt injured by a government act in breach of internationally guaranteed human rights norms voluntarily acquiesced in the violation of the right on the grounds that Muslims were not entitled to claim the same rights as other human beings or that rights protections were alien to Islamic culture.

17. Teson, "International Human Rights," 895.

18. Louis Munoz, "The Rationality of Tradition," *Archiv für Rechts und Sozial-philosophie* 68 (1981), 212.

19. Donnelly, *Universal Human Rights,* 117.

20. Ibid., 118.

21. Jack Donnelly, "Cultural Relativism and Universal Human Rights," *Human Rights Quarterly* 6 (1984), 411.

22. As an introduction to human rights organizations working in the Middle East, one can consult the *MERIP Middle East Report,* November-December 1987, and files kept by groups such as Amnesty International, Middle East Watch, and Africa Watch. See also Virginia N. Sherry, "The Human Rights Movement in the Arab World: An Active and Diverse Community of Human Rights Advocates Exists in Several Countries of the Region," *Human Rights Watch,* No. 4, Special Middle East Watch Issue (Fall 1990), 6–7.

23. In the French version of the 1989 constitution, Article 32 provides: "La défense individuelle ou associative des droits fondamentaux de l'homme et des libertés individuelles et collectives est garantie."

24. Ann Mayer, "Islam and the State," *Cardozo Law Review* 12 (1990), 1006–07. For example, the constitution begins with the phrase "In the name of Allah, the Merciful, the Clement," and Algeria is described as "a land of Islam." Quotes from 1006.

25. Malise Ruthven, *A Satanic Affair: Salman Rushdie and the Rage of Islam* (London: Chatto and Windus, 1990), 107–08.

26. Abdullahi An-Na'im, "Religious Minorities Under Islamic Law and the Limits of Cultural Relativism," *Human Rights Quarterly* 9 (1987), 5.

Chapter 2

1. Information on accessions is published in collections of UN instruments, and recent data can be found in Jean Bernard Marie, "International Instruments Relating to Human Rights," *Human Rights Law Journal* 10 (1989), 103–30.

2. Louis Henkin, "International Human Rights as Rights," in *Human Rights: NOMOS 23*, J. Roland Pennock and John Chapman, eds. (New York: New York University Press, 1981), 258–59.

3. Excellent introductions to the historical problems of establishing constitutional government in Iran can be found in Yann Richard, *Le Shi'isme en Iran. Imam et Révolution* (Paris: Maisonneuve, 1980); Abdul-Hadi Hairi, *Shi'ism and Constitutionalism in Iran* (Leiden: Brill, 1977); and Said Arjomand, ed., *Authority and Political Culture in Shi'ism* (Albany: SUNY Press, 1988).

4. Shaul Bakhash, *The Reign of the Ayatollahs* (New York: Basic Books, 1984).

5. For examples of how Muslims are meshing human rights ideas with the Islamic tradition, see Abdullahi An-Na'im, *Toward an Islamic Reformation: Civil Liberties, Human Rights and International Law* (Syracuse: Syracuse University Press, 1990); Abdullahi El-Naiem [An-Na'im], "A Modern Approach to Human Rights in Islam: Foundations and Implications for Africa," in *Human Rights and Development in Africa,* Claude Welch, Jr., and Ronald Meltzer, eds. (Albany: SUNY Press, 1984), 75–89; and "Religious Freedom in Egypt: Under the Shadow of the Islamic Dhimma System," in *Religious Liberty and Human Rights in Nations and Religions,* Leonard Swidler, ed. (Philadelphia: Ecumenical Press, 1986), 43–59. See also Subhi Mahmassani, *Arkan huquq al-insan* (Beirut: Dar al-'ilm li'l-malayin, 1979). The rethinking by contemporary Muslim feminists of the premodern norms of *shari'a* law affecting women, which is discussed in Chapter 6 in connection with the question of women's status, is another example of the trend toward harmonization of Islamic precepts with international rights norms.

6. For example, public comments evincing disagreement with the Iranian regime's policy of disregard for human rights were among the factors leading to the resignation of Ayatollah Montazeri, Khomeini's designated successor, on March 27, 1989. *Iran Focus* 1:3 (December 1988), 5; 2:3 (March 1989), 4. Not

coincidentally, Montazeri had continued to associate with members of Bazargan's Freedom Movement of Iran, the only liberal political opposition group still bold enough to try to combat the regime's repressive policies. *Iran Focus* 2:5 (May 1989), 4.

7. Suroosh Irfani, *Revolutionary Islam in Iran: Popular Liberation or Religious Dictatorship?* (London: Zed Books, 1983) (on unnumbered page preceding the dedication page).

8. Quoted by Edward Mortimer, "Islam and Human Rights," *Index on Censorship,* October 1983, 5.

9. The most extensive publications and documents are those compiled by the international human rights organization, Amnesty International. Materials on the human rights records of Iran, Pakistan, and the Sudan can be found under the respective country headings in the annual reports issued by Amnesty International and also in that organization's newsletter and other reports that are periodically published. Examples of special publications by Amnesty International dealing with human rights problems in these countries include *Torture in the Eighties,* 1984; *Violations of Human Rights in Pakistan,* April 1985; *Political Imprisonment in the Sudan,* October 1984; *Human Rights Violations in the Islamic Republic of Iran,* May 1980; *Iran Briefing,* 1987; *Iran. Violations of Human Rights. Documents Sent by Amnesty International to the Government of the Islamic Republic of Iran,* 1987; *Iran. Violations of Human Rights, 1987–1990,* 1990. Human Rights Watch and Middle East Watch publish periodic bulletins on human rights problems and monitor the rights situation in Muslim countries. The U.S. Department of State submits annual reports entitled *Country Reports on Human Rights Practices* that are published and that often have valuable information on human rights problems, even though U.S. foreign policy may influence the treatment of human rights violations in individual countries. The French human rights group, FIDH, or Fédération internationale des droits de l'homme, has documented human rights abuses in its reports, such as *Rapport de Mission. Iran: Mission au Kurdistan* (August 9–September 8, 1983); and *Rapport de Mission. Pakistan* (March 13, 1984), and also in its regular newsletter, *La Lettre de la FIDH.* Africa Watch has monitored the human rights situation in the Sudan. Examples of its reports include: *Sudan: Destruction of the Independent Secular Judiciary; Military Government Clamps Down on Press Freedom* (September 25, 1989); *Political Detainees in the Sudan* (October 24, 1989); *Sudan: Khartoum: Government to Execute Striking Doctors. The Provinces: Militia Killings and Starvation Policy Return* (December 6, 1989); *Sudan: Recent Developments in Khartoum, an Update* (December 13, 1989); *Political Detainees in Sudan: Academics* (January 22, 1990); *Sudan: The Massacre at el Jebelein* (January 23, 1990). The periodical *Index on Censorship* has included important articles and reports on human rights violations in these countries. For example, see the materials on political repression and censorship in Pakistan in Maleeha Lodhi, "Deterring Dissent in Education," *Index on Censorship,* April 1985, 28; Scriptor [pseud.], "Why the Press Is Tame, ibid., 31; Farhad [pseud.], "Curbing Free Thought," ibid., 33. The UNESCO Com-

mission on Human Rights has reviewed the human rights situation in Iran. See *Information Relating to Violations of Human Rights in Iran Under the International Convenant on Civil and Political Rights,* E/CN.4/1983/19 (February 22, 1983), UNESCO Commission on Human Rights, 39th Session, January 31–April 11, 1983. The UN Sub-Commission on Prevention of Discrimination and Protection of Minorities expressed concern about the persecution of Baha'is in Iran in ECOSOC E/CN 4/Sub.2/L779 (September 2, 1981).

10. The refusal of the Iranian government to cooperate with UN efforts to monitor the human rights situation and the concern that this provoked are documented in the report of the Economic and Social Council, "Situation of Human Rights in the Islamic Republic of Iran, Note by the Secretary General," A/41/787 (November 3, 1986), and Economic and Social Council, *Report on the Human Rights Situation in the Islamic Republic of Iran,* E/CN.4/1987/23 (January 28, 1987).

11. Both the Persian and the English texts of the Iranian Constitution of 1979 that are used here are taken from the collection *Constitutions of the Countries of the World,* Albert Blaustein and Gisbert Flanz, eds. (Dobbs Ferry: Oceana, 1986). The English translation was prepared by Changiz Vafai.

12. An English text of the declaration can be found in the British Broadcasting Company Summary of World Broadcasts, Part 4, "The Middle East, Africa and Latin America." See BBC SWB May 1, 1984, ME/7631/A/2.

13. BBC SWB May 1, 1984, ME/7631/A/8.

14. Ibid., ME/7631/A/9.

15. Ibid., ME/7631/A/9.

16. BBC SWB September 25, 1984, ME/7757/A/6.

17. The Transitional Constitution of the Republic of the Sudan, 1985, in *Constitutions of the Countries of the World,* Blaustein and Flanz, eds. Article 3 made constitutional principles supreme so that they would prevail over other laws; Article 5 said that the state shall strive to "eradicate racial and religious fanaticism"; Article 11, that the state and each person "shall be subject to the rule of law as applied by the courts"; and Article 17, that all persons would be equal before the law.

18. An excellent summary of relevant developments can be found in the Chronology section that is appended to the Constitution of the Islamic Republic of Pakistan in the collection *Constitutions of the Countries of the World,* Blaustein and Flanz, eds.

19. As noted, President Zia was allied with conservative Islamic groups like the Jama'at-i-Islami of Mawdudi. *Amir* is the term Mawdudi advocated for the leader of an Islamic government, which does not seem a coincidence in this context.

20. Political Plan Announced, Seventh Session of Federal Council. Address by President General Muhammad Zia ul-Haq. Islamabad, August 12, 1983. Constitution of the Islamic Republic of Pakistan, in *Constitutions of the Countries of the World,* Blaustein and Flanz, eds., 182.

Chapter 3

1. Leo Strauss, *Natural Right and History* (Chicago: University of Chicago Press, 1953), 181–82.

2. J. Roland Pennock, "Rights, Natural Rights, and Human Rights—A General View," in *Human Rights: NOMOS* 23, J. Roland Pennock and John W. Chapman, eds. (New York: New York University Press, 1981), 1.

3. A compilation may be found in *International Human Rights Instruments of the United Nations, 1948–1982* (London: Mansell, 1983).

4. Marcel Boisard, "On the Probable Influence of Islam on Western and International Law," *International Journal of Middle Eastern Studies* 11 (1980), 429–50.

5. The philosophy of Sufism, Islamic mysticism, does have elements of individualism, and it is a major component of the Islamic tradition. For a general account, see A. J. Arberry, *Sufism: An Account of the Mystics of Islam* (New York: Macmillan, 1950). Notwithstanding Sufis' concentration on dissolving the individual and achieving spiritual oneness with God, their focus on the perfection of the individual soul and their common disregard for Islamic law and ritual does tend to link them with currents of thought that would challenge authority—like that of Islamic clerics purporting to dictate definitive versions of Islamic law—and support individual freedom. However, to date Muslims do not appear to be mining the Sufi tradition for elements with which to construct rights theories. The otherworldly focus of Sufism, its concentration on spiritual matters, and its disregard for issues of positive law may have led to its potential relevance being overlooked.

6. This is not to say that this distinction is always made by Muslims. As a review of anti-individualistic perspectives maintained by proponents of Islamic human rights schemes will show (Chapters 5–8), contemporary Muslims often identify features of premodern culture that are reflected in medieval Islamic thought with Islam itself. They thus see individualism as incompatible with the Islamic religion.

7. The ideas of the *mu'tazila* are discussed in George Hourani, *Islamic Rationalism: The Ethics of 'Abd al-Jabbar* (Oxford: Clarendon Press, 1971); Majid Khadduri, *The Islamic Conception of Justice* (Baltimore: Johns Hopkins University Press, 1984), 41–53.

8. Khadduri, *The Islamic Conception of Justice,* 78–105.

9. The struggles between proponents of reason and Revelation in Islamic intellectual history are described in A. J. Arberry, *Revelation and Reason in Islam* (London: Allen & Unwin, 1957; Khadduri, *The Islamic Conception of Justice,* 39–34, 64–70; Mohamed El-Shakankiri, "Loi divine et loi humaine et droit dans l'histoire juridique de l'Islam," *Studia Islamica* 59 (1981), 161–82. Shi'i positions differ from Sunni ones, a critical difference between the sects being the Shi'i concept of the imamate. Problems were created for Twelver Shi'is by the last imam's going into occultation. A thorough exposition of Shi'i doctrines in this connection may be found in Abdulaziz Sachedina, *The Just Ruler (al-Sultan al-'adil) in Shi'ite Islam. The Comprehensive Authority of the Jurist in Imamite Jurisprudence* (New York: Oxford University Press, 1988).

10. Khomeini's views are presented in Farhang Rajaee, *Islamic Values and World View: Khomeyni on Man, the State, and International Politics* (Lanham, Md.: University Press of America, 1983), 42–45.

11. These points are made in Noel Coulson, "The State and the Individual in Islamic Law," *International and Comparative Law Quarterly* 6 (1957), 49–60.

12. In this, Islamic legal thought resembles aspects of the natural law approach to rights in Western civilization. See Myres McDougal, Harold Lasswell, and Lung-chu Chen, *Human Rights and World Order: The Basic Policies of an International Law of Dignity* (New Haven: Yale University Press, 1980), 68–71.

13. A useful introductory survey of this topic is Erwin J. Rosenthal, *Political Thought in Medieval Islam: An Introductory Outline* (Cambridge: Cambridge University Press, 1962).

14. Coulson, "The State and the Individual," 50.

15. Examples of works that document the humanism that was and continues to be part of the Islamic tradition are Mohammed Arkoun, *L'humanisme Arabe au iv*ᵉ*/v*ᵉ *siècle: Miskawayh, philosophe et historien* (Paris: J. Vrin, 1970); Marcel Boisard, *L'humanisme de l'Islam* (Paris: Albin Michel, 1979); Hisham Djait, *La Personnalité et le devenir arabo-islamiques* (Paris: Albin Michel, 1974); Joel Kraemer, *Humanism in the Renaissance of Islam. The Cultural Revival During the Buyid Age* (Leiden: Brill, 1986); Fazlur Rahman, *Islam and Modernity: Transformation of an Intellectual Tradition* (Chicago: University of Chicago Press, 1982); and the introductory section in *In Quest of an Islamic Humanism: Arabic and Islamic Studies in Memory of Mohamed al-Nowaihi*, Arnold Green, ed. (Cairo: American University Press, 1984).

16. Some examples are given in Franz Rosenthal, *The Muslim Concept of Freedom Prior to the Nineteenth Century* (Leiden: Brill, 1960), 100–01, 105, 144.

17. Elie Adib Salem, *Political Theory and Institutions of the Khawarij* (Baltimore: Johns Hopkins University Press, 1965); Khadduri, *The Islamic Conception of Justice*, 20–23.

18. The general ignorance of Kharijite doctrines is partly linked to the fact that the remnants of the original community fled under persecution to remote parts of the Muslim world. Thus, one finds them in places like Oman and in the mountains or isolated settlements in Algeria. Because so much of the writing by Kharijites was destroyed by their foes, the source materials on their ideas is quite limited.

19. For an examination of the case of Egypt, see Farhat Ziadeh, *Lawyers, the Rule of Law, and Liberalism in Modern Egypt* (Stanford: Hoover Institution, 1968).

20. A classic account of the changing political views of the Arab elite at the time that constitutionalist ideas were percolating through Muslim societies is in Albert Hourani, *Arabic Thought in the Liberal Age, 1798–1939* (Oxford: Oxford University Press, 1967.)

21. Examples can be found in Abdol Karim Lahidji, "Constitutionalism and Clerical Authority," in *Authority and Political Culture in Shi'ism,* Said Arjomand, ed. (Albany: SUNY, 1988), 133–58; and Hairi, *Shi'ism and Constitutionalism.*

22. Examples of Professor an-Na'im's work can be found in "A Modern Approach to Human Rights in Islam: Foundations and Implications for Africa," in *Human Rights and Development in Africa,* Claude Welch, Jr., and Roland Meltzer, eds. (Albany: SUNY Press, 1984), 75–89; his study of the religious reformer Mahmud Muhammad Taha, along with the translation of Taha's major work, *The Second Message of Islam,* Abdullahi an-Na'im, trans. (Syracuse: Syracuse University Press, 1987); and his *Toward an Islamic Reformation: Civil Liberties, Human Rights and International Law* (Syracuse: Syracuse University Press, 1990).

23. Mohammed Arkoun, *Pour une critique de la raison islamique* (Paris: Maisonneuve-Larose, 1984), and *L'Islam, morale et politique* (Paris: Desclee de Brouwer, 1986).

24. Sadiq Jalal al-'Azm, *Naqd al-fikr al-dini* (Beirut: Dar al-tali'a, 1972).

25. See, for example, Abu'l A'la Mawdudi, *Human Rights in Islam* (Leicester: Islamic Foundation, 1980), 39; Sultanhussein Tabandeh, *A Muslim Commentary on the Universal Declaration of Human Rights,* F. J. Goulding, trans. (Guildford: F. J. Goulding, 1970), 1, 85; and the first page of the English-language pamphlet version of the UIDHR.

26. This is particularly true in the case of the UIDHR, Tabandeh, and Mawdudi. They cite sources without attempting to show how the rights they purport to see in the text have been derived from the sources on which they are allegedly based. Examples will be offered subsequently.

27. The writings of Mawdudi epitomize these characteristics.

28. This methodological deficiency is not peculiar to Islamic legal thought. Following the natural law approach to rights in the Western tradition has led to similar confusion and arbitrariness in deriving rights principles. A treatise on human rights, in a discussion of the Western natural rights tradition, one in which rights are derived "from postulated norms achieved by techniques such as the revelation of divine will," concludes that "the abiding difficulty with the natural law approach is that its assumptions, intellectual procedures, and modalities of justification can be employed equally by the proponents of human dignity and the proponents of human indignity in support of diametrically opposed empirical specifications of rights." McDougal, Lasswell, and Chen, *Human Rights and World Order,* 70–71.

29. A. K. Brohi, "The Nature of Islamic Law and the Concept of Human Rights," in International Commission of Jurists, Kuwait University, and Union of Arab Lawyers, *Human Rights in Islam, Report of a Seminar Held in Kuwait, December 1980* (International Commission of Jurists, 1982), 43–60.

30. A. K. Brohi, "Islam and Human Rights," *PLD Lahore* 28 (1976), 148–60.

31. A. K. Brohi, "The Nature of Islamic Law and the Concept of Human Rights," *PLD Journal* 1983, 143–76.

32. Brohi, "The Nature of Islamic Law" (Kuwait seminar), 48.

33. Brohi, "Islam and Human Rights," 150.

34. Ibid., 151.

35. Ibid, 152.

36. Ibid., 159.

37. Abdul Aziz Said, "Precept and Practice of Human Rights in Islam," *Universal Human Rights* 1 (1979), 73.

38. Ibid., 74.

39. Ibid., 77.

40. M. F. al-Nabhan, "The Learned Academy of Islamic Jurisprudence," *Arab Law Quarterly* 1 (1986), 391–92. The article was originally published in the Kuwaiti magazine *al-'Arabi* in October 1983.

41. Taymour Kamel, "The Principle of Legality and Its Application in Islamic Criminal Justice," in *The Islamic Criminal Justice System,* Cherif Bassiouni, ed. (New York: Praeger, 1982), 169.

42. Cherif Bassiouni, "Sources of Islamic Law and the Protection of Human Rights," in *The Islamic Criminal Justice System,* 13–14.

43. Ibid., 23.

44. This failure to accord significance to the question of the rights of the individual vis-à-vis the state has a counterpart in the *shari'a* classification of rights in only two categories, those of the rights of God (to obedience from Muslims), *huquq Allah,* and the rights of the slaves (of God), or *huquq 'ibad.* The latter are rights that give individuals legal claims against other individuals. Coulson, *The State and the Individual in Islamic Law,* 50.

45. Abu'l A'la Mawdudi, *The Islamic Law and Constitution* (Lahore: Islamic Publications, 1980), 252. The original, in a more accurate translation, reads: "Hearing and obeying are the duty of a Muslim man both regarding what he likes and what he dislikes." *Mishkat Al-Masabih,* English Translation with Explanatory Notes, James Tobson, trans. (Lahore: Muhammad Ashraf, 1963), vol. 2, 780.

46. Jack Donnelly, "Human Rights as Natural Rights," *Human Rights Quarterly* 4 (1982), 391.

47. Mawdudi, *Human Rights,* 24.

48. Ibid., 24–25.

49. Ibid., 36.

50. Article 14, Azhar draft constitution.

51. Mawdudi, *Human Rights,* 37.

52. It is not unheard of, but highly unusual, to claim that the dead have human rights. If one adopted the view, based on a coherent philosophical approach, that the dead have human rights, one would be likely to propose other rights as well. See Raymond Belliotti, "Do Dead Human Beings Have Rights?" *Personalist* 60 (1979), 201–10.

53. Article 1.b, UIDHR.

54. Mawdudi, *Human Rights,* 18.

55. Ibid., 38.

56. Mawdudi, *Human Rights,* 22.

57. Article 14, UIDHR, Arabic version.

58. Mawdudi, *Human Rights*, 36.
59. Ibid., 17.
60. Ibid., 18.
61. Article 20.e, UIDHR.

Chapter 4

1. Rosalyn Higgins, "Derogations Under Human Rights Treaties," *British Yearbook of International Law* 48 (1976–77), 281.

2. Myres McDougal, Harold Lasswell, and Lung-chu Chen, "The Aggregate Interest in Shared Respect and Human Rights: The Harmonization of Public Order and Civic Order," *New York Law School Law Review* 23 (1977–1978), 183.

3. Ibid., 201–02.

4. Ibid., 202.

5. UDHR, Articles 1, 7, 10, and 16, respectively.

6. UDHR Article 17 and ICCPR Article 18.

7. UDHR Article 23 and ICESC Article 6.

8. UDHR Article 19, 20, and 21, respectively.

9. ICCPR Article 19, 21, 22, and 25, respectively.

10. ICCPR Articles 6 and 9, respectively.

11. Yves Linant de Bellefonds, *Traité de droit musulman comparé, Vol. 1, Théorie de l'acte juridique* (Paris: Mouton, 1965), 18–50; Noel Coulson, *A History of Islamic Law* (Edinburgh: Edinburgh University Press, 1964), 21–119. There is a large literature on this subject written by Islamic jurists from a very early period in Islamic legal history on.

12. The products of Islamic reformist thought are assessed in many studies, including Malcolm Kerr, *Islamic Reform* (Berkeley: University of California Press, 1966); Charles Adams, *Islam and Modernism in Egypt: A Study of the Modern Reform Movement Inaugurated by Muhammad Abduh* (New York: Russell & Russell, 1968); Aziz Ahmad, *Islamic Modernism in India and Pakistan, 1857–1964* (London: Oxford University Press, 1967).

13. Some treatments of more recent trends in Islamic thought and the ideologized versions of Islam that have emerged are Ali Dessouki [Dassuqi], ed., *Islamic Resurgence in the Arab World* (New York: Praeger, 1982); Michael Curtis, ed., *Religion and Politics in the Middle East* (Boulder, Colo.: Westview Press, 1981); James Piscatori, ed., *Islam in the Political Process* (New York: Cambridge University Press, 1983); John Esposito, ed., *Voices of Resurgent Islam* (New York: Oxford University Press, 1983); Nikki Keddie and Juan Cole, eds., *Shi'ism and Social Protest* (New Haven: Yale University Press, 1986); Emmanuel Sivan, *Radical Islam: Medieval Theology and Modern Politics* (New Haven: Yale University Press, 1985).

14. See Abdul-Hadi Hairi, *Shi'ism and Constitutionalism in Iran* (Leiden: Brill, 1977), which gives many examples of the objections raised by *'ulama* to the proposed constitution.

15. One eyewitness to a religious demonstration against the proposed constitution reported that religious students chanted, "We do not want liberty," and "We do not want a constitution," while a mullah proclaimed that merciful Allah could pardon drinking wine, gambling, adultery, murder, and every form of crime, but constitutionalists were to be killed in as great numbers as possible, egging on his followers to beat two constitutionalists to death. The naked mangled bodies of the constitutionalists were then displayed. Ibid., 218.

16. The phenomenon of *'ulama* misconstruing the purport of Western freedoms is examined in many parts of Hairi's book. A good example is the explanation that one religious scholar gave for supporting freedom of speech and freedom of the press. He seems to have understood this freedom to mean that writers and religious orators would be allowed to familiarize people with the truth regarding freedom in accordance with the *sunna* and the Qur'anic verse 16:125, "Call unto the way of thy Lord with wisdom and fair exhortation and reason with them in the better way." Ibid., 219.

17. Article 15 allowed persons to be dispossessed of property in cases where religious law authorized it. Although this could be read as a religious restriction on the right of private ownership, the traditional clerical interpretations of the *shari'a* afforded great protections for private property. Here, the "Islamic" grounds for interfering with the right would have been interpreted very narrowly, probably more narrowly than in many secular legal systems.

18. Shaul Bakhash, *The Reign of the Ayatollahs* (New York: Basic Books, 1984), 77.

19. Ibid., 78.

20. Ibid.

21. *Qavanin* (pl. of *qanun*) would normally refer to secular laws. However, with the modification by the adjective "Islamic," as here, *qavanin* seems to mean "Islamic principles." This application of the term contrasts with the use of *qavanin* in Article 4, where the reference can only be to secular law, since there it is stated that laws, *qavanin*, should be based on (and qualified by) "Islamic principles," *mavazin-e eslami*. In the context of Article 4, *qavanin* must logically refer to secular laws, since interpreting *qavanin* in that article to refer to Islamic law would result in the provision that Islamic principles should be based on Islamic principles.

22. For discussions of the political clampdown and the widespread rights abuses that followed the brief era of freedom after the shah's overthrow, the sources already cited on Iran's record of rights violations may be consulted. The annual reports of Amnesty International are particularly informative. One sees patterns of discrimination against women and minorities and even the active persecution of women and non-Muslims that are justified by the regime's version of Islam, and those who oppose the official religio-political line have suffered severe repression in the name of protecting Islam and the Islamic government from its enemies. The best jobs are reserved for male Muslims— and, then, only if they are deemed to be supportive of the regime. Freedom of expression and the press has been sharply curbed, and criticism of the government has led to criminal prosecution, protracted imprisonment, torture,

and even death. Perhaps the most dramatic illustration of the lack of freedom was seen in what happened to President Abolhassan Bani Sadr after he fell out with the ruling clique of conservative clerics in 1981. Despite the fact that he was then the president of the country and possessed of an overwhelming electoral mandate, his own newspaper was shut down and attempts were launched to arrest and prosecute him; these were thwarted only by his secret flight to the West, where he has been forced to live in exile. The many political parties that flourished in the immediate aftermath of the revolution were crushed after they opposed the policies of the dominant clerical faction. Public demonstrations of dissent or gatherings by opponents of the regime are no longer tolerated. The patterns of political repression have persisted, and recent developments are reported in *Iran. Violations of Human Rights, 1987–1990* (New York: Amnesty International, 1990).

23. An excellent illustration of how under Khomeini political expediency could override any concern for fidelity to *shari'a* law can be seen in the regime's support of the storming of the U.S. Embassy in Tehran and the taking of diplomats as hostages, measures in flagrant contravention of Shi'i law. For a learned discussion of the background of this case, see Roy Mottahedeh, "Iran's Foreign Devils," *Foreign Affairs* 38 (1980), 19–34. Later it became even more obvious that under Khomeini, raison d'Etat (political considerations) could overrride tenets of Islamic law. Ayatollah Khomeini stated on January 7, 1988, that his government was free to undertake any actions that it deemed in the interests of Islam. The statement is reported in FBIS-NES-88-004, January 7, 1988, 49–50. In his statement he claimed that Iran's Islamic government was among the most important divine institutions and had priority over such secondary institutions as prayers, fasting, and the pilgrimage—even though the latter are conventionally seen as fundamental pillars of the Islamic faith.

Khomeini's command on February 14, 1989, that Salman Rushdie, a British citizen living in Britain, be executed for apostasy, without his being brought to trial, with no opportunity for him to present a defense, and without allowing him any opportunity to repent showed a similar disregard for *shari'a* criteria of legality. I made this point in Ann Mayer, "Islam and the State," *Cardozo Law Review* 12 (1990), 1024–26. The Rushdie case is discussed in Chapter 8 as well.

24. Examples of the problems of translating the UIDHR can be seen in two attempts to provide literal translations of the Arabic version into English and French, which have resulted in inconsistent interpretations of important passages. *IslamoChristiana* 9 (1983), 103–20 (English), and 121–40 (French).

25. In the pamphlet version of the UIDHR in English published by the Islamic Council, these notes are placed on page 16 after the rights provisions.

26. It will be recalled that the Islamic qualifications included in Iranian constitutional rights provisions were similarly vague and open-ended.

27. In the Arabic counterpart of this article, one discovers that the article actually offers a "right" to propagate Islam.

28. *Al-intiqal* in the Arabic, but translated into English as "transfer."

29. See for example, Abu'l A'la Mawdudi, *Purdah and the Status of Women in Islam* (Lahore: Islamic Publications, 1979), 145–47, 200–09.

30. Sultanhussein Tabandeh, *A Muslim Commentary on the Universal Declaration of Human Rights,* F. J. Goulding, trans. (Guildford: F. J. Goulding, 1970), 20.

31. This position correlates with standards set in anti-Ahmadi legislation enacted in 1984 by the Zia government in Pakistan. The treatment of Pakistan's Ahmadi minority will be discussed in Chapter 8.

32. Tabandeh, *A Muslim Commentary,* 73.

33. Abu'l A'la Mawdudi, *Human Rights in Islam* (Leicester: Islamic Foundation, 1980), 28–29.

Chapter 5

1. A summary of the rules on personal status can be found in Joseph Schacht, *Introduction to Islamic Law* (Oxford: Clarendon Press, 1964), 24–33. A survey of sources dealing with inequality can be found in Ann Mayer, "Stratification, Authority and Justice in the Law of the Islamic Middle East," *BRISMES Bulletin* 4 (1977), 82–91, and 5 (1978), 3–19.

2. An example would be the condemnation of the principle of equality in the supplement to the first Iranian Constitution, signed by a number of prominent Shi'i clerics. Abdul-Hadi Hairi, *Shi'ism and Constitutionalism in Iran* (Leiden: Brill, 1977), 221–22, 232–33.

3. Abu'l A'la Mawdudi, *Human Rights in Islam* (Leicester: Islamic Publications, 1980), 28–29.

4. Ibid., 21.

5. Ibid., 32.

6. Jacobus Ten Broek, *The Antislavery Origins of the Fourteenth Amendment* (Berkeley: University of California Press, 1951).

7. For a discussion of this, see Oscar Garibaldi, "General Limitations on Human Rights: The Principle of Legality," *Harvard International Law Journal* 17 (1976), 525–26.

8. Illuminating descriptions of some aspects of early Muslim reactions to and interpretations of the principle of equality and equality before the law are in Hairi, *Shi'ism and Constitutionalism,* 224–34.

9. This was the interpretation of Na'ini, a leading Shi'i cleric, who supported the Iranian constitutionalist movement and endeavored to show that constitutional rights accorded with Islam. Ibid., 224.

10. For example, the Prophet is quoted as saying that there can be no superiority of the Arab over the non-Arab, of the red (meaning "white" in contemporary U.S. usage) over the black, of the black over the red save in piety, and the Prophet is quoted as saying that if his own daughter stole, her hand would be cut off like that of any other thief.

11. Nuri was active in organizing the revolutionary committees and the Revolutionary Guards, in the debates over the postrevolutionary constitution, and in the Majles after the revolution. This information was kindly provided by Hamid Algar.

12. Yahya Noori [Nuri], "The Islamic Concept of State," *Hamdard Islamicus* 3 (1980), 78.

13. Ibid., 83.

14. Ibid., 70–80.

15. One should not assume that cultural differences make Orwell's ideas inaccessible to Iranians or Muslims generally, or that they cannot perceive the inconsistencies and contradictions in Islamic rights formulations. A particularly interesting indication of the fact that Iranians perceive the relevance of Orwell's work to their current circumstances is the enormous popularity that Orwell's works have enjoyed in Iran since the clergy established their domination of political life. It seems not to be a coincidence that by 1984 a Persian translation of Orwell's *Animal Farm* had become one of Iran's best-selling books and George Orwell Iran's single best-selling author. "Book Boom in Tehran," *Index on Censorship,* October 1984, 9.

16. The texts cited are 3:64, "None of us shall take others for lords beside Allah," and 49:13, "We have created you male and female." These are not texts that were historically interpreted to mandate full legal equality—nor does Tabandeh, in his critique of the UDHR, interpret them to establish an Islamic principle of nondiscriminatory treatment of women and non-Muslims.

17. Sultanhussein Tabandeh, *A Muslim Commentary on the Universal Declaration of Human Rights,* F. J. Goulding, trans. (Guildford: F. J. Goulding, 1970), 15.

18. Ibid., 19.

19. Ibid., 20.

20. Because the Arabic and English categories of grounds on the basis of which it is impermissible to discriminate do not correspond and because the English translation is obviously only a very rough approximation of the Arabic, the English cannot be used to clarify the meaning of the particularly ambiguous terms *jins* and *'irq,* which potentially have overlapping meanings. At best, one could presume that in order to avoid redundancy, if *'irq* is taken to mean "race," *jins* should be taken to have some other meaning. The antidiscrimination language in the Preamble of the UIDHR is also not helpful in deciphering the precise meanings of the terms because of a lack of parallelism between the language it uses and that in Article 3.b. For example, the Preamble states that there can be no discrimination based on *asl* (origin or descent), *'unsur* (origin, race, or ethnic status), *jins* (the ambiguity of which has just been noted), color, language, or religion. Because other provisions of the UIDHR mandate sex-based discrimination, reading *jins* in Article 3.b to mean "sex," which would ordinarily be perfectly natural, entails internal inconsistencies in the UIDHR. To avoid such internal inconsistencies, one would tend to assume that *jins* should be assigned a meaning other than "sex." However, when one takes into account the frequent inconsistencies in the Islamic human rights literature, one cannot be sure that the authors of the UIDHR would have been troubled by including provisions barring sex-based discrimination and others mandating such discrimination.

21. *Ansar Burney v. Federation of Pakistan, PLD FSC,* 1983, 73.

22. Ibid., 93.

23. It is interesting to contrast the result of this Pakistani case with the law enforced in Iran after the Islamic Revolution that women must be excluded not just from the judiciary but also from studying law under the version of Islamic law that has been propounded by Iran's Shi'i clerical rulers. This will be discussed in relation to the status of women (Chapter 6), but it is mentioned here as yet another illustration of the differences among contemporary Muslims about women's status in Islam.

24. This same Qur'anic command is included in Article 6 of the Azhar draft constitution and Article 8 of the Iranian Constitution, but without any connection being made between it and a right of association.

25. It does not seem accidental that the Western reader, who, in most cases will not be able to translate the Arabic, is being given a very dissimilar version of the article, one that makes it look much more like familiar international human rights concepts. One sees in this provision yet another example of a pervasive pattern of discrepancies between the Arabic and English versions of the UIDHR where issues of equality are involved.

Chapter 6

1. Fazlur Rahman, "The Status of Women in the Qur'an," in *Women and Revolution in Iran,* Guity Nashat, ed. (Boulder, Colo.: Westview Press, 1983), 38.

2. A summary of these changes can be found in J.N.D. Anderson, *Law Reform in the Muslim World* (London: Athlone, 1976). See also Tahir Mahmood, *Personal Law in Islamic Countries* (New Delhi: Academy of Law and Religions, 1987).

3. See current discussions of these materials in Nawal El Saadawi, "Women and Islam," in *Women and Islam,* Azizah al-Hibri, ed. (Oxford: Pergamon Press), 194–202; Azizah al-Hibri, "A Study of Islamic Herstory," in ibid., 207–14; Naila Minai, *Women in Islam: Tradition and Transition in the Middle East* (New York: Seaview, 1981), 1–24; Jane Smith, "Women, Religion and Social Change in Early Islam," in *Women, Religion, and Social Change,* Yvonne Haddad and Ellison Findley, eds. (Albany: SUNY Press, 1985), 19–35.

4. al-Hibri, "A Study of Islamic Herstory," 207.

5. Rahman, "The Status of Women in the Qur'an," 37.

6. See the examination of disparities between the original sources and later interpretations in Barbara Stowasser, "The Status of Women in Early Islam," in *Muslim Women,* Freda Hussain, ed. (New York: St Martin's Press, 1984), 11–43.

7. Introductions to aspects of women's status in the *shari'a* can be found in Joseph Schacht, *Introduction to Islamic Law* (Oxford: Clarendon Press, 1964), 126–27; Yves Linant de Bellefonds, *Traité de droit musulman comparé, Vol. 2, Le Mariage. La Dissolution du mariage* (Paris: Mouton, 1965); Noel Coulson, *Succession in the Muslim Family* (Cambridge: Cambridge University Press, 1971); Jamal Nasir, *The Islamic Law of Personal Status* (London: Graham and

Trotman, 1986); Ghassan Ascha, *Du Statut inférieur de la femme en Islam* (Paris: L'Harmattan, 1987).

8. These developments are summarized in Anderson, *Law Reform in the Muslim World.*

9. A perfect embodiment of this response can be found in Abu'l A'la Mawdudi, *Purdah and the Status of Women in Islam* (Lahore: Islamic Publications, 1981). Many aspects of this literature are reviewed by Ascha, *Du Statut inférieur de la femme en Islam.*

10. Examples of the kinds of curbs on women's rights that are being proposed by conservatives in the name of "Islam" abound in Pakistan. See Khawar Mumtaz and Farida Shaheed, *Women of Pakistan. Two Steps Forward, One Step Back* (London: Zed, 1987), 77–122; Anita Weiss, "Implications of the Islamization Program for Women," in *Islamic Reassertion in Pakistan,* Anita Weiss, ed. (Syracuse: Syracuse University Press, 1986), 97–114.

11. See his comments in Abdullahi El-Naiem, "A Modern Approach to Human Rights in Islam: Foundations and Implications for Africa," in *Human Rights and Development in Africa,* Claude Welch, Jr., and Ronald Meltzer, eds. (Albany: SUNY Press, 1984), 82.

12. The feminist literature is currently burgeoning. Examples of what is currently being written can be seen in Freda Hussain and Kamelia Radwan, "The Islamic Revolution and Women: The Quest for the Qur'anic Model," in *Muslim Women,* Hussain, ed., 44–70; al-Hibri, "A Study of Islamic Herstory"; Fatna Sabbah [pseud.], *Women in the Muslim Unconscious* (New York: Pergamon, 1984); Fatima Mernissi, *Beyond the Veil* (New York: John Wiley, 1975); Farah Azari, *Women of Iran: The Conflict with Fundamentalist Islam* (London: Ithaca Press, 1983); Rashida Patel, *Women and the Law in Pakistan* (Karachi: Faiza Publications, 1979); Nashat, *Women and Revolution in Iran.*

13. This is a consistent theme of Mawdudi's writings. For an example of his arguments, see Mawdudi, *Purdah and the Status of Women,* 21–24.

14. Ibid., 24.

15. Ibid., 73–74.

16. One sign of this might be seen in the actual patterns of personal status–law reform and constitutional guarantees of women's rights in Muslim countries. Only Saudi Arabia maintains the premodern juristic rules unaltered, and only Turkey has entirely abandoned them to accord women equal legal rights. In all other Muslim countries the choice has been to compromise, keeping elements of the *shari'a* system of personal status but including many reforms improving the rights of women. See Anderson, *Law Reform in the Muslim World.*

17. Sultanhussein Tabandeh, *A Muslim Commentary on the Universal Declaration of Human Rights,* F. J. Goulding, trans. (Guildford: F. J. Goulding, 1970), 1.

18. See for example his comments on Article 16 of the UDHR, ibid., 41–45.

19. Ibid., 35.

20. Ibid., 41–45.

21. Ibid., 37–38.

22. Ibid., 38–39.

23. Ibid., 40.

24. Ibid., 58.

25. Ibid., 51.

26. Ibid., 57. The alliteration here, it should be recalled, is that of Tabandeh's translator.

27. Ibid., 52.

28. Abu'l A'la Mawdudi, *The Islamic Law and Constitution* (Lahore: Islamic Publications, 1980), 262–63; and *Purdah and the Status of Women in Islam,* passim, and on divorce, 151.

29. Ibid., 12.

30. Ibid., 12–15, 26–71.

31. Ibid., 15.

32. Ibid., 73.

33. Abu'l A'la Mawdudi, *Human Rights in Islam* (Leicester: Islamic Foundation, 1980), 18.

34. Ibid.

35. Indeed, restrictions on women's testimony in the *shari'a* rules of evidence can make it more difficult for a woman to prove such an offense and obtain the conviction of the offender because two female witnesses may be required or, in the cases of *hadd* crimes (those for which the penalty is set or implied in the text of the Qur'an), the testimony of women witnesses may be barred altogether.

36. The systematically conducted mass rape of Bengali women, perpetrated by soldiers who were largely from the Punjab in West Pakistan, attracted international attention and opprobrium. Prominent among those publicizing the sufferings of the victims was Germaine Greer. The effects of the rape were particularly traumatic and harsh because, due to the local concept of female honor, Bengali women became outcasts in their own societies after being raped, even though they were in no way to blame for their predicament. The lives of untold numbers of innocent women were ruined because they were deemed to have been defiled by the acts of their rapists, and the fate of those impregnated by the rapes was particularly deplorable. Naturally, in India, Pakistan's enemy, the sordid details of these incidents were publicized. See for example Amita Malik, *The Year of the Vulture* (New Delhi: Orient Longman, 1972).

37. According to the Preface, Mawdudi's human rights pamphlet is translated from a speech delivered on November 16, 1975, at the Civil Rights and Liberties Forum in the Flatties Hotel in Lahore. Mawdudi, *Human Rights,* 7.

38. This is because according to the choice-of-law rules in Islam and in the law of Muslim countries, Islamic criteria are used to judge the validity of a mixed marriage. The fact that the religious law of the husband allows such a marriage is treated as irrelevant. Relevant Islamic choice-of-law rules are discussed in Klaus Wähler, *Interreligiöses Kollisionsrecht im Bereich privatrechtlicher Rechtsbeziehungen* (Cologne: Carl Heymanns Verlag, 1978), 157–58. Muslim conservatives today share the view that the validity of a mixed marriage is to be judged under *shari'a* rules. See Mawdudi, *The Islamic Law and*

Constitution, 287. It is also a rule of public policy applied in Muslim countries even where the law does not ban such marriages. Nasir, *The Islamic Law of Personal Status,* 63–64.

39. Examples of such rules are discussed in Nasir, *The Islamic Law of Personal Status,* 56–58, 64.

40. These references are on p. 19 of the English version.

41. For example, see Mawdudi's invocation of this verse in his book *Purdah and the Status of Women,* 149.

42. Yves Linant de Bellefonds, *Traité de droit musulman comparé. Vol. 3. Filiation. Incapacités, liberalités entre vifs* (Paris: Mouton, 1965), 81–142.

43. In theory, the guardian could also marry off a male ward without his consent, but because of the ease with which a Muslim man could terminate an unwanted marriage, this had little practical effect or significance.

44. Public debate on this topic may be repressed. The extent of the phenomenon of forced marriages in contemporary Algeria, the sufferings of women compelled to marry against their wills, and the difficulties a Muslim feminist experienced in maintaining an open discussion of women's reactions to forced marriages are a topic in Fadela M'Rabet, *La Femme Algérienne Suivi de les Algériennes* (Paris: Maspero, 1969), 143–65.

45. Nasir, *The Islamic Law of Personal Status,* 46–48.

46. Some of the legal reforms that have been made in response to this problem are indicated in ibid., 117, 130–31.

47. See, for example, Mawdudi, *Purdah and the Status of Women,* 144–55.

48. Noel Coulson, *Succession in the Muslim Family* (Cambridge: Cambridge University Press, 1971), 214.

49. Linant de Bellefonds, *Traité de jurisprudence musulman comparé. Vol. 2,* 451–70.

50. Ibid.

51. Doreen Hinchcliffe, "The Iranian Family Protection Act," *International and Comparative Law Quarterly* 17 (1968), 516–21; Eliz Sanasarian, *The Women's Rights Movement in Iran: Mutiny, Appeasement, and Repression from 1900 to Khomeini* (New York: Praeger, 1982), 94–97.

52. Sanasarian, *The Women's Rights Movement in Iran,* 136–37.

53. Shahla Haeri, "The Institution of Mut'a Marriage in Iran: A Formal and Historical Perspective," in *Women and Revolution in Iran,* Nashat, ed., 231–52.

54. General works on this topic include Nashat, ed., *Women and Revolution in Iran;* Azar Tabari and Nahid Yeganeh, eds., *In the Shadow of Islam: The Women's Movement in Iran* (London: Zed, 1982); Sanasarian, *The Women's Rights Movement in Iran;* Azari, *Women of Iran.*

55. The incident described here was widely reported in the world's press, including the *Herald* (Harare) and the *New York Times* on January 22, 1986.

56. "Sudan: Threat to Women's Status from Fundamentalist Regime," *News from Africa Watch,* April 9, 1990.

57. *The Meaning of the Glorious Qur'an,* Marmaduke Pickthall, trans. (Beirut: Dar al-kitab al-lubnani, 1971).

58. See, for example, Tabandeh, *A Muslim Commentary,* 51–52; Mawdudi, *Purdah and the Status of Women,* 185–201.

59. Aspects of the traditional Arab concept of female honor, or *'ird,* and its manipulation to secure male dominance have been studied in the anthropological literature on the Middle East. See, for example, Peter Dodd, "Family Honor and the Forces of Change in Arab Society," *International Journal of Middle Eastern Studies* 4 (1973), 40–54. A recent critique of mechanisms of oppression in Arab society that analyzes how the concept of *'ird* has been used to deny women their humanity and basic rights can be seen in Nawal El-Saadawi, *The Hidden Face of Eve: Women in the Arab World* (Boston: Beacon, 1981), 7–90.

60. For examples of what the Pakistani campaign against obscenity and indecency involved and the constraints it meant for women, see Mumtaz and Shahid, *Women of Pakistan,* 81–83.

61. Tabandeh, *A Muslim Commentary,* 39.

62. Ibid., 41

63. Ibid., 51.

64. Ibid., 52.

65. Mawdudi, *Purdah and the Status of Women in Islam,* 113–22.

66. Ibid., 120.

67. Ibid., 121–22.

68. Javad Bahonar, "Islam and Women's Rights," *al-Tawhid* 1 (1984), 160.

69. Ibid., 161.

70. Ibid., 165.

71. Ibid., 161.

72. Ibid., 164. Of course, since he was trying to show the Islamic treatment of women in a positive light, Bahonar neglected to mention that women in the Islamic inheritance scheme receive only one-half the share of a male inheriting in the same capacity.

73. Mary Daly, *The Church and the Second Sex* (Boston: Beacon, 1985), 85.

74. Ibid., 88.

75. Ibid., 154.

76. Ibid., 115.

77. Ibid.

78. Ibid., 164.

79. Ibid., 87.

Chapter 7

1. Herbert Liebesny, "The Development of Western Judicial Privileges," in *Law in the Middle East,* vol. 1, Majid Khadduri and Herbert Liebesny, eds. (Washington, D.C.: Middle East Institute, 1955), 309–33.

2. Peter Holt, *Egypt and the Fertile Crescent, 1516–1922* (Ithaca: Cornell University Press, 1966), 167–72.

3. For accounts of this relationship see generally ibid.; Bernard Lewis, *The Middle East and the West* (New York: Harper, 1964), and the sources cited

therein; and Elizabeth Monroe, *Britain's Moment in the Middle East, 1914–56* (Baltimore: Johns Hopkins University Press, 1981).

4. The theme that European rule was needed to ensure impartial, fair government and administration of justice and to protect minorities from oppression permeated Lord Cromer [Evelyn Baring], *Modern Egypt*, 2 vols. (New York: Macmillan, 1908), especially vol. 2, 123–259.

5. These are themes that pervade Ayatollah Khomeini's influential writings and speeches. See Imam [Ruhollah] Khomeini, *Islam and Revolution. Writings and Declarations of Imam Khomeini*, Hamid Algar, trans. (Berkeley: Mizan Press, 1981).

6. See in this connection the reactions of Khomeini to Western criticisms of Iran's human rights record in a pamphlet put out by the Islamic Propagation Organization on the occasion of the Sixth Islamic Thought Conference. The pamphlet is entitled *Iran: The Cry of Justice. A Collection of the Statements of Imam Khomeini on Human Rights*.

7. Egypt provides an apposite example of the challenge to the legitimacy of the modern state mounted by groups calling for Islamization. See Johannes Jansen, *The Neglected Duty: The Creed of Sadat's Assassins* (New York: Macmillan, 1986).

8. The circumstances of the early community are described in W. Montgomery Watt, *Muhammad, Prophet and Statesman* (Oxford: Oxford University Press, 1971).

9. For background see A. S. Tritton, *The Caliphs and Their Non-Muslim Subjects. A Critical Study of the Covenant of Umar* (London: Cass, 1970); Antoine Fattal, *Le Statut légal des non-Musulmans en pays d'Islam* (Beirut: Imprimerie Catholique, 1958).

10. The law of *jihad* is thoroughly discussed in Majid Khadduri, *War and Peace in the Law of Islam* (Baltimore: Johns Hopkins University Press, 1955).

11. The evolution of *jihad* doctrines has been treated in Rudolph Peters, *Islam and Colonialism. The Doctrine of Jihad in Modern History* (The Hague: Mouton, 1979). See also a discussion of recent developments in Ann Mayer, "War and Peace in the Islamic Tradition and in International Law," in James Johnson and John Kelsay, eds., *Just War and* Jihad: *War, Peace, and Statecraft in the Western and Islamic Traditions* (Westport, Conn.: Greenwood Press, forthcoming).

12. Zoroastrians and Sabeans are sometimes also included in this category.

13. A useful review of the rules pertaining to the status of *dhimmi*s is in Fattal, *Le Statut légal des non-musulmans en pays d'Islam*.

14. Joseph Schacht, *Introduction to Islamic Law* (Oxford: Clarendon Press, 1964), 130–31.

15. For a survey of how the Muslim community interracted with non-Muslims in the Subcontinent, see Ishtiaq Husain Qureshi, *The Muslim Community of the Indo-Pakistan Subcontinent, 610–1947. A Brief Historical Analysis* (The Hague: Mouton, 1962).

16. See, for example, the studies in Benjamin Braude and Bernard Lewis, eds., *Christians and Jews in the Ottoman Empire*, 2 vols. (New York: Holmes & Meier, 1982).

17. On the treatment of Jews see generally Bernard Lewis, *The Jews of Islam* (Princeton: Princeton University Press, 1984).

18. Introductions to some of the changes in attitudes brought about by nationalism can be found in Albert Hourani, *Arabic Thought in the Liberal Age, 1798–1939* (London: Oxford University Press, 1962); Bernard Lewis, *The Emergence of Modern Turkey* (London: Oxford, 1961).

19. The implications of Islamization programs for religious minorities are emphasized in P. J. Vatikiotis, *Islam and the State* (London: Croom Helm, 1987). See also Ishtiaq Ahmad, *The Concept of an Islamic State. An Analysis of the Ideological Controversy in Pakistan* (New York: St. Martin's Press, 1987).

20. Subhi Mahmassani, *Arkan huquq al-insan* (Beirut: Dar al-'ilm li'-malayin, 1979), 260–64, 281.

21. Ibid., 260–64.

22. This approach is characteristic of chapters in S. M. Haider, ed., *Islamic Concept of Human Rights* (Lahore: Book House, 1978). In his chapter in this work, "Equality Before Law and Equal Protection of Laws as Legal Doctrines for the Prevention of Discrimination and Protection of Minorities," 213–37, Haider unequivocally endorsed the principle of full equality for all citizens regardless of religion.

23. Al-Bishri's ideas are discussed in detail in Leonard Binder, *Islamic Liberalism* (Chicago: University of Chicago Press, 1988), 246–92.

24. Ibid., 287–88.

25. Abdullahi El-Naiem, "A Modern Approach to Human Rights in Islam: Foundations and Implications for Africa" in *Human Rights and Development in Africa,* Claude Welch, Jr., and Ronald Meltzer, eds. (Albany: SUNY Press, 1984), 85.

26. Abdullahi An-Na'im applied his Islamic human rights norms to critique the treatment of non-Muslims in Egypt in "Religious Freedom in Egypt: Under the Shadow of the Islamic *Dhimma* System," in *Religious Liberty and Human Rights in Nations and Religions,* Leonard Swidler, ed. (Philadelphia: Ecumenical Books, 1986), 43–59.

27. Sultanhussein Tabandeh, *A Muslim Commentary on the Universal Declaration of Human Rights,* F. J. Goulding, trans. (Guildford: F. J. Goulding, 1970), 15.

28. Ibid., 18.

29. Ibid., 15.

30. Ibid., 17.

31. Ibid., 36.

32. Ibid.

33. Ibid., 37.

34. Ibid.

35. Ibid., 70.

36. Ibid., 71.

37. Abu'l A'la Mawdudi, *Human Rights in Islam* (Leicester: Islamic Publications, 1980), 30. It would seem that he did not feel that this inhibition prevented him from attacking the "heretical" Ahmadis, even though their

"heretical" views should have qualified them as non-Muslims, whose feelings Mawdudi said, must be respected.

38. Without such standards it would, for example, be difficult to tell whether the Iranian government's harsh denunciations of Baha'is would be deemed to violate Article 12.e.

39. See, for example, Shaul Bakhash, *The Reign of the Ayatollahs* (New York: Basic Books, 1984), 226.

40. Abu'l A'la Mawdudi, *Islamic Law and Constitution* (Lahore: Islamic Publications, 1980), 188–89, 274–76.

41. This conclusion is further strengthened by a reading of the section of the Preamble to the constitution that deals with the army. It provides that the goal of the army is "accomplishing an ideological mission, that is, the 'Jihad' for the sake of God, as well as for struggling to open the way for the sovereignty of the Word of God throughout the world." That is, this is an army with the mission to engage in combat on behalf of the Islamic cause.

42. Roger Cooper, *The Baha'is of Iran*, Minority Rights Group Report 51 (London: Minority Rights Group, 1982), 7–8, 10.

43. Ibid., 11.

44. Cooper, *The Baha'is of Iran;* Douglas Martin, "The Persecution of the Baha'is of Iran, 1844–1984," *Baha'i Studies* 12/13 (1984); Amnesty International annual reports; Economic and Social Council Commission on Human Rights, *Report on the Human Rights Situation in the Islamic Republic of Iran by the Special Representative of the Commission, Mr. Reynaldo Galindo Pohl, Appointed Pursuant to Resolution 1986/41,* E/CN.4/1987/23.

45. Mawdudi, *Human Rights,* 21–22.

46. Mawdudi, *Islamic Law,* 288–91.

47. Ibid., 191–93.

48. Ibid., 297–98.

49. Ibid., 276.

50. Ibid., 287.

51. A fascinating record of materials on the 1953 disturbances and the theological, ideological, and political views of both the Ahmadis and their opponents, including Mawdudi and his Jama'at, can be seen in *Report of the Court of Inquiry Constituted Under Punjab Act II of 1954 to Enquire into the Punjab Disturbances of 1953* (Lahore: Superintendent, Government Printing, Punjab, 1954).

52. The ordinance and the human rights violations that ensued pursuant to its demotion of Ahmadis to the status of imposters wrongfully claiming to be Muslims are discussed in "Pakistan Ordinance XX of 1984. International Implications on Human Rights," *Loyola of Los Angeles International and Comparative Law Journal* 9 (1987), 661–92. There was even one prosecution of an Ahmadi for praying and meditating in the Islamic fashion in the privacy of the defendant's own home. Rashida Patel, *Islamisation of Laws in Pakistan?* (Karachi: Faiza, 1986), 126–27; Amnesty International, *Pakistan: Violations of Human Rights,* April 1985, 6–7; *Human Rights Internet Reporter* 10 (1985), 384.

53. *Mujeeb-ur-Rehman v. Federal Government of Pakistan, PLD FSC,* 1984, 136.

54. Still not appeased by the measures that have been taken against the Ahmadis, Muslim conservatives demanded that further discriminatory and repressive restrictions be imposed on the Ahmadi community. Disheartened, many Ahmadis became resigned to emigrating from Pakistan to escape the pattern of discrimination.

Chapter 8

1. Sami Aldeeb Abu Sahlieh, "Les Droits de l'homme et l'Islam," *Revue générale de droit international public* 89 (1985), 636–37.

2. John Kelsay, "Saudi Arabia, Pakistan, and the Universal Declaration of Human Rights," in David Little, John Kelsay, and Abdulaziz Sachedina, *Human Rights and the Conflict of Culture: Western and Islamic Perspectives on Religious Liberty* (Columbia: University of South Carolina Press, 1988), 35–37.

3. Abu Sahlieh, *Les droits de l'homme et l'Islam,* 637.

4. These patterns are surveyed in Ann Mayer, "Law and Religion in the Muslim Middle East," *American Journal of Comparative Law* 35 (1987), 143–47.

5. For example, a Roman Catholic male, who was unable to divorce his wife under the rules of his faith, could change the applicable personal status rules by converting to Islam, where, under the premodern rules, the husband has an unfettered right to divorce. However, if he wished subsequently to return to his original faith, this would constitute apostasy from Islam.

6. Sultanhussein Tabandeh, *A Muslim Commentary on the Universal Declaration of Human Rights,* F. J. Goulding, trans. (Guildford: F. J. Goulding, 1970), 71.

7. Ibid., 59.

8. The author's translation of a French translation from the Arabic offered in Sami Aldeeb Abu Sahlieh, "Liberté religieuse et apostasie dans l'Islam," *Praxis juridique et religion* 23 (1986), 53.

9. Abu Sahlieh, "Liberté religieuse," 61–66.

10. Abu Sahlieh, "Les droits de l'homme et l'Islam," 644.

11. Abdulaziz Sachedina, "Freedom of Conscience and Religion in the Qur'an," in Little, Kelsay, and Sachedina, *Human Rights and the Conflicts of Culture: Western and Islamic Perspectives on Religious Liberty,* 53–90.

12. Subhi Mahmassani, *Arkan huquq al-insan* (Beirut: Dar al-'ilm li'l-malayin, 1979), 123–24.

13. Majid Khadduri, *The Islamic Conception of Justice* (Baltimore: Johns Hopkins University Press, 1984), 238.

14. Stefan Wild, "Gott und Mensch im Libanon," *Der Islam* 28 (1972), 242.

15. Tabandeh, *A Muslim Commentary,* 70.

16. Ibid., 71.

17. Ibid., 70–71.

18. Ibid., 71.

19. Ibid.

20. Ibid., 71–72. One can find similar defenses being offered by an Egyptian author for the application of the death penalty for apostasy. These are discussed in Abu Sahlieh, "Les droits de l'homme et l'Islam," 643–44.

21. Tabandeh, *A Muslim Commentary,* 72.

22. Ibid., 72–73.

23. Ibid., 59.

24. Ibid., 72.

25. It should be recalled that his intended audience consisted of persons attending an international human rights conference in Iran.

26. J. Roland Pennock, "Rights, Natural Rights, and Human Rights—A General View," in *Human Rights: NOMOS* 23, J. Roland Pennock and John Chapman, eds. (New York: New York University Press, 1981), 14.

27. The meaning of the phrase *takhdhil li'l-umma* is obscure. A related verb with the same root occurs in the Qur'an (3:160) in the sense of "forsake." However, the verbal noun *takhdhil* seems to mean something like incitement to neglect to aid companions or to be cowardly and weakhearted. Although one can predict that the prohibited speech targeted here would encourage something harmful to the Islamic community, just what could constitute this *takhdhil* is open to speculation.

28. An indication of how confusing this provision is can be seen in a protest that was made by the International Commission of Jurists (ICJ) over the 1985 execution of Mahmud Muhammad Taha as an apostate, an event that will be discussed in this chapter. The ICJ invoked the UIDHR provision on freedom of religion. *Human Rights Internet Reporter* 10, January–April 1985, 359. This was apparently in the mistaken belief that the UIDHR outlawed executions for apostasy. In fact, it has been drafted in such a way as to accommodate the application of premodern *shari'a* rules, including the imposition of the death penalty for apostasy.

29. *Report of the Court of Inquiry Constituted Under Punjab Act II of 1954 to Enquire into the Punjab Disturbances of 1953* (Lahore: Superintendent, Government Printing, Punjab, 1954), 218.

30. Roger Cooper, *The Baha'is of Iran,* Minority Rights Group Report 51 (London, Minority Rights Group, 1982), 13–15; Douglas Martin, "The Persecution of the Baha'is of Iran, 1844–1984," *Baha'i Studies* 12/13 (1984), 49, 54–56, 58, 65.

31. Martin, "The Persecution of the Baha'is," 54.

32. Cooper, "The Baha'is of Iran," 13–14; Economic and Social Council, *Report on the Human Rights Situation in the Islamic Republic of Iran,* E/CN.4/1987/20 (January 28, 1987), 20.

33. Economic and Social Council, "Report on the Human Rights Situation," 21.

34. The statements were discussed in front page articles in the *New York Times,* February 15 and 20, 1989.

35. Various representative reactions and comments, largely from Muslims, can be found in *Index on Censorship,* May 1989, 7–18. Responses to the order

to kill Rushdie are also discussed in *The Rushdie File,* Lisa Appignanesi and Sara Maitland, eds. (Syracuse: Syracuse University Press, 1990).

36. *The Rushdie File,* Appignanesi and Maitland, eds., 126–27.

37. In connection with the Rushdie affair it was noteworthy that the Islamic Council, which had produced the UIDHR, did not intervene on the public debates to insist that the principles of freedom of religion or freedom of speech would be violated by killing Rushdie, who himself had been an outspoken advocate of human rights and critic of governmental rights violations.

38. His views are set forth in a book that was recently translated by Professor Abdullahi Ahmed An-Na'im, *The Second Message of Islam by Ustadh Mahmoud Mohamed Taha* (Syracuse: Syracuse University Press, 1987).

39. Abu Sahlieh, "Liberté religieuse," 51.

40. This observation is based on the author's personal experiences in Khartoum in December 1984–January 1985.

41. Abdullahi An-Na'im, "The Islamic Law of Apostasy and Its Modern Applicability. A Case from the Sudan," *Religion* 16 (1986), 207.

42. BBC SWB ME/7714/A/10 (August 6, 1984).

43. A valuable discussion of this case can be found in An-Na'im, "The Islamic Law of Apostasy," 197.

44. Ibid., 209. It is significant for purposes of this study to note that the Muslim World League is the parent organization of the Islamic Council, which sponsored and published the UIDHR. According to one account, the Muslim World League actually congratulated Nimeiri for executing Taha. Abu Sahlieh, "Les droits de l'homme et l'Islam," 707.

45. BBC SWB ME/7853/A/1 (January 19, 1985).

46. Ibid.

47. Ibid.

48. These comments are based on a wide range of interviews conducted by the author in Khartoum in the summer of 1985.

Chapter 9

1. See the thorough examination of this phenomenon in Roger Bastide, *The African Religions of Brazil: Toward a Sociology of the Interpetration of Civilizations,* Helen Sabba, trans. (Baltimore: Johns Hopkins University Press, 1978).

2. These results were not duplicated in the elections in Pakistan in October 1990, but it is difficult to read the outcome of that vote. In the 1990 election, Bhutto's party got only 45 seats to the 105 won by the eight-party coalition known as the Islamic Democratic Alliance, and of the men contending for the prime ministership, the one chosen was a former ally of President Zia's, Nawaz Sharif. The relatively poor performance of Benazir Bhutto may have been due in part to her failure to live up to her campaign promises to repeal Zia's Islamization measures, but it seems that the main cause for voter disillusionment was the combination of her weak leadership and the rumors of the network of corruption that allegedly surrounded her. Her electoral performance

was also not helped by her having been dismissed from office in August by the president, ostensibly for nepotism and corruption, and then being denied an opportunity to defend herself in court, since she was not tried on the charges prior to the election.

3. Soundings by a researcher in an Iranian village have indicated that the reaction of at least some villagers has been very negative to repressive clerical rule. See Reinhold Loeffler, *Islam in Practice: Religious Beliefs in a Persian Village* (Albany: State University of New York Press, 1988).

4. *Iran. Violations of Human Rights, 1987–1990* (New York: Amnesty International, 1990), 38–39.

5. The record of the military dictatorship of General Omar Bashir is reviewed in *Denying "the Honour of Living." Sudan. A Human Rights Disaster, An Africa Watch Report* (New York: Africa Watch Committee, March 1990). Titles of other reports include: *Sudan: Destruction of the Independent Secular Judiciary; Military Government Clamps Down on Press Freedom* (September 25, 1989); *Political Detainees in the Sudan* (October 24, 1989); *Sudan: Khartoum: Government to Execute Striking Doctors. The Provinces: Militia Killings and Starvation Policy Return* (December 6, 1989); *Sudan: Recent Developments in Khartoum, an Update* (December 13, 1989); *Political Detainees in Sudan: Academics* (January 22, 1990); *Sudan: The Massacre at el Jebelein* (January 23, 1990).

6. Sultanhussein Tabandeh, *A Muslim Commentary on the Universal Declaration of Human Rights,* F. J. Goulding, trans. (Guildford: F. J. Goulding, 1970), 57. This position was echoed in comments by Khomeini. After denouncing Muslims who wanted to Westernize everything and after condemning Western human rights advocates for their hypocrisy, Khomeini railed against the idea that Muslims should measure Islam "in accordance with Western criteria." Instead, he argued, Muslims should be loyal to Islam. Imam [Ruhollah] Khomeini, *Islam and Revolution. Writings and Declarations of Imam Khomeini,* Hamid Algar, trans. (Berkeley: Mizan Press, 1981), 270–72.

7. The issues discussed here are not, of course, unique to the Muslim world. They relate to the search for cultural identity going on in many Third World societies. A valuable study of the problems of establishing cultural identity in dependent countries is Borhan Ghalioun, "Identité, culture et politique culturelle dans les pays dépendants," *Peuples Méditerranéens* 16 (1981), 31–50.

8. Abu'l A'la Mawdudi, in *Purdah and the Status of Women in Islam* (Lahore: Islamic Publications, 1979), cited figures such as "Judge Ben Lindsey, President of the Juvenile Court of Denver," 59, "Dr. Kraft Ebing [sic]," 116, and "Wester Marck [sic]," 127, to show that there is a scientific justification for *shari'a* rules. Even statements in the popular U.S. monthly *Reader's Digest* are deemed worthy of citation to establish that *shari'a* rules are correct. See 45.

9. Tabandeh, *A Muslim Commentary,* 51.

10. International Commission of Jurists, Kuwait University, and Union of Arab Lawyers, *Human Rights in Islam. Report of a Seminar Held in Kuwait, December 1980* (International Commission of Jurists, 1982), 9. See also remarks on 11 and 34.

11. A. K. Brohi, "The Nature of Islamic Law and the Concept of Human Rights," in ibid., 54.

12. Tabandeh, *A Muslim Commentary,* 85.

13. Abu'l A'la Mawdudi, *Human Rights in Islam* (Leicester: Islamic Foundation, 1980), 15.

14. Ibid., 39.

15. Presumably, these are meant to be like the ones in the scheme of drastically circumscribed and watered-down Islamic human rights that he set forth in his human rights pamphlet.

16. Iraq is an excellent example of how a dictator can now entirely dominate a country. A thoughtful analysis of the degree of oppression that it was possible for Saddam Hussain to achieve in Iraq can be found in Samir al-Khalil, *Republic of Fear: The Inside Story of Saddam's Iraq* (New York: Pantheon Books, 1989).

17. For example, see Mawdudi, *Human Rights,* 15, 17–22.

18. International Commission of Jurists, *Human Rights in Islam,* 7.

19. Ibid., 49–55.

20. *MERIP Middle East Report,* November-December 1987, discusses a number of the indigenous human rights groups. See also Virginia N. Sherry, "The Human Rights Movement in the Arab World: An Active and Diverse Community of Human Rights Advocates Exists in Several Countries of the Region," *Human Rights Watch,* No. 4, Special Middle East Watch Issue (Fall 1990), 6–7.

21. The declaration from the meeting is presented in German translation in Bassam Tibi, "Bericht über das Kolloquium arabischer Wissenschaftler und Schriftsteller: *Multaqa Tunis ath-thaqafi 'an al-hurriyat al-dimuqratiya fi al-'alam al-'arabi*/Das kulturelle Tunis-Kolloquium über die demokratischen Freiheiten in der arabischen Welt im Centre Culturel de Hammamet," April 1–3, 1983, *Orient* 24 (1983), 398–99.

22. *al-Dimuqratiya wa huquq al-insan fi al-watan al-'arabi,* Ali Hilal [Dassuqi], ed. (Cairo: Markaz dirasat al-wahda al-'arabiya, 1983).

23. Mawdudi made a very similar assertion, claiming, "When we speak of human rights in Islam we mean those rights granted by God. Rights granted by kings or legislative assemblies can be withdrawn as easily as they are conferred; but no individual and no institution has the authority to withdraw the rights conferred by God." Mawdudi, *Human Rights,* 15.

Chapter 10

1. Louis Henkin, "The Universality of the Concept of Human Rights," *Annals* 506 (November 1989), 12, 14–15.

2. Fang Lizhi, "Keeping the Faith," *New York Review of Books* 36 (December 21, 1989), 43–44.

3. Henkin, "The Universality of the Concept of Human Rights," 13.

4. Ibid., 15.

About the Book and Author

Does the philosophy and practice of Islam stand in the way of realizing human rights? In this book Ann Elizabeth Mayer offers a critical assessment of recent human rights schemes proposed by Muslim conservatives as alternatives to the International Bill of Human Rights. She argues that these schemes possess no direct antecedents in the premodern Islamic tradition but are legal hybrids of Islamic and international principles.

Dr. Mayer contrasts the position of Muslim conservatives with that of Muslims who endorse international human rights standards as fully compatible with Islam and offers evidence that the provisions of Islamic human rights schemes tend to dilute and nullify rights guaranteed by international law. In addition, she evaluates the political significance of Islamic rights schemes by examining the actual patterns of rights deprivations in Muslim countries and the policies of governments that have pursued Islamization campaigns. Dr. Mayer persuasively demonstrates that it is not Islamic tradition that discourages respect for human rights but the selective interpretation and application of Islamic law and tradition by Muslim groups who are threatened by the demand for democratic freedoms throughout the Muslim world.

Ann Elizabeth Mayer is associate professor of legal studies at the Wharton School of the University of Pennsylvania. She holds a Ph.D. in Middle Eastern history, a Juris Doctor, and a certificate in Islamic and comparative law from the School of Oriental and African Studies, University of London. She is a member of the Bar of the State of Pennsylvania. Her numerous publications have focused on Islamic law in contemporary societies, problems of jurisprudence, law and social structure, comparative law, Islamic banking and taxation, and human rights issues.

Index